I0010838

Ext JS Application Development Blueprints

Develop robust and maintainable projects that exceed client expectations using Ext JS

Colin Ramsay

PUBLISHING

BIRMINGHAM - MUMBAI

Ext JS Application Development Blueprints

Copyright © 2015 Packt Publishing

All rights reserved. No part of this book may be reproduced, stored in a retrieval system, or transmitted in any form or by any means, without the prior written permission of the publisher, except in the case of brief quotations embedded in critical articles or reviews.

Every effort has been made in the preparation of this book to ensure the accuracy of the information presented. However, the information contained in this book is sold without warranty, either express or implied. Neither the author, nor Packt Publishing, and its dealers and distributors will be held liable for any damages caused or alleged to be caused directly or indirectly by this book.

Packt Publishing has endeavored to provide trademark information about all of the companies and products mentioned in this book by the appropriate use of capitals. However, Packt Publishing cannot guarantee the accuracy of this information.

First published: April 2015

Production reference: 1170415

Published by Packt Publishing Ltd.
Livery Place
35 Livery Street
Birmingham B3 2PB, UK.

ISBN 978-1-78439-530-8

www.packtpub.com

Credits

Author
Colin Ramsay

Reviewers
Govinda Sambamurthy
Vincent Stanislaus

Acquisition Editor
Kevin Colaco

Content Development Editor
Arwa Manasawala

Technical Editor
Shashank Desai

Copy Editor
Relin Hedly

Project Coordinators
Danuta Jones
Purav Motiwalla

Proofreaders
Simran Bhogal
Stephen Copestake
Safis Editing

Indexer
Hemangini Bari

Graphics
Disha Haria

Production Coordinator
Melwyn D'sa

Cover Work
Melwyn D'sa

About the Author

Colin Ramsay is a software developer and writer with 15 years of coding experience. From .NET to Ruby, JavaScript, and CSS, he has worked with a range of technologies and local and international clients. His company, Go Tripod Ltd., is based in Cornwall, UK. This company works with multinational clients to implement exciting JavaScript products and ideas. He has coauthored *Learning Ext JS* and *Learning Ext JS 3.2*, both by Packt Publishing. Colin also writes on various topics on his personal blog at `http://colinramsay.co.uk/`.

His main hobby is to make mischief.

I'd like to thank all the people who listened to the ideas, updates, and complaints while I was writing this book; you have the patience of saints and I love you for it.

About the Reviewers

Govinda Sambamurthy is a software development manager in the Oracle Fusion Applications team at Bangalore. He is responsible for building highly available and highly scalable enterprise products. Govinda has more than 13 years of experience in the IT industry and has played the roles of a developer, consultant, technical lead, and manager. He has extensive experience in software development for banking, financial, retail, and telecom verticals as well as product development and in building enterprise solutions that are deployed in high-availability architectures. He was part of various development teams in Oracle, including Enterprise Manager, Enterprise Content Management, WebCenter, and Fusion Applications. His areas of interest include data modeling, middleware diagnostics, cloud computing, the Semantic Web, analytics, and next generation UI.

He is the coauthor of *Oracle Enterprise Manager Grid Control 11g R1: Business Service Management*, *Packt Publishing*.

I would like to thank the author and Packt Publishing for giving me this opportunity to be a reviewer. I would also like to thank my mother, Padma, my wife, Nithya, and my toddler, Anirudh, for letting me spend precious family time in the review process. I would also like to thank my managers, Huan Tran and Reza Bfar, at Oracle for approving my request to be a formal reviewer of this book.

Vincent Stanislaus is an ICT professional with more than 18 years of industry experience; since the past 10 years, he has been working with a global wealth management investment banking firm; his other areas of Industry expertise include Superannuation, Banking, Insurance, Student Management, and Government Divisions (Education/Housing).

Vincent's current areas of focus is Information Security, Technology Risk, and Change/Release Management. He currently manages releases for core applications that are designed using various technologies, such as Sencha GXT, GWT, Oracle Fusion Middleware (Forms/Reports), Oracle WebLogic, and Apache/Tomcat.

Prior to this, his focus was on enforcing standards for the development team and ensuring they were adhered to by developers. He loves reviewing code prepared by developers, highlights any issues, and prevents them from being released to production in order to mitigate outages.

He has reviewed the book *Oracle Application Express 4.0 with Ext JS* and the e-video *Oracle APEX Techniques*, both by Packt Publishing.

He resides in Melbourne, Australia with his wife, Robina, and two lovely children, Jonathan and Marilyn.

www.PacktPub.com

Support files, eBooks, discount offers, and more

For support files and downloads related to your book, please visit www.PacktPub.com.

Did you know that Packt offers eBook versions of every book published, with PDF and ePub files available? You can upgrade to the eBook version at www.PacktPub.com and as a print book customer, you are entitled to a discount on the eBook copy. Get in touch with us at service@packtpub.com for more details.

At www.PacktPub.com, you can also read a collection of free technical articles, sign up for a range of free newsletters and receive exclusive discounts and offers on Packt books and eBooks.

https://www2.packtpub.com/books/subscription/packtlib

Do you need instant solutions to your IT questions? PacktLib is Packt's online digital book library. Here, you can search, access, and read Packt's entire library of books.

Why subscribe?

- Fully searchable across every book published by Packt
- Copy and paste, print, and bookmark content
- On demand and accessible via a web browser

Free access for Packt account holders

If you have an account with Packt at www.PacktPub.com, you can use this to access PacktLib today and view 9 entirely free books. Simply use your login credentials for immediate access.

Table of Contents

Preface

In times gone by, JavaScript was used to provide minor enhancements to the Web in order to decorate pages with amusing effects or to validate user input. Slowly but surely, as browsers implemented faster JavaScript engines and new features and as developers and engineers came up with new techniques and ideas, JavaScript became near-ubiquitous in providing the functionality that end users have come to expect. With Ext JS, you have a toolset that allows you to build advanced JavaScript applications, but with great power comes great responsibility.

An application architect is the guiding hand of a project. They help to ensure that client expectations are met, timescales are achieved, and costs are contained. While juggling these requirements, the architect must provide the foundations for a technically successful project consisting of high quality, understandable code.

In *Ext JS Application Development Blueprints*, we'll go through the theory and practice of designing and building Ext JS applications. Over the next 11 chapters, you'll learn how Ext JS gives developers the key to a professionally designed software project and how to take this knowledge and use it in a range of real-world scenarios.

What this book covers

Chapter 1, Introduction, describes why software architecture is important and how this book will help you learn it.

Chapter 2, MVC and MVVM, introduces two classic patterns in software development and how they're implemented in Ext JS.

Chapter 3, Application Structure, shows how the various parts of an Ext JS application can be organized into a form that eases the development process.

Chapter 4, Sencha Cmd, looks at the way Sencha's command-line tools act as a powerful companion for your developers, enabling a leaner product that is delivered on schedule.

Chapter 5, Practical – a CMS Application, shows how to design and build a simple CMS application and how to start employing the ideas you've learned so far.

Chapter 6, Practical – Monitoring Dashboard, involves the creation of a log viewer dashboard using charts and grids that adapt to user input.

Chapter 7, Practical – an E-mail Client, shows off the responsive features of Ext JS 5 while continuing to demonstrate advanced use of the MVVM pattern.

Chapter 8, Practical – Questionnaire Component, uses Sencha Cmd to demonstrate code reuse by designing and building a wizard component.

Chapter 9, A Shopping Application, brings all the techniques from previous chapters to bear on a tablet-centric shopping app.

Chapter 10, Debugging and Performance, teaches you advanced techniques to diagnose a range of problems in development and production.

Chapter 11, Application Testing, provides you with techniques to build automated tests that allow for the kind of robust application expected from an application architect.

What you need for this book

The code samples in this book were developed for Ext JS 5.0.1 and the equivalent version of Sencha Cmd. The server-side APIs for the practical chapters were written using Node.js. For more information, refer to `http://www.sencha.com/products/sencha-cmd/download` and `http://nodejs.org/download/`.

Who this book is for

If you're already working with Ext JS and are looking to extend your knowledge as a team leader, or are simply looking to understand how to design and structure your applications, this book is for you. We won't stop and explain every little facet of Ext JS, and we'd expect that you have a good grasp of the fundamentals of the framework. We'll encourage problem solving, rather than coding-by-numbers, so a positive attitude and desire to learn is essential!

Conventions

In this book, you will find a number of text styles that distinguish between different kinds of information. Here are some examples of these styles and an explanation of their meaning.

Code words in text, database table names, folder names, filenames, file extensions, pathnames, dummy URLs, user input, and Twitter handles are shown as follows: "This should be familiar to a seasoned Ext JS developer: we use `Ext.define` to create a class called `MyApp.SessionManager`."

A block of code is set as follows:

```
Ext.define('MyApp.SessionManager', {
    login: function(username, password) {
            User.login(username, password, {
                    success: Ext.bind(this.loginSuccess, this)
            });
    },

    loginSuccess: function() {
            this.isLoggedIn = true;
    }
});
```

Any command-line input or output is written as follows:

```
[INF] [echoproperties] app.output.js=app.js
[INF] [echoproperties] app.output.js.compress=false
[INF] [echoproperties] app.output.js.enable=true
[INF] [echoproperties] app.output.js.optimize=false
```

New terms and **important words** are shown in bold. Words that you see on the screen, for example, in menus or dialog boxes, appear in the text like this: "Clicking on **Record** again allows you to analyze the results."

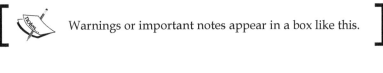

> Warnings or important notes appear in a box like this.

> Tips and tricks appear like this.

Reader feedback

Feedback from our readers is always welcome. Let us know what you think about this book—what you liked or disliked. Reader feedback is important for us as it helps us develop titles that you will really get the most out of.

To send us general feedback, simply e-mail feedback@packtpub.com, and mention the book's title in the subject of your message.

If there is a topic that you have expertise in and you are interested in either writing or contributing to a book, see our author guide at www.packtpub.com/authors.

Customer support

Now that you are the proud owner of a Packt book, we have a number of things to help you to get the most from your purchase.

Downloading the example code

You can download the example code files from your account at http://www.packtpub.com for all the Packt Publishing books you have purchased. If you purchased this book elsewhere, you can visit http://www.packtpub.com/support and register to have the files e-mailed directly to you.

Errata

Although we have taken every care to ensure the accuracy of our content, mistakes do happen. If you find a mistake in one of our books—maybe a mistake in the text or the code—we would be grateful if you could report this to us. By doing so, you can save other readers from frustration and help us improve subsequent versions of this book. If you find any errata, please report them by visiting http://www.packtpub.com/submit-errata, selecting your book, clicking on the **Errata Submission Form** link, and entering the details of your errata. Once your errata are verified, your submission will be accepted and the errata will be uploaded to our website or added to any list of existing errata under the Errata section of that title.

To view the previously submitted errata, go to https://www.packtpub.com/books/content/support and enter the name of the book in the search field. The required information will appear under the **Errata** section.

Piracy

Piracy of copyrighted material on the Internet is an ongoing problem across all media. At Packt, we take the protection of our copyright and licenses very seriously. If you come across any illegal copies of our works in any form on the Internet, please provide us with the location address or website name immediately so that we can pursue a remedy.

Please contact us at copyright@packtpub.com with a link to the suspected pirated material.

We appreciate your help in protecting our authors and our ability to bring you valuable content.

Questions

If you have a problem with any aspect of this book, you can contact us at questions@packtpub.com, and we will do our best to address the problem.

1
Introduction

Learning how to understand a single line of code, building that first "Hello World" script, and experiencing the thrill when it works as you expect are the small steps that draw us into the world of programming. This book is about the projects we can build in this world using Sencha's Ext JS 5 and how to ensure you're building on a strong foundation.

In this chapter, we're going to examine why strong application architecture is important from a theoretical and practical point of view. We'll introduce the rest of the book and answer the following questions:

- What is application architecture?
- How is it important?
- How does Ext JS help with application design?
- How will this book help your software architecture?

Let's start with talking about what we mean by software architecture and why it's important for a successful project.

Humble beginnings

As coders, many of us would have started our development career by writing scripts or code that we found helpful, which helped out with a hobby. That buzz, the insight that you can create something practical and useful, that's where the passion starts. It's from these hastily assembled first few lines on which many of us have built a career.

In those early days, we found ourselves writing code that spanned hundreds of lines, but with no regard for how it might look if we came back to it in six months. Would it be understandable? Can a feature be added without breaking something else? Also, what if we want to share it with a friend or on the Internet? Trying to work out the cause of a bug is going to rapidly become a nightmare.

In fact, the Internet is littered with such code. Why is this a problem? Let's say you got roped into building a simple shopping cart for a friend. You knew enough to get it working, but also enough to be dangerous. A shopping cart is responsible for taking payment for goods, and a single security hole could result in someone being out of pocket. Suddenly, your favor for a friend has become something that has caused them to lose face and money.

Fortunately, in my case, there were no drastic ramifications for my lack of development expertise as a newcomer to coding. I created a PHP script. This script generated a photo gallery for a website. It started off as a list of photos and expanded to include thumbnail generation, pagination, and an administration/upload facility. It was an example of traditionally bad PHP with HTML mixed in with logic code and spaghetti loops to try and make the thing work the way I wanted.

With time, the solution comes organically; we start to break our work into smaller chunks that make sense for the application. It will slowly become clear that there are sensible ways of working, which make life easier, as your codebase grows. In the photo gallery example, I could start to extract very simple aspects (such as headers, footers, and pagination links) in order to focus on the core functionality.

Of course, not everyone starts this way. Developing a hobby into a career is just one path by which the coding community develops its skillset. University or online courses, books, and forums contribute to our learning process. The important thing to bear in mind is that neither coder nor architect was born into the world knowing everything and it's okay, even essential, to admit when there's a gap in your knowledge. From a senior consultant to hobbyist hacker, we're going to try and fill some of these gaps, as you build larger and more complex applications.

Growing up

Rather than writing code that is for a hobby or side project, we're now writing applications that help run businesses. Someone is paying for this development time, and someone's livelihood is relying on it. As professional software developers, we need to adopt a professional mindset and skillset to match. Rather than coming up with an idea and sitting down to code it immediately, we need to carefully consider how our application is constructed. We need to ensure that it will work as expected when real-world users get their hands on it; this will provide a strong platform for future developers to build on.

As software developers, we can be responsible for tens of thousands of lines of code—and in many cases more—and may be working in a team comprising a range of other individuals. At this scale, badly designed applications can become unwieldy, unreliable, and difficult to test.

It's unwieldy because without a strong design, functionality is tacked on as it's required, building on an already shaky foundation; unreliable because this shaky foundation has cracks crawling with bugs, and difficult to test because the system's parts are so intertwined that each component doesn't have a clear set of responsibilities and capabilities.

This is the danger of taking an idea and running with it; you may be creating code that grows out of control like a weed in a garden. A design is the key because it allows you to be the gardener (carefully tending each facet of the system as it grows). We want to create a clear, positive structure for our team members to start from and build on.

The structure we want to create in an application should give us clear delineation between one component and another. Each part of the system should be responsible for itself and nothing more (a small part in a larger machine). The layers of our code (from data to presentation and all the wiring in between) should also be clear-cut because no one wants to see a template talking directly to a backend service.

This is a classic example of overlapping concern. In this presentation, code should never have to worry about fetching data, only how to present it. This, and many more such issues, can be easily avoided with a strong structure and application design that is implemented from the start.

The shoulders of giants

Many have gone on this journey of scalability before us. It's worth remembering that there are many formal metrics to help us determine whether our code is too complex. "Cyclomatic complexity" is one example, a technique that evaluates details (such as code cohesion and branching depth) and can be tied into automated systems that raise a warning when a threshold for complexity is crossed.

In reality though, such metrics are a method of firefighting complexity rather than planning to avoid it. By looking at ways in which we can structure our code for success, we can minimize the need for such automated checks.

The first stop must be **object-orientated programming (OOP)**. By encouraging a piece of functionality to be encapsulated in a class, we immediately impose a sense of separation in our application. Just as splitting our multi-hundred-line script into separate chunks made sense, here we can formalize this approach by creating classes that take responsibility for a single piece of functionality.

With the photo gallery, the pagination is a great example of where concerns could overlap. My original implementation just had a lot of loops and conditional statements wrapped up with the HTML. Instead, we can have one class that does the logic of the pagination (for example, whether the "next" link is available) and another class responsible for generating the HTML based on this data.

In Ext JS 4, Sencha brought in a new class system that allows you to better create objects that encapsulate application functionality as well as a strong application framework. Ext JS 5 builds on this and adds some extra features to make the Ext JS application architecture ideal for everyone (from individual developers to large teams). The structured approach that it makes available allows you to scale a code base while keeping its foundations strong.

What is application architecture?

Most people have a general idea of the role of a traditional architect, creating precise diagrams to pass on to the builders and other craftsmen who will undertake construction. More than this, an architect needs to consider the materials used, the aesthetics of a building, and oversee the construction process.

In the world of software, the architect has a similar role: design and supervision. We need to invest in the role of an architect and ensure that we make it an end-to-end process that ensures we take responsibility of the quality of the final product. Design and supervision requires a comprehensive knowledge of the product requirements, the technologies involved, and the available resources. The architecture of a software program (our "raison d'etre") is multifaceted, from the quality of the up-front documentation that dictates how the project will be built, to the finesse of the end product, which users will love to work with.

Requirement analysis

A software project should never begin without a list of requirements from the customer, client, or other stakeholder. This is often in the form of a detailed specification document. Requirement analysis involves the architect understanding the problem that needs to be solved and applying what they've learned to the next stages of the process.

Here's a short example:

Users should be able to log in, log out, register, and request a new password. Login should be persistent across browser sessions.

The architect reads this and the developers (in turn) end up with the following code to handle user logins:

```
Ext.define('MyApp.SessionManager', {
    login: function(username, password) {
        User.login(username, password, {
            success: Ext.bind(this.loginSuccess, this)
        });
    },
    loginSuccess: function() {
        this.isLoggedIn = true;
    }
});
```

This should be familiar to a seasoned Ext JS developer: we use `Ext.define` to create a class called `MyApp.SessionManager`. The login method contains an invocation of a login method on the `User` class and triggers a callback if it succeeds. Using `Ext.bind`, we set the scope of the success callback to the `SessionManager` class and when it's called, we set the `isLoggedIn` value to `true`. Further code would then redirect the authenticated user to the rest of the application.

The problem is that the architect has not correctly processed the requirements. They have missed the second part (the part that mandates that logins should be persistent across sessions). In this code sample, we store the login state in memory. To support the requirements, we should use a cookie, `localStorage`, or some other storage mechanism to make the login available between browser sessions. What will this code look like? Let's tweak this class a little, change one method, and add a few more methods:

```
loginSuccess: function(userDetails) {
    this.setUser(userDetails);
},

isUserLoggedIn: function() {
    return window.localStorage.getItem('user') === null;
},

setUser: function(userDetails) {
```

```
        window.localStorage.setItem('user', Ext.encode(userDetails));
    },

    getUser: function() {
        return Ext.decode(window.localStorage.getItem('user'));
    }
```

The replacement `loginSuccess` method passes off to `setUser`, which makes use of `localStorage` to persist user details across browser sessions. We also provide an additional `isUserLoggedIn` method to check `localStorage` for any user details and a `getUser` method to grab these details. Note the use of `Ext.encode` and `Ext.decode` to convert JavaScript objects to strings that can be inserted into `localStorage`.

This is a more realistic implementation of this functionality that needs to be better specified at a higher level. Without translating this requirement from the client's stipulations through to the developer's instructions, we'd be omitting an important part of the application's feature set.

Data design

As with much of the application architecture, it will be a collaborative effort between the architect, developers, database administrators, and other members of the technical team. Data design is the result of a discussion about the data you need to store, where it will be stored, and how this will be reflected in the stores and models in your Ext JS. Let's look at a theoretical requirement for an application:

After three failed login attempts, the user account will be locked for 30 minutes.

This means that we need to record the number of failed login attempts and the last login attempt in the `User` model or some other persistence method (such as a server-side database). Without it, we wouldn't be able to create the correct client-side logic and UI to support this requirement.

Code design

Perhaps, the bulk of an architect's work comes from structuring the application's code base. Depending on the size of the team, the architect may or may not be involved in writing the code itself, but they will have intimate knowledge of the application at a higher level (almost certainly at the class level and in important situations at the method level). In many cases, UML or other diagramming tools will be used to provide a way of recording and sharing the design, as shown in the following diagram:

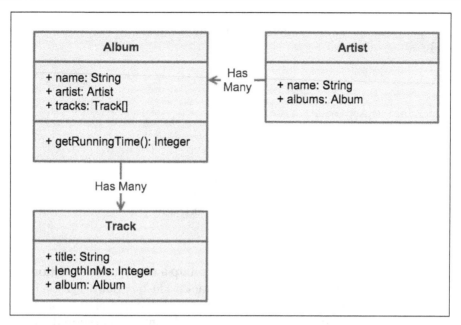

A UML-like diagram showing the models in a theoretical music application

The `Album` class that comes from this would look like the following code:

```
// model/Artist.js
Ext.define('MyApp.model.Artist.', {
    extend: 'Ext.data.Model',

    fields: [
        { name: 'name', type: 'string' }
    ]
});

// model/Album.js
Ext.define('MyApp.model.Album', {
    extend: 'Ext.data.Model',

    fields: [
        { name: 'name', type: 'string' },
        { name: 'artist', reference: 'Artist' }
    ],
```

```
        getRunningTime: function() {
            return this.tracks().sum('lengthInMs');
        }
    });

    // model/Track.js
    Ext.define('MyApp.model.Track.', {
        extend: 'Ext.data.Model',

        fields: [
            { name: 'title', type: 'string' },
            { name: 'lengthInMs', type: 'integer' },
            { name: 'album', reference: 'Album' }
        ]
    });
```

We define fields with the `reference` config to set up a many-to-one relationship between artists and albums, and albums and tracks. The `getRunningTime` method, which was shown in the previous class diagram, is an example of an area that an architect might not get involved in (they can leave the implementation details of this method to a developer).

This is the key aspect of architecture that we'll be covering in this book.

Technology evaluation

In this book, we will discuss Ext JS 5, so our technology choice should be fairly straightforward! Nonetheless, it's important for an architect to evaluate all of the relevant parts of their technology stack to ensure that it supports the product requirements. Here are some technology questions that are still relevant in our situation:

- Do we need to cater to various form factors (such as mobile and tablet)?
- Do we need to support Internet Explorer 8?
- Do we need to talk to a SOAP service?

All of these have potential ramifications that an architect must evaluate while planning a project.

Code standards and practices

In the same way that a building architect must make sure the design they create adheres to building code and safety regulations as well as ensuring the materials they use will create a pleasing finish, software architects must also take steps to guarantee the quality of the finished product.

Naming conventions, formatting guidelines, a process to deploy the application — all these contribute to having a professional workflow that makes it easy for the developers and project to succeed. The architect is the guiding hand, bringing the customer something that exceeds their expectations.

Documentation

There are many reasons why documenting the development process is a good idea. For example:

- Transparency between team members
- Providing a point of reference during development
- Offering a comparison for post-project review

Having a single point of reference for the design documents helps in a large team and assists with bringing new team members up to speed. It's a very bad idea for the architect to hold all of their ideas in their head, and it's a very good idea for this knowledge to be shared, discussed, and recorded. Such documentation might come in a variety of forms:

- Class diagrams
- UI wireframes
- User stories
- Coding standards
- Code documentation

Code documentation will often be automatically created as part of a build process, but an architect will be responsible for mandating this code to be documented and instituting a build step to generate it. Other forms will be part of a manual process and can involve the client, the development team, and the architect.

 These definitions are up for discussion! Wikipedia's software architecture page is extensive and offers multiple points of view at http://en.wikipedia.org/wiki/Software_architecture.

In the next few pages, we'll look at how software and software developers can find themselves in possession of an unwieldy code base, what makes it unwieldy, why it's a problem. We'll also look at the attributes that make for a well-architected software product.

Ext JS

Before version 4 of Ext JS, Sencha didn't try to impose any kind of structure on our applications. Components were split across multiple files, but other than this, we didn't have any guidance on how they should communicate or how they are pieced together to form an application. Ext JS began with version 1.0 on April 15, 2007 as a library of user interface widgets—buttons, trees, grids, and features (such as layouts) to help them all hang together, but not much more than this.

At the time, this didn't seem to matter much. The idea of a single page application written in JavaScript still felt like the technology of the future, and while it was starting to happen, it certainly wasn't as ordinary as it was in 2014. Augmenting existing web pages with slick Ajax-powered widgets was more than enough.

As time went on, with lots of widgets and dynamic parts of the website all needing to interact, the requirement for a formal mechanism for intercommunication became obvious. People were using Ext JS to build enterprise-level applications that specified high levels of availability and therefore rigorous testing regimes. Spaghetti code just wasn't going to cut it anymore.

The world that was

Let's take a look at a classic piece of example code from back in the days of Ext 3.4:

```
// View a working version at https://fiddle.sencha.com/#fiddle/90s

// Basic JSON sample data
var sampleData = { data: [
    { "firstName": "Jack", "surname": "Slocum" },
    { "firstName": "Shea", "surname": "Frederick" },
    { "firstName": "Colin", "surname": "Ramsay" },
    { "firstName": "Steve", "middle": "Cutter", "surname":
"Blades" },
    { "firstName": "Nigel", "surname": "White" },
] };
```

```
// Create a store to hold our JSON data
var userStore = new Ext.data.JsonStore({
    data: sampleData,
    root: 'data',
    fields: ['firstName', 'middle', 'surname']
});

// Grid panel using the store, setting the columns to match the
incoming data
var grid = new Ext.grid.GridPanel({
    store: userStore,
    colModel: new Ext.grid.ColumnModel({
        defaults: {
            width: 120,
            sortable: true
        },
        columns: [
            { header: 'First Name', dataIndex: 'firstName' },
            { header: 'Middle', dataIndex: 'middle' },
            { header: 'Surname', dataIndex: 'surname' }
        ]
    }),
    viewConfig: {
        forceFit: true
    },
    width: 600,
    height: 300,
    frame: true
});

// Event handler to do something when the user clicks a row
grid.on('rowclick', function(g, idx) {
    Ext.Msg.alert('Alert', 'You clicked on the row at index ' +
idx);
});

// Render the grid to the viewport
grid.render(document.body);
```

This block of code should be familiar to the reader as something that generates a populated grid:

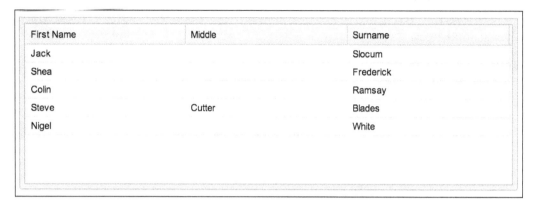

First Name	Middle	Surname
Jack		Slocum
Shea		Frederick
Colin		Ramsay
Steve	Cutter	Blades
Nigel		White

When a row on the grid is clicked on, an alert box appears showing the index of the target row. This is all well and good. It represents a fairly typical example of what you'd have seen in the Ext JS documentation at the time of Ext JS 3.4.

So, what's the problem? The problem is that this code does everything. It sets up our data store, drawing JSON from either a remote or local source. It creates the grid itself along with its many configuration options. It sets up event handling code to pop up the alert box. And after all that's been done, it finally renders the grid to the screen.

Within a simple piece of code like this, the problem is less pronounced. Although, when more functionality is added, such as paging or a detail window popping up with further information about a record and tying all of this into a larger application with server-side interaction, multiple screens, and so on, then things start to get tricky.This is the type of issue that Sencha tried to resolve by introducing defined architectural practices in Ext JS 4. Rather than putting everything together and mixing all these different concerns, the idea was that they could be pulled apart into more logical, concise, and distinct objects.

State of the art

The **model-view-controller** (**MVC**) pattern was the choice of the new wave of web developers. Ruby on Rails had already popularized MVC and many other major frameworks had brought their own ideas to the table.

While MVC has often been used in web development over recent years, it's used elsewhere in software development and, indeed, was originally developed for desktop GUI coding. Learning about MVC as a general concept is outside our scope, but there's plenty of information and examples on the Web.

Ext JS 4.0 was released on April 26, 2011, over 4 years after v1.0, and many developers were already comfortable with using the MVC pattern in their server-side apps. Frameworks (such as Backbone.js) had slowly begun to give developers the tools to use such architectural patterns in their client-side code. Ext JS 4 needed to do the same and it delivered.

Mostly very cool

Prior to version 4, Ext JS had stores and records (the "model" in MVC). It had components or widgets (the "view" in MVC). The architectural issue was twofold; how did models and views talk to each other? How did we avoid making our views bloated with logic code?

One answer was to introduce the controller concept. This allowed us to create a layer of glue to create stores, hook them up to components, and use events to manage communication between all of these parts of the application.

In version 5 of Ext JS, a couple of extra features fully answered our architectural questions with ViewControllers and ViewModels. ViewControllers allow us to separate out logic code in our views into a distinct class, ensuring that both the view and ViewController can focus on their own set of responsibilities.

Supporting cast

As well as building classes into the Ext JS framework to help us build complicated applications, Sencha has also provided a number of supplementary tools that assist with the development process. In particular, Sencha Cmd is a powerful command-line tool that introduces some indispensable facilities.

From the beginning, Sencha Cmd can help by generating the directory structure of your application with a best practice layout, specifically created to help with the new Ext JS 5 cross-device support. You can add new models, controllers, and so on, all from the command line.

As you're developing, Sencha Cmd can help you by compiling theme files, slicing and dicing images, and running a development web server to run your code locally. Also, during testing and deployment, it can package your code into an optimized bundle to give your users the minimum amount of code to download in their browser.

Sencha Cmd is a great example of a product that is growing up. It represents a key piece of your development infrastructure and a fantastic complement to the Ext JS framework itself.

Getting ready

We know about the issues we'd like to address and how we're going to learn to do so. So, now let's look at some of the non-architectural aspects of an application that you might want to think about even before starting to put pen to paper on the design. While everything we've discussed so far talks about the overarching method to shape the development of an application, the other parts of the puzzle can often be just as important.

The specification

How do you design an application without knowing what it is you're designing? This is what a specification provides. A document or series of documents that describe in exacting detail how the features that make up your software should behave. It's a continuing mistake in the software business that we don't collect the requirements of our users and clients before we start writing code. In the same way that it's irresponsible to build an application without architecting it correctly, it's irresponsible to build an application without being as certain as possible that you're creating the correct thing for a paying customer. What sort of issues can a specification avoid? Some of them are as follows:

- Missed deadlines
- Cost overruns
- Developer stress
- Customer dissatisfaction

This reads as a fairly generic list of things we don't want during our project.

More importantly for the purposes of this book, a specification allows you to have all of the information needed to create your application design. It doesn't necessarily mean our design will be right, but without a specification, you can guarantee the design will be wrong.

A good match

Part of creating both a specification and a design is understanding the customer requirements; understanding the "problem domain" that represents their business. It's really hard to write a piece of computer software for a shipping business unless you understand at least a little bit about shipping, for example the way they calculate rates in relation to cargo weight and the distance it's travelling.

In regard to Ext JS, we may be working with an external SOAP API that provides these shipping rates. Well, Ext JS supports working with SOAP (with a Sencha Complete license), but if it didn't, this would probably affect our design—we'd have to write more code to talk to the SOAP API—and therefore our timings.

We're writing a content management system, but it needs to be very closely tied with the customer's branding due to agreements with third parties. Will the Ext JS theming system allow us to incorporate the extensive customization needed for the project?

We started working on a sales portal for a new client when the Finance Director reveals that all his work outside the office is done on an iPad mini. We now have to work backwards to incorporate touchscreen support. If we'd have consulted all of the stakeholders at the right time, we'd have saved weeks of work.

These examples are somewhat contrived, but serve to highlight that application design is not only about software, but also a fusion of consulting the people involved, evaluating your resources, understanding the problem domain, and creating a software architecture. These requirements don't exist in isolation.

How we work

Consider bringing a new developer or tester in your team. How quickly can they get up and running with the latest build of your code? How can they track down the code change that resulted in a bug they're working on and then find the developer responsible for the bug? Is there a particular way in which automated tests should be created and new code should be written?

These are all highly important questions when creating a successful application because they reduce the barrier between creating and improving the existing code base and keeping the quality of the resulting code high. Joel Spolsky, of Microsoft and Fog Creek fame, wrote a blog article back in 2000 that is still highly relevant today. Titled *The Joel Test: 12 Steps to Better Code*, it asked twelve questions of development houses based on Joel's extensive experience working with a variety of coding teams and projects (from Microsoft Excel to Fog Creek's own Trello). The whole article's well worth a read, but we're going to take a fresh look at it with regards to Ext JS development.

In safe hands

Joel's first question, "Do you use source control?"

Step one when a new developer arrives is where is your code kept? We're long past shared network drives and manually copying the code of other developers on your team, so you should be using some form of source control. This is definitely a situation in which something is better than nothing, so we won't specifically discuss the alternatives, but in my case, I'm using Git, which is created as the source control system for the Linux kernel and is now extremely popular in software development.

Each member of your team can now grab code from each other, roll back their mistakes, track changes, and find the origin of bugs. However, a source repository is not just a giant hole in which everyone's files is up. There are some that are unique to each developer (such as configuration files for an IDE), and there are some that are automatically generated by a build process or other script. With Git, we'd use a `.gitignore` file to exclude several items that simply create a message of your repository and commits:

```
# sample gitignore for extjs5
# The build directory can be recreated by developers using Sencha
Cmd - it should be excluded from the repo
build/

# Changes every time a build is run
bootstrap.js
bootstrap.css

# Temporary files created when compiling .scss files
.sass-cache/

# Some team members may use Sencha architect - exclude so they
keep their custom settings
.architect

# It's possible to create reusable packages using Sencha Cmd
but depending on your preference you might want to exclude this
directory. Packages are discussed in chapter 3.
packages/
```

There will be a lot more than this in a `.gitignore` file if your Ext JS application shares a directory with any server-side code. Most large projects will have a heavily customized `.gitignore` file. Moreover, not all source control systems will have a similar feature and setting it up at the start of the project will keep your application history neat and tidy.

If you build it, they will come

Joel's second question, "Can you make a build in one step?"

We mentioned earlier that it needs to be easy for developers and testers to build a final version of your application from the raw source code. This could be the process that compresses your CSS and JavaScript so that your users can download it more quickly. The key is that you want to be testing your work against the same final build as your users to avoid bugs creeping through.

In Ext JS 5, we can use the Sencha Cmd to create development, testing, and production builds and it can even be used to create a packaged version of your application for deployment on touch devices. In doing so, it gives a unified mechanism for your whole team to work from the same build with a single command, making Joel very happy. This also ties into his third question, "Do you make daily builds?" With the tools we've described so far, an automated build system can grab the latest and greatest code from source control, build it using the Sencha Cmd, and deploy it to a testing or beta server for evaluation.

Managing your time

Joel's fourth question, "Do you have an up-to-date schedule?" and his fifth question, "Do you have a spec?"

Of course, neither of these is specific to Ext JS applications, but they're tightly related to the theme of this book. We've discussed having a specification that informs your application design, but it's an up-to-date schedule that goes hand in hand. By designing your application correctly, you are dividing it into sections that can be scheduled by yourself, your team, or your management.

A single controller with its associated views and the required models could be scheduled to take a month to complete, so an app designed to have three controllers could take three months. Joel's sixth question's a little bit more specific than this though, he asks for an up-to-date schedule. This means examining your work to ensure you're meeting your schedule and adjusting accordingly. It also means learning from a slipping schedule and realizing that your design may have been flawed in some ways. A more complex view with lots of interaction will clearly take more time than a simple view, so it's not as straightforward as our "one month per controller" suggestion.

You can buy fashion, but you can't buy style

The rest of Joel's questions are more general, so we'll skip them and talk about another important facet of setting up your development process: style. Not what your developers are wearing, but the way in which they write code. There are two things to consider here, the ones related to JavaScript and the ones specific to Ext JS.

The developers of Twitter Bootstrap caused upset in 2012 by opting not to use semicolons at the end of lines of JavaScript and combining that with some slightly obtuse syntax. Refer to https://github.com/twbs/bootstrap/issues/3057.

In truth, it doesn't matter too much whether you use semicolons or not in most circumstances due to JavaScript's automatic semicolon insertion. Refer to http://ecma262-5.com/ELS5_Section_7.htm#Section_7.9.

The more important point is that whatever you do, do it consistently and make sure everyone working on your application is doing it too. Not doing this will have severe consequences for the maintainability of your application as it's developed (imagine having files with two or three different styles of commenting, string quoting, and conditional statements).

Ext JS itself has a couple of conventions that will make your life much easier if you adhere to them. When a controller requires a store, you can do it like this:

```
Ext.define('MyApp.controller.MyController', {
    extend: 'Ext.app.Controller',

    requires: [
        'MyApp.store.Albums'
    ],

    getAlbumsStore: function() {
        return this.getStore('Albums');
    }
});
```

This is equivalent to:

```
Ext.define('MyApp.controller.MyController', {
    extend: 'Ext.app.Controller',

    stores: ['Albums']
});
```

As the `Store` class was defined as `'MyApp.store.Albums'`, we can refer to it with the `'Albums'` shortcut. Likewise, controllers should always have "controller" as the middle part of the class name, "model" for models, and "view" for views.

This is partially covered in the naming conventions segment of the Ext JS 5 Core Concepts guide. What isn't explicitly mentioned is the way that these shortcuts are pervasive across Ext JS and how they can make your code much clearer.

Summary

Although a lot of this book discusses the bigger picture of designing an application, there are many different criteria for developing a successful product. Attention must be paid to the smaller things that we've already mentioned (such as semicolon style or naming conventions) in order to not only provide a solid foundation for your code, but also to ensure everyone who is working with it feels invested and on the same page. You're not only painting a picture of a well-architected application, but you're also building an intricate machine with hundreds of moving parts. All of them need to be well oiled for your project to succeed.

In the next chapter, we'll start to talk about the theory of application structure and discuss design patterns that will help shape our code base. We'll frame this in the context of Ext JS and show how it provides a strong set of features that build on these patterns and enable us to begin setting up the architecture for a robust application.

2
MVC and MVVM

The problem with software development is that we're always looking for the right way to do things. Each software shop will have their own set of guidelines that indicate how their developers should operate. This is the way that software works: we build a set of ideas that reflect our best thoughts on how things should be developed and the software community learns from these ideas and builds on them. They are formalized into patterns of working and these patterns are shared throughout the development community. In this chapter, we'll talk more about this concept, specifically:

- The MVC pattern
- The MVVM pattern
- The way Ext JS uses both
- The evolution of Ext JS from MVC to MVVM
- The benefits of design patterns in the current version of Ext JS

Discussions about design patterns are often very dry. In this chapter, we'll use some practical examples to illustrate why they're so important and how they can help you kick-start your architecture efforts.

Diary of always

In the beginning, there was a giant mess. Well, maybe not quite, but in modern software development, we've got lots of design and architectural patterns that we can draw on to help us shape an application and ensure we're not reinventing the wheel. Each of these is the result of decades of their work, which is constantly reviewed and put into practice, and we all hope that the most elegant and useful work will bubble to the top. Along the way, we've seen clumsy patterns being overtaken by more elegant ones. Hopefully, our mess has become a little bit less tangled.

A key development in the way we build graphical interfaces was **model-view-controller** (**MVC**), which was invented at the near-legendary Xerox PARC in the 1970s by Norwegian computer scientist Trygve Reenskaug. It was first publicly incorporated in Smalltalk, a programming language developed by a cast of computer scientists including Alan Kay. It brought together a host of ideas, which influenced nearly all the object-oriented languages we use today. It was a pretty big deal and created by some pretty big guns.

Connelly Barnes, assistant professor of computer science at University of Virginia, gives us a great way of viewing MVC:

> *"The model is the data, the view is the window on the screen, and the controller is the glue between the two."*

It was first in describing software constructs in terms of their responsibilities, for example, the View is responsible for presentation. In *Chapter 1, Introduction*, we talked about its importance in creating strong application architecture.

It can be difficult for us to look back on innovations (such as Smalltalk and MVC) and understand why they were so important. We could spend many pages reviewing what went before and why the advent of MVC has been described as a seminal insight. What really matters though is that it was a new way of looking at organizing graphical user interface-based software, a new paradigm in computing science that would prove to stand the test of time for the next thirty years:

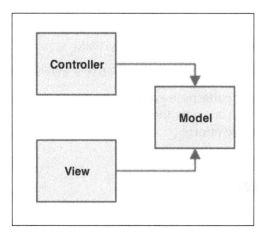

Martin Fowler's bare-bones MVC

There are several differences between the MVC implementation that Ext JS uses (the one that Ruby on Rails brought to prominence) and the original implementation in Smalltalk. It has constantly been honed and tweaked since its inception, tailored for the various environments in which it has been used.

Bringing MVC to the Web

Smalltalk's MVC implementation was created with traditional desktop GUI systems in mind. The separation of responsibilities that it represents makes a lot of sense for web-based software; the model is the representation of the business and persistence layers, the controller is the server-side glue, and the view is the HTML rendered for the client browser.

However, in traditional MVC, the view observes changes in the model in order to reflect its current state by responding to events that the model issues. In a standard HTTP request/response situation, this isn't viable.

Model 2 is a derivative of MVC that was implemented in the Java Struts framework, which introduced a potential solution to this issue. Rather than the view and model directly communicating, the controller becomes a marshaling point for changes. It responds to changes in the view and passes them to the model and vice versa, as shown in the following diagram:

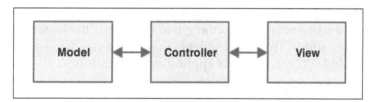

MVC/Model 2 on the Web

This is the way in which Ruby on Rails implements MVC and in turn inspired a multitude of similar MVC frameworks for the Web (such as ASP.NET MVC).

This is in contrast to web technologies (such as Classic ASP, PHP, and Cold Fusion), where it's standard practice to create a page that combines logic, rendering, and database access. This can be described (although rarely is) as Model 1 with the MVC implementation as its logical successor. A Model 1 approach leads to the problems, which we described at the beginning of *Chapter 1, Introduction*, and so the popularization of MVC, in particular the simplified approach that Ruby on Rails took, begins to provide a strong basis for a well-constructed application.

MVC on the Web might follow this request flow:

1. The browser makes a request that is passed on to a controller.
2. The controller consumes the request parameters.
3. It retrieves a model (typically from a database) based on these parameters.
4. Finally, it renders a view based on the model and passes it back to the browser.

Of course, with the advent of Ajax, WebSockets, and fully client-side MVC frameworks, this is a very simplified example. It does serve to show how MVC can easily be adapted for the Web and, in fact, suits the Web very well.

Ext JS and MVC

We've looked at the origins of MVC and the way it was adapted for traditional server-side web applications. How does it work when we use it with the kind of JavaScript-heavy application we'd typically build using Ext JS?

The whole MVC concept moves entirely into the browser. As far as we're concerned, the server can use any technology it wants. It'll generally just provide and consume data to and from the browser. We move back to an MVC implementation that is a little more like the Smalltalk version (different UI elements you see on-screen are views) and each can have their own controller.

Again, this is about breaking down responsibility. Instead of having a single controller take care of an entire page, we can have a search controller, a list controller, and a detail controller (anything that represents the logical units that make up our application). This is a key detail in how the step from server-side MVC to client-side MVC can help our application architecture.

We already know that Ext JS Components are our views, and Ext JS models are well named to fit right in. We're left with one important question: what are controllers actually supposed to do? It's probably easier to remove the things we know they don't do and see what's left. We know that models deal with data, but they're also responsible for the calculations and logic around this data. Calculations and rules, for example, belong in a model, but not in a controller.

 This is a generalization. In many cases, you'll have other classes that do this logic work in order to further break down your application. The important thing to take away is that you do not want domain logic in your controller!

We also know views deal with presentation. You could build up an HTML string in your controller and pass it to the browser for rendering, but this would involve the controller in something which is the view's responsibility.

What are we left with? In truth, not much. All your controllers need to do is be in charge of your views and models. That's it. They look at the request the user is making, fetch a model, and use it to render the view to the browser.

In fact, if your controller is doing more than this, you need to take this as a bad sign. A controller should be the conductor of your orchestra, not the one making the music.

Examples of Ext JS MVC

The following screenshot shows our Ext JS v4 MVC test application:

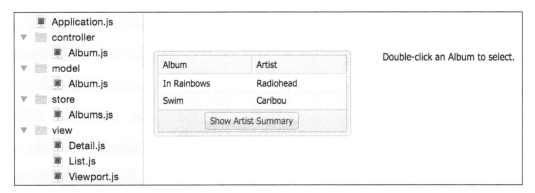

We've generated a stock Ext JS v4 application here, which sticks to the MVC structure and then we've amended it to suit our needs. In this small app, there's a grid of music albums on the left. When you click on the button on the grid, it generates a summary of the artists who are mentioned in the grid, and when you double-click on a row, it puts the album information in the right-hand pane. It's a toy application, but it's useful to demonstrate how MVC works. Later, we'll compare it with a similar application written with Ext JS v5. Let's take a look at the code:

```
// view/List.js
Ext.define('MvcEx1v4.view.List', {
    extend: 'Ext.grid.GridPanel',
    alias: 'widget.app-list',
    store: 'Albums',
    forceFit: true,
    frame: true,
    requires: ['Ext.Msg'],

    columns: [
        { text: 'Name', dataIndex: 'name' },
        { text: 'Artist', dataIndex: 'artist' }
    ],

    initComponent: function() {
        this.bbar = [
```

```
            '->',
                { xtype: 'button', text: 'Show Artist Summary',
    handler: this.onShowSummary, scope: this },
                '->'
            ];

            this.callParent(arguments);
        },

        onShowSummary: function() {
            var summary = this.getStore().collect('name').join(', ');

            Ext.Msg.alert('Artists', summary);
        }
    });
```

Here's our `MvcEx1v4.view.List` class in `view/List.js`. It's a fairly straightforward grid that uses a store called `'Albums'` and a button on the bottom toolbar to generate the artist summary. Notice that the event handler to generate this summary is included in the view:

```
// view/Detail.js
Ext.define('MvcEx1v4.view.Detail', {
    extend: 'Ext.Container',
    alias: 'widget.app-detail',
    html: 'Double-click an Album to select'
});
```

Our second view is `MvcEx1v4.view.Detail` in `view/Detail.js`. This is just a simple container with some placeholder HTML. Finally, we have the application viewport that holds our views:

```
// view/Viewport.js
Ext.define('MvcEx1v4.view.Viewport', {
    extend: 'Ext.container.Viewport',
    requires:['MvcEx1v4.view.List'],
    layout: 'hbox',
    defaults: {
        width: 250,
        margin: 20
    },
    items: [{ xtype: 'app-list' }, { xtype: 'app-detail' }]
});
```

Again, there are a few surprises here. Notice that we refer to our views using the values we defined in their individual "alias" configuration options: app-detail and app-list. We've taken care of the "V" in MVC, so let's move on to "M" and see where our data comes from, as shown in the following code:

```
// model/Album.js
Ext.define('MvcEx1v4.model.Album', {
    extend: 'Ext.data.Model',

    fields: [
        { name: 'name', type: 'string' },
        { name: 'artist', type: 'string' }
    ]
});
// store/Albums.js
Ext.define('MvcEx1v4.store.Albums', {
extend: 'Ext.data.JsonStore',

    model: 'MvcEx1v4.model.Album',

    data: [
        { name: 'In Rainbows', artist: 'Radiohead' },
        { name: 'Swim', artist: 'Caribou' }
    ]
});
```

For easier reading, I've combined the code for the model and the store that consumes it. The data for this application is added inline using the data configuration option (just to avoid messing around with server-side Ajax calls). Let's look at the final facet of MVC, the controller:

```
// controller/Album.js
Ext.define('MvcEx1v4.controller.Album', {
    extend: 'Ext.app.Controller',

    refs: [{
        ref: 'detail',
        selector: 'app-detail'
    }],

    init: function() {
        this.control({
            '.app-list': {
                itemdblclick: this.onAlbumDblClick
```

```
            }
        });
    },

    onAlbumDblClick: function(list, record) {
            var html = Ext.String.format('{0} by {1}',
    record.get('name'), record.get('artist'));

            this.getDetail().getEl().setHTML(html);
    }
});
```

Here's where things start to deviate from the straightforward view to data implementation you'd typically see in an Ext JS v3 application. We're introducing a new class that brings in a new architectural construct. But to what end?

The answer is communication. The controller, as we know, is the glue that sticks together the "M" and the "V". In our simple example here, it's giving us a mechanism to let the list view talk to the detail view without either of them having to be aware of each other. The control feature is used to determine what to do when the list view (aliased as app-list) fires an itemdblclick event.

We supply the onAlbumDblClick method to respond to this event. In here, we want to talk to our detail view (aliased as app-detail). We previously used the refs configuration option to help with this. Let's break it down:

```
refs: [{
    // We give our ref the name "detail". This autogenerates
    // a method on the controller called "getDetail" which
    // will enable us to access the view defined by the selector.
    ref: 'detail',

    // The selector is passed to Ext.ComponentQuery.query,
    // so any valid component query would work here. We're
    // just directly referencing the app-detail alias we
    // set up in the view's configuration
    selector: 'app-detail'
}]
```

Long story short, the refs feature gives us a shorthand way to access a view. In the onAlbumDblClick handler, we use the autogenerated this.getDetail() method that refs provides. This gives us a reference to the view. We can then set HTML of its view's element based on the event data provided by the list view.

How does it help your application

Let's recap. How are we better off than in Ext JS 3 before we had any of this MVC stuff involved?

- We've got clear separation of presentation and data with views and models
- We have a way of orchestrating different parts of our application using controllers
- We've got a way of splitting our app into logic units by using multiple controllers with associated views

Not only does this lend itself to a good design by keeping different bits of functionality very separate from the outset, but it also gives us a good platform for maintainability purposes because it imposes a very specific way of working.

MVC and the illusion of choice

Given everything we've just covered, you'd think that MVC was the holy grail of development. It's tried and tested, adaptable, and supported by Ext JS. In fact, there are some cases in which it's useful to go a little further and augment MVC.

To use Ext JS-specific examples, let's look at what happens when you start writing a more complicated application. Your controllers can react to the events that your views fire, orchestrate interactions between different views, and even stores other controllers. So, does this mean that you put your event handlers in your controllers, your views, or a combination of both?

This is a key question, which can be answered simply by being very strict with your development process from the beginning. MVC provides the "illusion of choice"; in this, it offers a large variety of ways to set up your application, but only a few that will result in a healthy application.

How about when you have a central source of data, but different views that consume it? You might want to have this data in slightly different forms for each view. Does the view itself take responsibility for shaping this data?

Ext JS 5 implements a pattern called **model-view-viewmodel (MVVM)** that tries to address these questions.

Introducing MVVM

MVVM can be seen as an augmentation of MVC. Introducing the view model concept, it recognizes that not every view concerned with a dataset will be using this data in the same way. It adds a layer of indirection between a view and a model, called a view model, to solve this issue. It also keeps separation of concerns to the fore; why should the model, which is dealing with our data be concerned about anything to do with our view, which is dealing with presentation?

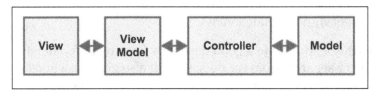

A typical representation of MVVM

How does Ext JS use MVVM?

With Ext JS 5, MVVM is wholeheartedly embraced. The sample application structure that Sencha Cmd generates will provide a `ViewModel` class alongside the `View` class. This has tight integration into the `View` class via new configuration options, which make it a first-class citizen when trying to solve the common problems that arise in a large MVC application, as we discussed earlier.

In addition, a `ViewController` class is created to encapsulate the logic you'd normally put in a view or in a standard controller. It removes the question of where to put event handlers that are concerned with things internal to the view, rather than event handlers that will be passing off events to other parts of your application.

Getting our MVVM started

We started by generating an Ext JS 5 application template using Sencha Cmd and used it as a basis to build an implementation of our example album list application. The default Ext JS 5 template uses an MVVM implementation as follows:

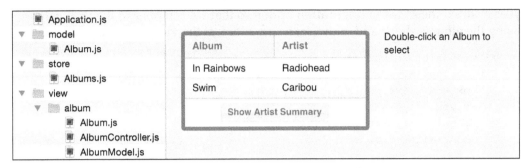

Our example app ported to Ext JS 5's MVVM architecture

The most immediate difference you'll notice is that we've lost our controllers directory and there's a lot more going on in the views directory. Let's break it down:

```
// model/Album.js
Ext.define('MvvmEx1v5.model.Album', {
    extend: 'Ext.data.Model',

    fields: [
        { name: 'name', type: 'string' },
        { name: 'artist', type: 'string' }
    ]
});
```

The album model is identical to the previous example, although note that we've changed the application name to MvvmEx1v5. The store is only very slightly different:

```
// store/Albums.js
Ext.define('MvvmEx1v5.store.Albums', {
    extend: 'Ext.data.JsonStore',

    model: 'MvvmEx1v5.model.Album',

    data: [
        { name: 'In Rainbows', artist: 'Radiohead' },
        { name: 'Swim', artist: 'Caribou' }
    ]
});
```

We've added the `alias` configuration option so that we can refer to the store later using the albums shorthand. Now, let's take a look at the views directory:

```
// view/album/Album.js
Ext.define('MvvmEx1v5.view.album.Album', {
    extend: 'Ext.container.Container',
    xtype: 'app-album',
    requires: ['Ext.grid.Panel'],
    controller: 'album',
    layout: 'hbox',
    defaults: {
        width: 250,
        margin: 20
    },
    items: [
        {
            xtype: 'grid',
            reference: 'list',
            viewModel: 'album',
            bind: '{albums}',
            forceFit: true,
            frame: true,
            margin: '20 10 20 20',
            columns: [
                { text: 'Album', dataIndex: 'name' },
                { text: 'Artist', dataIndex: 'artist' }
            ],
            bbar: [
                '->',
                { xtype: 'button', text: 'Show Artist Summary',
handler: 'onShowSummary' },
                '->'
            ],
            listeners: {
                rowdblclick: 'onAlbumDblClick'
            }
        },
        { xtype: 'container', margin: '20 10', reference:
'detail', width: 150, html: 'Double-click an Album to select' }
    ]
});
```

We've combined the previous `app-list` and `app-detail` views into a single `app-albums` view, and whereas before we had the logic to build the album summary in the view, we now define only the event handler and the logic goes elsewhere. This view is now 100 percent presentation and defers all the complicated stuff to other classes.

Note that we have a `controller` configuration option that defines the view controller to use for this view class. Our grid component has several interesting configuration options too:

- `reference`: We use this later to get hold of this component from the view controller.
- `viewModel`: This is the alias of the view model this component will use.
- `bind`: This defines how the view talks to the view model. We're using the simplest binding (the grid's default `bindProperty` is store), so here we're essentially just setting the store `config` to `'albums'`.

Now, let's move on to our album view model:

```
// view/album/AlbumModel.js
Ext.define('MvvmEx1v5.view.album.AlbumModel', {
    extend: 'Ext.app.ViewModel',
    alias: 'viewmodel.album',

    requires: [
        'MvcEx1.store.Albums'
        'Ext.Msg'
    ],
    stores: {
        albums: {
            type: 'albums'
        }
    },

    buildSummary: function() {
        return this.getStore('albums').collect('name').join(', ');
    }
});
```

Also, here we have one of these places that now contain this logic. A view model takes data from a model (or stores) and presents it in a way suitable for its matching view. In this case, we take the data from the `'albums'` store (referenced in the `type` configuration option by the albums alias we mentioned earlier). It provides a `buildSummary` method that transforms the stored data into a string ready to be used in the UI as follows:

```
// view/album/AlbumController.js
Ext.define('MvvmEx1v5.view.album.AlbumController', {
    extend: 'Ext.app.ViewController',
    alias: 'controller.album',

    onShowSummary: function() {
        var summary =
this.lookupReference('list').getViewModel().buildSummary();

        Ext.Msg.alert('Artists', summary);
    },

    onAlbumDblClick: function(list, record) {
        var html = Ext.String.format('{0} by {1}',
record.get('name'), record.get('artist'));
        this.lookupReference('detail').getEl().setHtml(html);
    }
});
```

Finally, we have our view controller, which is where any logic that manages our view should go. Event handlers defined in the view controller will automatically be available to the matching view.

Are we better off?

Yes, we're better off because we're more organized. We know where all of our application bits go, and although we've got a lot more files than a straightforward one-class Ext JS application, we'll always know where to look to change the configuration of a view, where to find our logic for the albums, or where to shape the information we pull from a store.

One important point about this example is that we forego the overarching controller from the first example in favor of a view controller. Here, this makes sense; we want this view controller to be concerned only with albums, not with other parts of the application. However, a higher-level controller is still a valid piece of the Ext JS MVVM architecture and can be reintroduced in situations that require a way to coordinate an application at a higher level than a view controller.

A brief interlude regarding stores

Throughout this entire chapter, we've talked a lot about models, but never specifically about stores despite using them in our example applications. Why isn't it "SVC" or "SVVM"?

In Ext JS, a store is a specific class, which brings specific functionality and is tightly bound into your application. However, in a simple MVC or MVVM implementation, the "store" could just be an array of models, rather than being a separate architectural feature. So, a store is really just a way of collecting models together and Ext JS happens to be the place where we can do lots of extra things (such as sorting, filtering, and batching).

Inter-communication

We've shown how to create a simple application that uses several moving parts to create a logical unit. Thanks to the MVVM pattern, we have a methodology that allows the parts of this unit to communicate without having to be explicitly tied to the implementation details of other parts.

When we extend our application, we'll have several of these logical units, perhaps, an artist section in addition to an album section. Now, these have to communicate with each other in turn. This represents one of the main problems in software architecture: how to allow albums and artists to talk to each other without contaminating either component with details of the other. It's a problem that scales in direct proportion to the size and complexity of an application.

The main event

One approach to this problem is to allow your application parts to fire off custom events, each containing a payload that can be consumed by any other part of your application that might be interested in them.

In fact, we see this in action all the time in web development. Event handlers are an integral part of JavaScript programming as we bind functions to the events thrown by user interface elements (such as buttons) or to browser events (such as `window.onload`). We've touched on this in our example code already; our view fired off a `rowdblclick` event that was handled by our view controller.

In complex applications, developers will often implement a feature called an event bus, a way of taking the events that application components fire off and transporting them to various subscribers. Since Ext JS 4.2, event domains have allowed developers to incorporate a similar feature into their code base.

Event domains

Event domains allow controllers to react to events from various different sources in your application. The default sources are:

- **Components**: These are events fired from components. This is essentially the functionality that `Ext.app.Controller.control()` provides by handling events from classes that extend `Ext.Component` and bind them to event listeners.

- **Global**: These are events fired from a single global source and used to bind arbitrary application-wide events.

- **Controller**: These are events fired from other controllers.

- **Store**: These are events fired from a store.

- **Direct**: These are events fired from classes that extend `Ext.direct.Provider`. This is only used if you require `Ext.direct.Manager` in your application.

Some event domains allow you to filter the received events by a selector (usually the ID associated with the source), but in the Component case, you can use a full-blown `Ext.Component` query. This allows you to have finer-grained control on how to subscribe to events.

An event domain example

Let's go back to our MVVM album example we created earlier. Our view had handler and listener configurations that tied view events to event handlers that we put in our view controller. However, event domains allow us to remove this tie and give all of the control to the view component. In `view/album/Album.js` in our previous example, we can remove the listener config on the grid and the handler on the button and then add the following code to `view/album/AlbumController.js`:

```
init: function() {
    this.listen({
        component: {
            'app-album grid': {
                'rowdblclick': 'onAlbumDblClick'
            },
            'app-album button': {
                'click': 'onShowSummary'
            }
        }
    });
},
```

This is slightly more verbose, so look at what exactly is happening here. We pass an object to `this.listen`, which contains a component property; this indicates we are configuring the Component Event Domain. Inside here, we use two selectors, one for the grid itself and one for the summary button, and inside these definitions we specify the event we are binding to and the event handlers.

This gives us the ability to remove anything clever from the view and put it all in the view controller. The view deals purely with presentation and the view controller deals with the logic.

Using custom events

We've shown how event domains can be used to separate our code concerns even further, but now, you'll see how they can help orchestrate interactions at a higher level. For this, let's take a look at a theoretical situation in which our application has grown to incorporate multiple views and view controllers:

```
// view/search/SearchController.js
Ext.define('EventDomain1.view.search.SearchController', {
    extend: 'Ext.app.ViewController',
    alias: 'controller.search',

    init: function() {
        this.listen({
            component: {
                'app-search button': {
                    'click': 'onSearchSubmit'
                }
            }
        });
    },

    onSearchSubmit: function() {
        var val = this.lookupReference('searchfield').getValue();
        this.fireEvent('search', val);
    }
});
```

We've created a new `SearchController`, which is the view controller for a new `Search` view. We use `this.listen` to listen for events on the component event domain and filter them using the selector `'app-search button'` (a button within our new `Search` view). When the button is clicked on, we trigger an event handler method called `onSearchSubmit`.

We extract the search term that the user entered and then fire a second event, passing the search term as the event data. The event we fire is called `'search'` and rather than being tied to a button or other UI component, it can be subscribed to by other parts of the application as a pure application event. Let's take a look at how it could be consumed:

```
// partial /view/album/AlbumController.js
init: function() {
    this.listen({
        controller: {
            '*': {
                'search': 'onSearch'
            }
        }
    });
}
```

This is a snippet of the `AlbumController` we've seen before with some extra goodness. With `this.listen`, we use the `'*'` selector to allow all controllers on the event domain. Then, we specify that we want to handle the search event with the `onSearch` handler method. This should all be feeling pretty familiar by now! The handler method could be as simple as the following code:

```
onSearch: function(searchTerm) {
    var list = this.lookupReference('list');
    list.getViewModel().search('searchTerm');
}
```

Assume that we created a `search` method on the view model. With just a small amount of code, we allowed two distinct parts of our application to communicate using information about our application rather than information about themselves. This is key to keeping the search part of this code unaware about the albums part and allows very clear-cut divisions between them. This provides easier testing through separation of concerns, better maintainability, and easier comprehension of how the application is structured.

Summary

MVC and MVVM are key architectural constructs that we need to firmly understand before starting on a new project. Given that they're so embedded in Ext JS, it's even more important to have a good grasp of the ideas behind them and why implementing such patterns will assist in the way we construct our code base. In the next chapter, we'll move on to more practical examples of structuring an Ext JS application, incorporating MVVM concepts with a variety of other ideas that set out a strong platform to build on.

3
Application Structure

We previously discussed how growing an application organically without any sense of architecture could result in an unmaintainable mess of spaghetti code. One of the great things about imposing structure is that it automatically gives predictability (a kind of filing system with in which we immediately know where a particular piece
of code should live).

The same applies to the files that make up your application. Certainly, we could put all of our files in the root of the website, mixing CSS, JavaScript, configuration and HTML files in a long alphabetical list, but we'd be losing out on a number of opportunities to keep our application organized. In this chapter, we'll look at:

- Ideas to structure your code
- The layout of a typical Ext JS application
- Use of singletons, mixins, and inheritance
- Why global state is a bad thing

Structuring your application is like keeping your house in order. You'll know where to find your car keys, and you'll be prepared for unexpected guests.

Ideas for structure

One of the ways in which code is structured in large applications involves namespacing (the practice of dividing code up by naming identifiers). One namespace could contain everything relating to Ajax, whereas another could contain classes related to mathematics. Programming languages (such as C# and Java) even incorporate namespaces as a first-class language construct to help with code organization.

Separating code from directories based on namespace becomes a sensible extension of this:

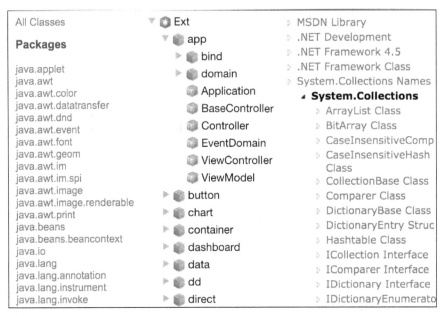

From left: Java's Platform API, Ext JS 5, and .NET Framework

A namespace identifier is made up of one or more name tokens, such as "Java" or "Ext", "Ajax" or "Math", separated by a symbol, in most cases a full stop/period. The top level name will be an overarching identifier for the whole package (such as "Ext") and will become less specific as names are added and you drill down into the code base.

The Ext JS source code makes heavy use of this practice to partition UI components, utility classes, and all the other parts of the framework, so let's look at a real example. The `GridPanel` component is perhaps one of the most complicated in the framework; a large collection of classes that contribute to features (such as columns, cell editing, selection, and grouping). These work together to create a highly powerful UI widget. Take a look at the following files that make up `GridPanel`:

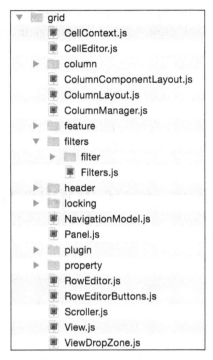

The Ext JS grid component's directory structure

The `grid` directory reflects the `Ext.grid` namespace. Likewise, the subdirectories are child namespaces with the deepest namespace being `Ext.grid.filters.filter`.

The main `Panel` and `View` classes: `Ext.grid.Grid` and `Ext.grid.View` respectively are there in the main director. Then, additional pieces of functionality, for example, the `Column` class and the various column subclasses are further grouped together in their own subdirectories. We can also see a `plugins` directory, which contains a number of grid-specific plugins.

 Ext JS actually already has an `Ext.plugins` namespace. It contains classes to support the plugin infrastructure as well as plugins that are generic enough to apply across the entire framework. In the event of uncertainty regarding the best place in the code base for a plugin, we might mistakenly have put it in `Ext.plugins`. Instead, Ext JS follows best practice and creates a new, more specific namespace underneath `Ext.grid`.

Going back to the root of the Ext JS framework, we can see that there are only a few files at the top level. In general, these will be classes that are either responsible for orchestrating other parts of the framework (such as EventManager or StoreManager) or classes that are widely reused across the framework (such as Action or Component). Any more specific functionality should be namespaced in a suitably specific way.

As a rule of thumb, you can take your inspiration from the organization of the Ext JS framework, though as a framework rather than a full-blown application. It's lacking some of the structural aspects we'll talk about shortly.

Getting to know your application

When generating an Ext JS application using Sencha Cmd, we end up with a code base that adheres to the concept of namespacing in class names and in the directory structure, as shown here:

The structure created with Sencha Cmd's "generate app" feature

We should be familiar with all of this, as it was already covered when we discussed MVVM in Ext JS. Having said that, there are some parts of this that are worth examining further to see whether they're being used to the full.

/overrides

This is a handy one to help us fall into a positive and predictable pattern. There are some cases where you need to override Ext JS functionality on a global level. Maybe, you want to change the implementation of a low-level class (such as `Ext.data.proxy.Proxy`) to provide custom batching behavior for your application. Sometimes, you might even find a bug in Ext JS itself and use an override to hotfix until the next point release. The `overrides` directory provides a logical place to put these changes (just mirror the directory structure and namespacing of the code you're overriding). This also provides us with a helpful rule, that is, subclasses go in `/app` and overrides go in `/overrides`.

/.sencha

This contains configuration information and build files used by Sencha Cmd. In general, I'd say try and avoid fiddling around in here too much until you know Sencha Cmd inside out because there's a chance you'll end up with nasty conflicts if you try and upgrade to a newer version of Sencha Cmd. Fortunately, *Chapter 4, Sencha Cmd*, is all about Sencha Cmd, where we'll dive deep into this folder.

bootstrap.js, bootstrap.json, and bootstrap.css

The Ext JS class system has powerful dependency management through the `requires` feature, which gives us the means to create a build that contains only the code that's in use. The bootstrap files contain information about the minimum CSS and JavaScript needed to run your application as provided by the dependency system. As we'll see in *Chapter 4, Sencha Cmd*, you can even create custom bootstrap files depending on your requirements.

/packages

In a similar way to how Ruby has RubyGems and Node.js has npm, Sencha Cmd has the concept of packages (a bundle which can be pulled into your application from a local or remote source).

This allows you to reuse and publish bundles of functionality (including CSS, images, and other resources) to reduce copy and paste of code, and share your work with the Sencha community. This directory is empty until you configure packages to be used in your app.

/resources and SASS

SASS is a technology that aids in the creation of complex CSS by promoting reuse and bringing powerful features (such as mixins and functions) to your style sheets. Ext JS uses SASS for its theme files and encourages you to use it as well. We'll look at this in *Chapter 4, Sencha Cmd.*

index.html

We know that index.html is the root HTML page of our application. It can be customized as you see fit (although, it's rare you'll need to). There's one caveat and it's written in a comment in the file already:

```
<!-- The line below must be kept intact for Sencha Cmd to build
your application -->
<script id="microloader" type="text/javascript"
src="bootstrap.js"></script>
```

We know what bootstrap.js refers to (loading up our application and starting to fulfill its dependencies according to the current build), so heed the comment and leave this script tag well alone!

/build and build.xml

The /build directory contains build artifacts (the files created when the build process is run). If you run a production build, then you'll get a directory inside /build called production and you should use only these files when deploying. The build.xml file allows you to avoid tweaking some of the files in /.sencha when you want to add some extra functionality to a build process. If you want to do something before, during, or after the build, this is the place to do it. We'll come back to the build process when we look at Sencha Cmd in *Chapter 4, Sencha Cmd.*

app.js

This is the main JavaScript entry point to your application. The comments in this file advise avoiding editing it in order to allow Sencha Cmd to upgrade it in the future. The Application.js file at /app/Application.js can be edited without fear of conflicts and will enable you to do the majority of things you might need to do.

app.json

This contains configuration options related to Sencha Cmd and booting your application. We'll cover this more in *Chapter 4, Sencha Cmd*.

When we refer to the subject of this book as a JavaScript application, we need to remember that it's just a website composed of HTML, CSS, and JavaScript as well. However, when dealing with a large application that needs to target different environments, it's incredibly useful to augment this simplicity with tools that assist in the development process. At first, it may seem that the default application template contains a lot of cruft, but they are the key to supporting the tools that will help you craft a solid product.

Cultivating your code

As you build your application, there will come a point at which you create a new class and yet it doesn't logically fit into the directory structure Sencha Cmd created for you. Let's look at a few examples.

I'm a lumberjack – let's go log in

Many applications have a centralized `SessionManager` to take care of the currently logged in user, perform authentication operations, and set up persistent storage for session credentials. There's only one `SessionManager` in an application. A truncated version might look like this:

```
/**
 * @class CultivateCode.SessionManager
 * @extends extendsClass
 * Description
 */
Ext.define('CultivateCode.SessionManager', {
    singleton: true,
    isLoggedIn: false,

    login: function(username, password) {
        // login impl
    },


    logout: function() {
        // logout impl
    },
```

```
        isLoggedIn() {
            return isLoggedIn;
        }
    });
```

We create a singleton class. This class doesn't have to be instantiated using the new keyword. As per its class name, `CultivateCode.SessionManager`, it's a top-level class and so it goes in the top-level directory. In a more complicated application, there could be a dedicated `Session` class too and some other ancillary code, so we'd create the following structure:

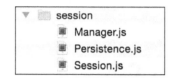

The directory structure for our session namespace

What about user interface elements? There's an informal practice in the Ext JS community that helps here. We want to create an extension that shows the coordinates of the currently selected cell (similar to cell references in Excel). In this case, we'd create an ux directory — user experience or user extensions — and then go with the naming conventions of the Ext JS framework:

```
Ext.define('CultivateCode.ux.grid.plugins.CoordViewer', {
    extend: 'Ext.plugin.Abstract',
    alias: 'plugin.coordviewer',

    mixins: {
        observable: 'Ext.util.Observable'
    },

    init: function(grid) {
        this.mon(grid.view, 'cellclick', this.onCellClick, this);
    },

    onCellClick: function(view, cell, colIdx, record, row, rowIdx,
e) {
        var coords = Ext.String.format('Cell is at {0}, {1}',
colIdx, rowIdx)

        Ext.Msg.alert('Coordinates', coords);
    }
});
```

It looks a little like this, triggering when you click on a grid cell:

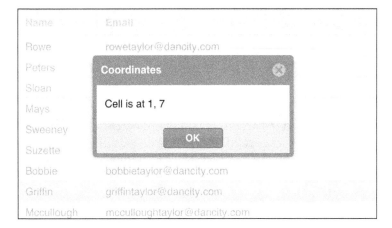

Also, the corresponding directory structure follows directly from the namespace:

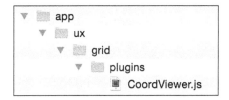

You can probably see a pattern emerging already.

 We've mentioned before that organizing an application is often about setting things up to fall into a position of success. A positive pattern like this is a good sign that you're doing things right.

We've got a predictable system that should enable us to create new classes without having to think too hard about where they're going to sit in our application. Let's take a look at one more example of a mathematics helper class (one that is a little less obvious).

Again, we can look at the Ext JS framework itself for inspiration. There's an `Ext.util` namespace containing over 20 general classes that just don't fit anywhere else. So, in this case, let's create `CultivateCode.util.Mathematics` that contains our specialized methods for numerical work:

```
Ext.define('CultivateCode.util.Mathematics', {
    singleton: true,
```

```
        square: function(num) {
            return Math.pow(num, 2);
        },

        circumference: function(radius) {
            return 2 * Math.PI * radius;
        }
    });
```

There is one caveat here and it's an important one. There's a real danger that rather than thinking about the namespace for your code and its place in your application, a lot of stuff ends up under the `utils` namespace, thereby defeating the whole purpose. Take time to carefully check whether there's a more suitable location for your code before putting it in the `utils` bucket.

This is particularly applicable if you're considering adding lots of code to a single class in the `utils` namespace. Looking again at Ext JS, there are lots of specialized namespaces (such as `Ext.state` or `Ext.draw`). If you were working with an application with lots of mathematics, perhaps you'd be better off with the following namespace and directory structure:

```
Ext.define('CultivateCode.math.Combinatorics', {
    // implementation here!
});
Ext.define('CultivateCode.math.Geometry', {
    // implementation here!
});
```

The directory structure for the math namespace is shown in the following screenshot:

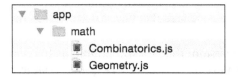

This is another situation where there is no definitive right answer. It will come to you with experience and will depend entirely on the application you're building. Over time, putting together these high-level applications, building blocks will become second nature.

Money can't buy class

Now that we're learning where our classes belong, we need to make sure that we're actually using the right type of class. Here's the standard way of instantiating an Ext JS class:

```
var geometry = Ext.create('MyApp.math.Geometry');
```

However, think about your code. Think how rare it's in Ext JS to actually manually invoke `Ext.create`. So, how else are the class instances created?

Singletons

A singleton is simply a class that only has one instance across the lifetime of your application. There are quite a number of singleton classes in the Ext JS framework. While the use of singletons in general is a contentious point in software architecture, they tend to be used fairly well in Ext JS.

It could be that you prefer to implement the mathematical functions (we discussed earlier) as a singleton. For example, the following command could work:

```
var area = CultivateCode.math.areaOfCircle(radius);
```

However, most developers would implement a circle class:

```
var circle = Ext.create('CultivateCode.math.Circle', { radius:
radius });
var area = circle.getArea();
```

This keeps the circle-related functionality partitioned off into the circle class. It also enables us to pass the circle variable round to other functions and classes for additional processing.

On the other hand, look at `Ext.Msg`. Each of the methods here are fired and forgotten, there's never going to be anything to do further actions on. The same is true of `Ext.Ajax`. So, once more we find ourselves with a question that does not have a definitive answer. It depends entirely on the context.

 This is going to happen a lot, but it's a good thing! This book isn't going to teach you a list of facts and figures; it's going to teach you to think for yourself. Read other people's code and learn from experience. This isn't coding by numbers!

The other place you might find yourself reaching for the power of the singleton is when you're creating an overarching manager class (such as the inbuilt `StoreManager` or our previous `SessionManager` example). One of the objections about singletons is that they tend to be abused to store lots of global state and break down the separation of concerns we've set up in our code, as follows:

```
Ext.define('CultivateCode.ux.grid.GridManager', {

    singleton: true,
    currentGrid: null,
    grids: [],

    add: function(grid) {
        this.grids.push(grid);
    },

    setCurrentGrid: function(grid) {
        this.focusedGrid = grid;
    }
});
```

No one wants to see this sort of thing in a code base. It brings behavior and state to a high level in the application. In theory, any part of the code base could call this manager with unexpected results. Instead, we'd do something like this:

```
Ext.define('CultivateCode.view.main.Main', {
    extend: 'CultivateCode.ux.GridContainer',

    currentGrid: null,
    grids: [],

    add: function(grid) {
        this.grids.push(grid);
    },

    setCurrentGrid: function(grid) {
        this.currentGrid = grid;
    }
});
```

We still have the same behavior (a way of collecting together grids), but now, it's limited to a more contextually appropriate part of the grid. Also, we're working with the MVVM system. We avoid global state and organize our code in a more correct manner. A win all round.

As a general rule, if you can avoid using a singleton, do so. Otherwise, think very carefully to make sure that it's the right choice for your application and that a standard class wouldn't better fit your requirements. In the previous example, we could have taken the easy way out and used a manager singleton, but it would have been a poor choice that would compromise the structure of our code.

Mixins

We're used to the concept of inheriting from a subclass in Ext JS—a grid extends a panel to take on all of its functionality. Mixins provide a similar opportunity to reuse functionality to augment an existing class with a thin slice of behavior. In *Code Complete Second Edition*, Steve McConnell, Microsoft Press US, Section 6.3, McConnell says:

> *"Think of containment as a "has a" relationship. A car "has an" engine, a person "has a" name, etc."*

> *"Think of inheritance as an "is a" relationship. A car "is a" vehicle, a person "is a" mammal, etc."*

An Ext.Panel "is an" Ext.Component, but it also "has a" pinnable feature that provides a pin tool via the Ext.panel.Pinnable mixin.

In your code, you should be looking at mixins to provide a feature, particularly in cases where this feature can be reused. In the next example, we'll create a UI mixin called shakeable, which provides a UI component with a shake method that draws the user's attention by rocking it from side to side:

```
Ext.define('CultivateCode.util.Shakeable', {
    mixinId: 'shakeable',

    shake: function() {
        var el = this.el,
            box = el.getBox(),
            left = box.x - (box.width / 3),
            right = box.x + (box.width / 3),
            end = box.x;

        el.animate({
            duration: 400,
            keyframes: {
                33: {
                    x: left
                },
```

```
        66: {
            x: right
        },
        100: {
            x: end
        }
    }
  });
 }
});
```

We use the `animate` method (which itself is actually mixed in `Ext.Element`) to set up some animation keyframes to move the component's element first left, then right, then back to its original position. Here's a class that implements it:

```
Ext.define('CultivateCode.ux.button.ShakingButton', {
    extend: 'Ext.Button',
    mixins: ['CultivateCode.util.Shakeable'],
    xtype: 'shakingbutton'
});
```

Also it's used like this:

```
var btn = Ext.create('CultivateCode.ux.button.ShakingButton', {
    text: 'Shake It!'
});
btn.on('click', function(btn) {
    btn.shake();
});
```

The button has taken on the new shake method provided by the mixin. Now, if we'd like a class to have the `shakeable` feature, we can reuse this mixin where necessary.

In addition, mixins can simply be used to pull out the functionality of a class into logical chunks, rather than having a single file of many thousands of lines. `Ext.Component` is an example of this. In fact, most of its core functionality is found in classes that are mixed in `Ext.Component`.

This is also helpful when navigating a code base. Methods that work together to build a feature can be grouped and set aside in a tidy little package. Let's take a look at a practical example of how an existing class could be refactored using a mixin. Here's the skeleton of the original:

```
Ext.define('CultivateCode.ux.form.MetaPanel', {
    extend: 'Ext.form.Panel',
```

```
    initialize: function() {
        this.callParent(arguments);
        this.addPersistenceEvents();
    },

    loadRecord: function(model) {
        this.buildItemsFromRecord(model);
        this.callParent(arguments);
    },

    buildItemsFromRecord: function(model) {
        // Implementation
    },

    buildFieldsetsFromRecord: function(model){
        // Implementation
    },

    buildItemForField: function(field){
        // Implementation
    },

    isStateAvailable: function(){
        // Implementation
    },

    addPersistenceEvents: function(){
        // Implementation
    },

    persistFieldOnChange: function(){
        // Implementation
    },

    restorePersistedForm: function(){
        // Implementation
    },

    clearPersistence: function(){
        // Implementation
    }
});
```

This MetaPanel does two things that the normal FormPanel does not:

- It reads the Ext.data.Fields from an Ext.data.Model and automatically generates a form layout based on these fields. It can also generate field sets if the fields have the same group configuration value.

- When the values of the form change, it persists them to localStorage so that the user can navigate away and resume completing the form later. This is useful for long forms.

In reality, implementing these features would probably require additional methods to the ones shown in the previous code skeleton. As the two extra features are clearly defined, it's easy enough to refactor this code to better describe our intent:

```
Ext.define('CultivateCode.ux.form.MetaPanel', {
    extend: 'Ext.form.Panel',

    mixins: [
        // Contains methods:
        // - buildItemsFromRecord
        // - buildFieldsetsFromRecord
        // - buildItemForField
        'CultivateCode.ux.form.Builder',

        // - isStateAvailable
        // - addPersistenceEvents
        // - persistFieldOnChange
        // - restorePersistedForm
        // - clearPersistence
        'CultivateCode.ux.form.Persistence'
    ],

    initialize: function() {
        this.callParent(arguments);
        this.addPersistenceEvents();
    },

    loadRecord: function(model) {
        this.buildItemsFromRecord(model);
        this.callParent(arguments);
    }
});
```

We have a much shorter file and the behavior we're including in this class is described a lot more concisely. Rather than seven or more method bodies that may span a couple of hundred lines of code, we have two mixin lines and the relevant methods extracted to a well-named mixin class.

The solution to pollution

In essence, we're striving to make sure that a newcomer to a project is never surprised by what they see. Everything should be clearly labeled, decisions should have logic behind them, and code should be in a place that makes sense for its functionality. We've briefly touched on how a namespace (such as utils) can become a "bucket" for code that doesn't immediately fit. There are a couple of other situations in which we find ourselves creating a dumping ground for functions that nobody knows what to do with.

A global solution to a local problem

Our hero, the plucky programmer with a lot of heart and a burgeoning talent, is writing their latest application when they realize something.

I'm going to need this function a lot; potentially, in most of my UI components.

Worried, they consider the best way to implement it, then the best place for it to fit in the existing code base.

I need to call it from anywhere in the application. Also, my application class is already available from everywhere in the app; I'll hang it off there. MyApp.myFunc(), here we come!

And so our hero starts down the road to madness. MyApp.isUserLoggedIn(), they ask? MyApp.isProduction() or MyApp.isStaging(), they wonder? Also, for convenient access to configuration, we have the MyApp.validNames and MyApp.apiUrl arrays.

Look on my global state ye mighty, and despair!

A little melodrama to get the point across. It's very easy to use your application singleton as an easy catch-all as shown here:

```
Ext.define('CultivateCode.Application', {
    extend: 'Ext.app.Application',

    name: 'CultivateCode',
```

```
        searchCfg: {
            mode: 'beginsWith',
            dir: 'asc'
        },

        isLoggedIn: false,
        isSecure: false,

        launch: function () {
            this.setupAjaxOverrides();
            this.performCookieCheck();

            Ext.apply(Ext.util.Format, {
                defaultDateFormat: 'd F Y'
            });
        },

        setMasked: function(mask) {
            // Implementation
        },

        setupAjaxOverrides: function() {
            // Implementation
        },

        onAjaxError: function(connection, resp, opt) {
            // Implementation
        }

        performCookieCheck: function() {
            // Implementation
        }
    });
```

What would be the right thing to do here? Well, searchCfg needs to be moved to the place it's used, perhaps a search model or view model, maybe on the UI component responsible for search.

The Ajax overrides and error handling could be moved to the /overrides folder and positioned within their correct namespaces, making them much more discoverable.

The cookie check, which makes sure users have cookies enabled on their browser, could probably be retained in the application class, simply because in this app, cookies could be a requirement.

Things such as `isLoggedIn` would be best taken care of by a `SessionManager`, as we previously discussed. Still in a singleton, but a singleton that is in a more discoverable and logical place for this functionality.

In another place, we can take our cue from the Ext JS framework: `setMasked`. Rather than having this as a method on the application, Ext JS provides it as a method on each `Ext.Container`, meaning you can call it directly on panels and grids. This means that the code that masks components will no longer jump up to the global application scope and hope that it's targeting the correct container. Instead, you can be certain that you're affecting the component you're interested in and nothing more, and all without polluting your global application class.

Summary – mind your own beeswax

In this chapter, we drove several points home.

When it comes to structuring your application, make life easy for yourself. Go for the principle of least surprise and don't pile all of your classes in a single namespace.

Keep your code in manageable blocks using architectural devices such as mixins. When you look in a class, you don't want to see thousands of meandering lines, but want a concise logical unit.

Use the Ext JS framework as structural inspiration. It may not be 100 percent, but it does show us something very important, which should inform every aspect of your application architecture: having a system is always better than not having one and you should be consistent at all times.

In the next chapter, we will look at Sencha Cmd, a tool that goes hand in hand with Ext JS to help us generate, develop, and deploy our applications.

4
Sencha Cmd

In *Chapter 3*, *Application Structure*, we described the nature of an Ext JS application as, essentially, a collection of HTML, JavaScript, and CSS. Just a web page. However, taking this point of view not only oversimplifies the issue, but it also means that your application won't reach its full potential; you'll be ignoring things like dependency management, code optimization, and many other matters that a high-quality application should incorporate.

> Remember that application architecture, just like building architecture, isn't just about piecing together parts of a whole. It's about brick-and-mortar, the materials used in construction, and the methodology used to construct the final product.

Sencha Cmd can be an important part of architecting your project. It gives you a strong foundation, a smooth workflow, and a polished final product. In this chapter, we'll look at:

- What Sencha Cmd actually is
- Why Sencha Cmd is important in your development process
- The way in which it helps you build an initial application template and then assists with adding new pieces of functionality
- How it provides useful tools for the ongoing development process
- The deployment process — producing optimized builds for various platforms and customizing the build process for more specific requirements

At the end of the chapter, you will understand how and why an application built with Sencha Cmd is significantly easier to develop and deploy. You'll have a strong understanding of the various parts of Sencha Cmd and how to configure and augment it to fit your requirements.

What is Sencha Cmd?

In short, Sencha Cmd is an executable that provides a series of further commands to assist with your Sencha application development. Under the hood, it comprises a number of third-party utilities and scripts that combine to provide this functionality. Here are a few of the things it bundles in its installation:

- **PhantomJS**: This is used to manipulate web pages without using a browser interface
- **VCDIFF**: This is a tool to work out the differences between a set of files
- **Closure Compiler**: This is a tool to optimize and minify the JavaScript code
- **Jetty**: This is a tool that provides a simple HTTP server

All of this is tied together with some custom glue from Sencha, supported by Apache Ant—a build tool commonly used in the Java world.

The result is a complex yet powerfully customizable tool. The use of Ant allows almost all of the features of Sencha Cmd to be tweaked and extended, while Sencha's additions provide a straightforward command-line interface to this power.

For the application architect, Sencha Cmd provides a centralized workflow for your developers and a reproducible build process. It can speed up development time and provides a way to add customer- or business-specific deployment tasks to your team's toolset.

Why is it important?

While Ext JS was developed under the assumption that its users will most likely work with Sencha Cmd too, there's no hard and fast rule that dictates that it must be used.

 We're not going to cover the installation of Sencha Cmd here. The latest installer is available on the Sencha website (`http://www.sencha.com/`) and should be a straightforward process.

In the next few pages, we'll create a small application without using Sencha Cmd and examine a couple of sticking points we'll hit on the way.

The act of creation

One of these sticking points comes up straightaway. With Sencha Cmd, creating a new application is as easy as the following command:

```
sencha -sdk ~/<path-to-ext-sdk> generate app MyApp ./my-app
```

Within seconds, Sencha Cmd creates a new directory called `my-app` containing the following:

- The specified Ext JS SDK
- An app directory containing model, controller, store, and view directories
- The `app.js`, `app.json`, and `Application.js` files
- The `index.html` file
- The Bootstrap files
- A sass directory with configuration files
- The `.sencha` directory and a `build.xml`

Now, much of this is part of the Sencha Cmd support infrastructure that we can discard. We're going to have to manually create a lot of the preceding detailed items. Let's get started.

Let's create the application directory and copy the Ext JS SDK in here:

Bare-bones application directory

Next up is the `index.html` page. We can create a standard HTML5 page and need to hook up the JavaScript and HTML for Ext JS. In an application generated by Sencha Cmd, we'd have the Bootstrap files to help us here. They go through your application's dependency tree and autoload files accordingly. Without Sencha Cmd, we have to include these files manually. So, we end up with the following code:

```
<!DOCTYPE HTML>
<html>
<head>
    <title>NoCMD</title>
    <link rel="stylesheet" type="text/css"
href="ext/build/packages/ext-theme-neptune/build/resources/ext-
theme-neptune-all.css">
    <script type="text/javascript" src="ext/build/ext-
all.js"></script>
```

```
    <script type="text/javascript" src="ext/build/packages/ext-
theme-neptune/build/ext-theme-neptune.js"></script>
    <script type="text/javascript" src="Application.js"></script>
</head>
<body></body>
</html>
```

We can now begin to build our application, starting with a small "Hello World"
that displays a message box:

```
// Application.js
Ext.application({
    name: 'NoCMD',
    launch: function() {
        Ext.Msg.alert('Welcome', 'To our Command-free
application!');
    }
});
```

Next step is to turn this into an MVVM application. Once we've built the directory
structure by adding app, app/model, app/store, and app/view, we can add our first
view. Remember that everything we've done so far would have been created with a
single call to Sencha Cmd.

Here's the code for our view classes; the view model comes first:

```
Ext.define('NoCMD.view.main.MainModel', {
    extend: 'Ext.app.ViewModel',
    alias: 'viewmodel.main',
    data: {
        introText: 'Welcome to the Command-free MVVM
application!',
        buttonText: 'Click Me!'
    }
});
```

This is entirely standard and is followed by the view itself:

```
Ext.define('NoCMD.view.main.Main', {
    extend: 'Ext.Panel',
    requires: ['NoCMD.view.main.MainModel',
'NoCMD.view.main.MainController'],
    viewModel: 'main',
    controller: 'main',
    items: [
        { xtype: 'component', bind: { html: '{introText}' } },
```

```
        { xtype: 'button', bind: { text: '{buttonText}', handler:
    'onClickButton' } }
        ]
    });
```

Note that in comparison with our previous apps, we have to explicitly require the view model and view controller. We'll come back to this in a moment. Finally, here's the view controller:

```
Ext.define('NoCMD.view.main.MainController', {
    extend: 'Ext.app.ViewController',

    requires: [
        'Ext.MessageBox'
    ],

    alias: 'controller.main',

    onClickButton: function () {
        Ext.Msg.alert('Confirm', 'Are you sure?');
    }
});
```

Let's go back to the `requires` option. When working with Sencha Cmd, the `viewModel` and controller configuration options are parsed as auto-dependencies. When we run the meta-command (or another command such as build that calls the meta-command), it compiles your code and produces Bootstrap files that tell Ext JS how to load your application.

Without Sencha Cmd, we have no autodependencies, so they must be specified explicitly with the `requires` option. That's another couple of lines of code that we could have avoided.

Not to mention the fact that all of these view-related files could have been generated with just one command:

sencha generate view main.Main

We're already seeing how setting up our application and adding new features is simplified with Sencha Cmd. Let's look briefly at the other end of the process: deployment.

We want to ensure that our users have a production build as slim as possible to minimize download times. With Sencha Cmd, we can use the `build` command to create a set of files for deployment that meet our requirements. Sencha Cmd will parse our JavaScript files and metadata and create a minimized JS file that only contains the classes we're actually using in our application. It does this by examining the requirements that each class has and building a tree of dependencies that can be combined into a single download.

Without Sencha Cmd, where are we? Here are the steps we'll need to take on each production build:

1. Make a list of all the files used by our application (including those in the Ext JS framework itself).

2. Combine them together and then minimize them. Replace the JavaScript files we reference in `index.html` with this new file.

Remember, this is only for JavaScript! Sencha Cmd can perform a similar process for CSS and compile the application's Sass files into a single download.

 Ext JS uses `Ext.Loader`, a class that ensures the classes you require are loaded, and if not, requests the relevant files using Ajax and parses them – all on the fly. It also means that a file could be loaded from anywhere in your code that requires it – there's no single point of reference.

In truth, the nature of an Ext JS application is such that performing this kind of production optimization becomes a lengthy process and is prone to errors. In the rest of this chapter, we'll show how your builds and the rest of your workflow will become quicker, easily reproducible, and result in a higher-quality end product.

Setting up your application

Sencha Cmd supports an advanced concept described as workspaces. In complex projects, there may be the need for multiple pages or sections, in essence, applications within the larger app. Workspaces allow you to share common code (such as session management, custom UI components, and helper classes across these various subapplications). It also avoids the need to duplicate framework code (that is, the Ext JS source) across the subapps.

 The Sencha Cmd documentation has detailed documentation on workspaces at `http://docs.sencha.com/cmd/5.x/workspaces.html`.

Generating a workspace can be done with the following command:

```
sencha generate workspace ./my-workspace
```

This simply adds some configuration files for the workspace. The extra magic comes when you generate an application for this workspace:

```
sencha -sdk ~/<path-to-sdk>/ext generate app MyApp ./my-workspace/my-app
```

The key difference here is that the SDK will be held at the workspace root rather than the application root. So, the subapplications will all use the same SDK.

Alternatively, you can use Sencha Cmd to generate just an application, which we've already touched on:

```
sencha -sdk ~/<path-to-sdk>/ext generate app MyApp ./my-app
```

This will build on the standard application template we've used many times before.

While workspaces are a useful method to organize your code and promote code reuse, we're going to focus on single applications for the rest of the book. All the ideas we're discussing can be implemented on an application level without the distraction of a workspace.

The generation game

From here, we can quickly build out the skeleton of our application. The key MVVM classes are controllers, models, and views (with their associated view controllers and view models). Sencha Cmd can assist with quickly creating all of these classes.

> The generation of code using a command-line tool is often known as "scaffolding" and was popularized by Ruby On Rails. For more on the subject, refer to http://en.wikipedia.org/wiki/Scaffold_(programming).

For controllers, it's simple:

```
sencha generate controller MyController
```

The preceding command produces:

```
// app/controller/MyController.js
Ext.define('MyApp.controller.MyController', {
    extend: 'Ext.app.Controller'
});
```

Then, the model generator invoked looks like this:

`sencha generate model MyModel fullName:string,age:int`

`MyModel` is the name of the model straightforward. The next parameters allow generation of fields in the model (provided as a comma-separated list of `name:type` field pairs). In this case, we're creating two fields: `fullName` of type string and `age` of type integer. This gives us the following code:

```
// app/model/MyModel.js
Ext.define('MyApp.model.MyModel', {
    extend: 'Ext.data.Model',
    fields: [
        { name: 'name', type: 'string' },
        { name: 'age', type: 'int' }
    ]
});
```

Finally, there's the following view generator:

`sencha generate view my.MyView`

This creates a few files for us, as shown here:

```
// app/view/my/MyView.js
Ext.define("MyApp.view.my.MyView",{
    "extend": "Ext.panel.Panel",
    "controller": "my-myview",
    "viewModel": {
        "type": "my-myview"
    },
    "html": "Hello, World!!"
});

// app/view/my/MyViewController.js
Ext.define(MyApp.view.my.MyViewController', {
    extend: 'Ext.app.ViewController',
    alias: 'controller.my-myview'
});

// app/view/my/MyViewController.js
Ext.define('MyApp.view.my.MyViewModel', {
    extend: 'Ext.app.ViewModel',
    alias: 'viewmodel.my-myview',
    data: {
        name: 'MyApp'
    }
});
```

With this command, as we're creating multiple files, we have the opportunity to create a directory and corresponding namespace to contain them. In this case, we created the `my` directory at `app/view/my` for these three files.

 Pay attention to the case of names of your models, views, and controllers here. Sencha Cmd doesn't do anything special to correct the case to keep with expected naming conventions. So, whatever you type will be directly carried over to the class.

There are two more commands we can run with generate: `theme` and `package`, but we'll cover these in more detail later in *Chapter 9, A Shopping Application*, when we build a packaged component with a custom theme.

Develop in style

Now that we're up and running with a Sencha Cmd-powered application, we can start to look at the ways Sencha Cmd can ease our ongoing development process. These range from generating application metadata to compiling theme files.

Here to serve – a website

A standard HTML web page can be run directly from your computer without requiring a web server. The browser just reads the files directly from your local drive. With the increasing popularity of JavaScript-based web applications, browsers have introduced a variety of security restrictions to prevent malicious sites from reading your local filesystem.

This causes issues with Ext JS because when developing, `Ext.Loader` will dynamically load and parse the JavaScript files your application depends on from your application directory.

The best way to solve this issue is to simply run your code through a web server as the browser normally expects. Fortunately, to avoid having to configure a full-blown web server on your development machine, Sencha Cmd gives you a simple way of starting up a lightweight server in the current directory. Simply run the following command:

```
sencha web start
```

You should get an output along these lines:

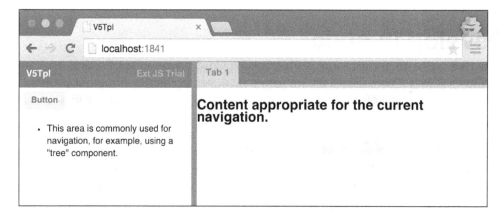

And sure enough, visit `http://localhost:1841` in your web browser and your application will be ready and waiting:

Note that we can override the port the server uses. In order to start it on port `1999`, we will issue the following command:

```
sencha web -port 1999 start
```

The Bootstrap process

Sencha Cmd's JavaScript compiler isn't just a way of concatenating and minifying. It understands your code and will process certain parts in order to simplify dependency management.

For example, a wildcard `requires` option such as `Ext.grid.*` will be expanded so that all of the files and classes under `Ext.grid` will be included. Certain configuration options, such as controller or ViewModel, will be converted into their full class reference. This is the Bootstrap process—the way in which dependency information is converted into a list of actual files to be loaded.

This metadata trickery comes with a small price. In certain situations, you need to refresh the Bootstrap data in order for Ext JS to load your application successfully. One way of doing this is to run the following command:

```
sencha app refresh
```

This will quickly rebuild the files needed to Bootstrap your app. However, we can go one step further and kill two birds with one stone by running a development web server that refreshes the app when needed. It's as simple as running the following command:

```
sencha app watch
```

With this, we have the same web server functionality as web start combined with a process that watches for metadata changes and alterations to Sass files. It will automatically rebuild Bootstrap data and CSS when it detects a change.

Care for the environment

Sencha Cmd supports the concept of environments to allow different behavior depending on the stage of your workflow. We've already mentioned that Sencha Cmd leverages the power of the Ant build system to allow customization of the process. The different environments simply define variables that are consumed by Ant and passed into the build process to enable, disable, or amend a part of the build.

You can see the default build variables by running the following command:

```
sencha ant .props
```

This produces something that includes the following code along with a million and one other variables:

```
[INF] [echoproperties] app.output.js=app.js
[INF] [echoproperties] app.output.js.compress=false
[INF] [echoproperties] app.output.js.enable=true
[INF] [echoproperties] app.output.js.optimize=false
```

Here the variable `app.output.js` has the value `app.js`.

> Note that build variables and configuration variables are two separate things. Configuration variables are used by Sencha Cmd as a whole, not just the build process. We'll only be discussing configuration variables, as they're most commonly used and provide the most "bang for your buck". We just don't have space to cover every variable.

We're going to take a closer look at environments now. They are used with the `app build` subcommand and give us a lot of power to customize our code for production.

The final product

When creating a production build, we want to make our code as lean as possible, removing logging, debugging, and making sure that we compress JavaScript and CSS and use all optimizations available. Let's look at the overrides for the product environment:

```
// Defined in .sencha/app/production.defaults.properties
build.options.logger=no
build.options.debug=false
build.compression.yui=1
build.optimize=true
enable.cache.manifest=true
enable.resource.compression=true
build.embedded.microloader.compressor=-closure
```

Let's look at each option in turn, ignoring the comment on the first line:

1. Disable Ext JS framework logging.
2. Tell the compiler to remove code designated as debug code.
3. Use the YUI Compressor to minify the JavaScript code.
4. Enable custom optimizations (such as removing the `requires` option) that are no longer needed when the dependency tree is already known. This can result in a slightly smaller code base.
5. Generate an HTML cache manifest file. This instructs the browser to cache the application's `index.html` file to reduce network activity.
6. Compress the CSS files and other resources.
7. Compress the "microloader" JavaScript that boots our application.

Along with the huge range of other configuration options, we have a mechanism to tailor our final build to suit our needs. For tracking production issues, you may wish to enable logging to the browser console, so you can toggle this option.

You could even create a custom environment that skips parts of the build for a quicker process. It's worth poring through the output that `sencha ant .props` creates in order to see where you can tailor the process for the needs of your team.

Before the build

Back in *Chapter 3, Application Structure,* we touched on the `build.xml` file that Sencha Cmd generates as part of an application template. Now, we'll take a closer look to see how we can use this file to hook into the build process and leverage it for our own purposes.

We've already mentioned that Sencha Cmd uses Ant, an XML-based build system at its core. A key concept of Ant is that of "targets", a term that describes a bundle of tasks that perform a part of the build process from the Ant manual:

> *"A target is a container of tasks that cooperate to reach a desired state during the build process."*

In our case, Sencha Cmd comes with a set of pre-existing targets that we can use to hook into various parts of the build process. The `build.xml` file contains stubs for these targets as well as some comments on what they do. We're going to hook into one of these and implement a task that will halt the build process if certain conditions are not met.

When we discussed the role of the architect, we speculated that there may be a requirement to enforce coding standards on the development team. We can use automated tools to make sure that best practice is used in a code base. Here, we'll use JSHint: a JavaScript code quality tool.

Ant is widely used and, as such, has many community-created additions. For JSHint, developer Phil Mander has created a task to use it in an Ant target. For more information, refer to `https://github.com/philmander/ant-jshint`.

To begin with, we need to download the Java JAR containing the new task at `http://git.io/VSZvRQ`.

I simply placed it in the application root along with the `build.xml` file, but if you've got a lot of extra tasks, it's definitely worth creating a new directory.

We can now configure our `build.xml` file to use this new task as follows:

```xml
<?xml version="1.0" encoding="utf-8"?>
<project name="MyApp" default=".help">

    <import file="${basedir}/.sencha/app/build-impl.xml"/>

    <!-- Expose the new task using the ant-jshint jar file -->
    <taskdef name="jshint" classname="com.philmander.jshint.
JsHintAntTask"
```

```
                classpath="${basedir}/ant-jshint-0.3.6-SNAPSHOT-deps.jar"
    />

        <!-- Hook into the before-init target -->
        <target name="-before-init">
            <!-- JSHint is now fully exposed via XML -->
            <jshint dir="${basedir}/app" includes="**/*.js"
    globals="Ext:true" options="strict=false">
                <!-- Output a report to a file called jshint.out -->
                <report type="plain" destFile="${basedir}/jshint.out"
    />
            </jshint>
        </target>
    </project>
```

There are several steps to hook up this new task:

- Add a `taskdef` element to make Ant aware of the `ant-jshint` task
- Add the target element with a name `–before-build`
- Add a `jshint` element configured as per the documentation on GitHub

There's only one really special thing to note about the way we've configured the JSHint task and that's the need to add Ext to the `globals` setting. As `ant-jshint` hasn't been told where the Ext JS framework is, we tell it to assume that a global variable called Ext is defined elsewhere.

We can now run `sencha app build` again and JSHint will parse through our code and check it against its rule set. If our code doesn't pass, the whole build will fail and a file called `jshint.out` will be created in the root of our application and will show the details of any JSHint errors and the lines on which they occurred.

With only ten minutes work, we've already created a low-friction method of ensuring buggy or low-quality code is less likely to reach production.

This is just one example of a prebuild check. You could also:

- Run a test suite
- Run code-complexity checks

By preventing a build from being created if these checks don't pass, you're enforcing a standard way of working across the board and forcing developers to check all of the little things that go towards creating a quality product.

Code complete

Once our quality checks have passed, we want to look at deploying the application. Again, we have an opportunity to codify some practices to make sure your team performs the same actions time and time again.

Let's set out a typical process that represents a deployment to production:

1. Quality checks such as tests and coding standards.
2. Minification and other optimization.
3. Bump the application version number.
4. Push to production server.

Number one was taken care of by our `before-init` step. Minification and optimization is taken care of by Sencha Cmd's build-in tasks. We're left with three tasks that we'd like to complete before pushing to production, so we'll look at them in turn, but first, let's have a brief interlude and talk about Ant.

An application for Ant

In effect, the next few pages are a tutorial for Ant, rather than Sencha Cmd or application architecture. There are many, many resources for Ant online and in print form, so why go over old ground?

Remember that this book isn't a list of facts and figures or code listings to type in line by line. It's supposed to get the brain thinking about the application from a top-down perspective and see how you can help your team build a strong product for your client.

An architect isn't just there to draw pictures of the house. They are there to make sure a beautiful house is built and the homeowner walks away happy.

Version numbers

Back to Ant. There are multiple reasons why you want to label an application with a build or version number—a key one is to let stakeholders know the version they're reviewing to see whether it contains the bug fixes they'd expect.

Versioning the application is a two-step process:

1. Generate a new build number.
2. Insert it in a JavaScript file for display on the UI.

Ant provides a task to make step one fairly simple:

```
<propertyfile  file="app.properties">
          <entry key-"build.number" type="int" operation="+"
value="1"/>
</propertyfile>
```

We use the `propertyfile` task to specify that a file called `app.properties` will contain an entry called `build.number`. Every time we run the task, it triggers an operation to increment `thisentry` by one as follows:

```
<property file="app.properties"/>
<replace file="${build.classes.file}" token="{VERSION}"
value="${build.number}"/>
```

Next, we read the `app.properties` file to understand how to use the property task, which makes the properties it contains available to further tasks.

Finally, we do a search and replace in the generated JS for a `{VERSION}` token and replace it with the `build.number` property. Let's see it as a full `build.xml`:

```
<?xml version="1.0" encoding="utf-8"?>
<project name="MyApp" default=".help">

    <import file="${basedir}/.sencha/app/build-impl.xml"/>

    <target name="-after-page">
        <propertyfile  file="app.properties">
            <entry key="build.number" type="int" operation="+"
value="1"/>
        </propertyfile>

        <property file="app.properties"/>
        <replace file="${build.classes.file}" token="{VERSION}"
value="${build.number}"/>
    </target>
</project>
```

Note that we're using the `after-page` target as a hook. This fires after Sencha Cmd has assembled all of the application's dependencies and created a single file to contain them. This is the file we do our search and replace on, which means that our original source files remain intact. You could have a JavaScript file such as this:

```
// app/Application.js
Ext.define('MyApp.Application', {
    extend: 'Ext.app.Application',
```

```
    name: MyApp',
    version: '{VERSION}'
});
```

Also, the `{VERSION}` token would be replaced, enabling you to use the version number across your application, perhaps in a footer or an **About** screen.

From release to production

Our code is neat and tidy, we know what version we're releasing. The next step is to push it to a production server. We'll use SFTP to transfer files to a remote server:

```
<target name="-after-build">
    <input
        message="Please enter SFTP username:"
        addproperty="scp.user" />
    <input
        message="Please enter SFTP password:"
        addproperty="scp.password" />
    <scp remoteTodir="${scp.user}@sftp.mysite.com:/path/to/myapp/dir"
password="${scp.password}">
        <fileset dir="build/production"/>
    </scp>
</target>
```

We use the `afterbuild` target, which means that all other aspects of the build are complete and the final production files have been built. As it's a really bad idea to hardcode security credentials, we use the input task to request input from the user on the command line. The resulting input gets assigned to the property specified in `addproperty`.

The `scp` task's `remoteToDir` attribute should be customized according to your needs, but the `scp.username` and `scp.password` values will be filled with the previous user input. In the `fileset` task, we specify that the whole `build/production` directory will be pushed up to the remote server.

We've shown how we can leverage the power of Ant to hook into key aspects of the Sencha Cmd build process, converting error-prone manual tasks to automated ones that can be easily shared with your development team.

The best of the rest

We've barely touched the surface of what Sencha Cmd can do. We're looking at Sencha Cmd from the perspective of a highly interested architect, but an architect needs a strong awareness of the full stack of tools available to their developers. Let's do a whistle-stop tour of some of the features that Ext JS developers can use to ease their work on the details of an application.

Packages

Packages are a way of reusing code between projects. Sencha Cmd and Ext JS recognize packages as fleshed out concepts in the Sencha ecosystem, so developers should be aware that they're available for use. The workspace concept, which we discussed earlier, assists with development of packages, but they can be consumed at the application level, providing a tidy bundle of CSS, JavaScript, and other resources for an app to consume from a local or remote source.

 The Sencha documentation at `http://docs.sencha.com/cmd/5.x/cmd_packages/cmd_creating_packages.html` provides instructions on creating packages.

At an enterprise level, packages are a key method to provide reusable logic and user interface elements that can be shared between teams. Code reuse is something that needs to be considered at an architectural level to avoid reinventing the wheel, so packages can be an important tool when looking at the bigger picture.

Themes

There are two approaches to working with CSS and images in Ext JS: first there's the full-blown theme option in which you create a package of images, Sass files, and JavaScript customization to build an entirely bespoke look and feel for your application. In many cases, some minor tweaks to the standard Ext JS components combined with some extra styles for your own UI elements are all that are needed. In this case, Sencha Cmd provides `sencha compass compile` to transform Sass files into CSS that is included in your app. Don't forget that `sencha app watch` also takes care of this step automatically.

Compilations

Command's build process relies on a subcommand called compile, which is responsible for parsing the files that make up your application. This subcommand can be invoked independently and could be used to create a list of application dependencies that could be further processed by tools other than Sencha Cmd.

In the greater JavaScript ecosystem, there are a growing number of build tools (such as Grunt and Gulp) that your developers may be more familiar with. By using a small portion of Sencha Cmd's features, your team could continue to leverage these tools while working with the Ext JS framework.

Summary

Standards and process are key responsibilities of a software architect and Sencha Cmd is an indispensable tool to help fulfill these responsibilities. We saw how it can touch all parts of the application lifecycle, from quickly getting up and running with a template to bolting on segments of a developing code base, to creating a final optimized product.

More than this, the various hooks with Sencha Cmd provides flexibility. It works with you and your team to help ease the development process and save time that would otherwise be wasted with manual tasks.

In the next few chapters, we'll look at how we can piece together everything we've learned so far about Ext JS application architecture and use some practical examples to further demonstrate how to build fantastic products for your clients.

5
Practical – a CMS Application

In previous chapters, we explored the more theoretical side of application architecture as well as the cast of tools we'll use to support us. We've reviewed design patterns, methods of structuring our application. Now, it's time to understand how these can fit together to create a well-structured application.

In this chapter, we'll create a basic user interface for a **content management system** (**CMS**). While many businesses will work with an off-the-shelf CMS (such as Joomla! or Drupal), the vastly varying requirements from business-to-business means that a bespoke content management system is a fairly common project.

It's also a deceptively-complicated proposition. With such a range of business-specific requirements, the basic CMS can quickly become a complex application with modules and interface elements that are tailored for the problem at hand. This makes it even more important that the basics are taken care of, for example, code structure and naming conventions.

In reflection of this, we'll only be creating a basic starter-level CMS. We'll be:

- Designing a data structure and the corresponding Ext JS model and store implementation
- Building a full class structure and mapping the interactions between them
- Sketching out pseudocode for some more complex interactions
- Fleshing out our design into a full implementation

This is also the general pattern that the next few chapters will take. In this particular chapter, our application will contain:

- A hierarchical treeview of website structure
- The search feature

- A form panel showing page detail
- A create, update, read, and delete functionality

By the end of the chapter, we'll have put our knowledge to test in a basic real-world application using Ext JS 5's MVVM architecture to structure our code in a way that's clean and understandable.

A content-managed system

We're going to be producing a bare-bone, but usable implementation of a CMS, which uses some of the Ext JS architectural concepts we've already touched on, such as view models and view controllers, event listeners, and data binding. Here's a look at the desired final product:

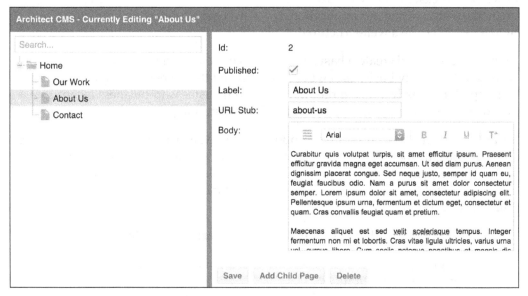

Architecture CMS: our first example application

Long before we get to this point, we need to go through the requirements for the application, design its various application layers, and come up with a design. Only then can we start talking about the code level. Let's get started with checking out our client's request.

The requirements

We receive two documents as our project brief from the client: a wireframe and a set of criteria to meet. A wireframe is the layout of our application in broad strokes, as shown here:

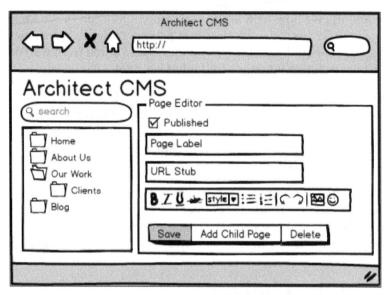

Wireframe graphic for "Architecture CMS"

Immediately, we know that this is a very simple single-page application with a tree view, editor panel, and a search bar. The criterion fleshes out as follows:

- REST backend API provided
- The treeview to show all pages
- Search that will highlight the matching page in the treeview
- The required HTML editor
- URLs that must be customizable
- Pages that can be published or unpublished
- User must be able to create, view, update, and delete pages

Let's assess these criteria in terms of Ext JS. Firstly, we know that REST support is available in Ext JS via `Ext.data.proxy.Rest`, which we can use through our models and stores. However, note that the second point requires a tree view representing the hierarchical structure. While Ext JS provides a `TreePanel` component and there's a dedicated `TreeStore` to handle hierarchical data, there may be a possibility that loading this kind of nested data via a REST API could have some complications.

At this point, we could consult with our team and even write some prototype code to investigate this REST issue before getting fully underway with development. It's important to resolve any uncertainty before moving forward.

With this cleared up, we now look at the requirement for search. We know that `Ext.data.NodeInterface`, the class that powers nodes in a `TreePanel`, has a `findChildBy` method that allows you to traverse a tree from the root and perform an arbitrary action when we find what we need.

The customer specified that an HTML editor is required, which is fine as Ext JS ships with a well-featured WYSIWYG HTML editor in `Ext.form.field.HtmlEditor`. For the URL customization, we don't have to do anything special other than be aware that the client has asked for this field to be included when editing; likewise the same with the published/unpublished flag.

Finally, we know the operations that the customer would like to perform on pages, which dictates how our application will interact with the existing backend. Given the REST API available to us, supporting the required **create, read, update, and delete (CRUD)** actions should be trivial with an implementation of `Ext.data.Model`.

Accepting the challenge

As we've reviewed the client's criteria against the tools available to us, we can confidently accept the challenge laid down for us. Without performing due diligence on customer requirements, we could begin a project without being 100 percent certain of whether we could complete it, potentially risking the success of the project and costing valuable time and money.

Starting at the bottom

The client stated that we have a REST API available to us. In fact, they have other Ext JS applications to be built on top of this API and so we're lucky. The data is returned as JSON that can be easily consumed by `Ext.data`. The customer provided documentation on how the API operates:

```
API Endpoint: http://localhost:3000

GET /pages
Accepts: n/a
Returns: [{ id: 1, text: 'label', children: [] }, { id: 2, text:
'', children: [] }]
```

```
PUT /page
Accepts: {"published":true,"stub":"our-work","body":"Our
Work.","id":"5e30c0a3-729a-4719-a17f-7e2286576bda"}
Returns: {"success":true}

POST /page
Accepts: {"label":"New Page","text":"New
Page","leaf":true,"id":"Unsaved-1","parentId":"5e30c0a3-729a-4719-
a17f-7e2286576bda","published":true,"stub":"new-page","body":"A
New Page."}
Returns: [{"clientId":"Unsaved-1","id":"2ae28c61-cc6e-4a98-83ee-
f527f4b19f1e","text":"New Page","body":"A New
Page.","published":true,"stub":"new-page","leaf":true}]

DELETE /page
Accepts: {"id":2}
Returns: {"success":true}
```

At this point, your developers will be dancing a little jig because not only do you have documentation, but also the API is very straightforward supports only a few operations.

Our part of the data implementation becomes easy now. We know that we want to implement a treeview. The data coming back from /pages is already formatted correctly for this with an array of children and both ID and text properties. We only need one model to represent a page, so it'll look something like this in pseudo-UML:

```
ArchitectureCms.model.Page: extends Ext.data.TreeModel
- id
- stub
- published
- body
- [] children
```

Then, we'll have a super simple store to collect these models together:

```
ArchitectureCms.store.Pages: extends Ext.data.TreeStore
```

There's no custom logic hanging off the store so that's literally our full definition, although we know that our implementation will be configured to use our `ArchitectureCms.model.Page`.

The data layer is the one through which everything will be built on. Although our design for this layer is super simple for this application, it's worth writing it in case we see any glaring issues. We can now look at how these data classes will interact with the user interface and glue classes in the rest of our application.

Work your way up

Controllers are the glue that binds your application together; it's often useful to look at our wireframe again and break down the aspects that represent view classes and will need a controller to orchestrate their actions. The basic wireframe can be seen in the following screenshot:

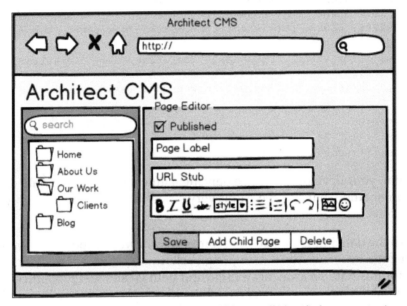

The wireframe broken down: yellow, green, and blue are all identified as separate views

In this application, as we have a very straightforward layout and set of interactions between components, we can get away with a very simple architecture.

While it's important to create a strong starting structure in the early days of an application, you should always strive to build something that is clearly designed and doesn't contain classes that have been added just in case they are needed.

> **You Aren't Going To Need it (YAGNI)** is a popular term with some software developers who believe that less is more—don't write code based on some far-future assumption about what you might need. Instead, iterate on your architecture with every addition and take as much care with these additions as you would at the start of a project.

In the Ext JS MVVM architecture, a top-level controller is used to mediate interactions between other controllers. Here, we've elected to create just one controller (a view controller called `Main`) that will coordinate all of the actions of the views within its namespace.

Let's take a look at how these new classes will look when working together and in association with our data layer:

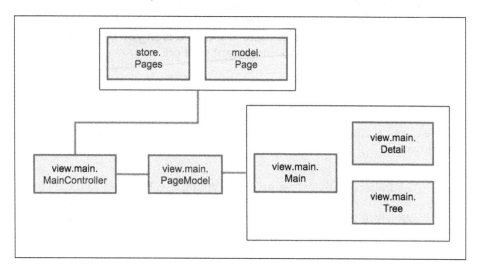

The preceding diagram clearly shows how data flows through our application (from the data layer that interfaces with the client's API to controllers and then down to views via view models). We can now flesh out each of these classes by naming them and specifying their methods and properties:

```
ArchitectCms.view.main.MainController: extends
Ext.app.ViewController
 - onAddClick
 - onDeleteClick
 - onSaveClick
 - onPageSelect
ArchitectCms.view.main.PageModel: extends Ext.app.ViewModel
 - pages
 - currentPage
 - isUnsavedPage
 - searchTerm
ArchitectCms.view.main.Main: extends Ext.panel.Panel
ArchitectCms.view.main.Detail: extends Ext.form.Panel
ArchitectCms.view.main.Tree: extends Ext.tree.Panel
 - searchFor
```

Let's break this down a bit and talk about the reasons we've designed the application in this way.

The devil is in the detail

It's immediately clear that the controller is where most of the interesting stuff is happening, but it's important to remember to keep your controllers slim. If you find yourself with lots of methods in there, it's a good sign you need another controller — look for the logical place one might split off.

In our case, a future iteration of the application might have separate view controllers for the tree and for the detail panel with an overarching controller to enable communication between the two. For now though, we just don't need this. All we have in our `MainController` class is four methods that will handle actions from our views.

 Controllers are there to support everything else. Focus on your data first, then your views, and use the controllers to connect them. As such, work out which events your views are going to fire and your controller will pretty much write itself — all it'll be doing is handling these events and passing off the hard work somewhere else.

This is a great opportunity to put implementation details to one side for a moment and think about how these classes would look if they were designed to make our life easy.

For example, the view model called `PageModel` has a method called `isUnsavedPage`, which allows you to ensure that the user doesn't navigate away before they save a new page, ensuring they won't lose any data.

Designing like this up front enables us to think about all of the great features that make for a good user experience without having to get worked up about the code that will make it happen. Of course, every situation is different. We need to make sure that we don't let our imagination run away with itself and start dreaming up features that aren't required!

There's a short discussion to be had with regard to the `searchFor` method on the `Tree` class. In controllers, we pull together a few parts of our application and hand off the real work to them, not to the controller itself. That's exactly what we're doing here. Think of this method in the same way you would use the `expandPath` method on the `Ext.tree.Panel` base — a method that acts on the tree interface without breaking out and interacting with anything else. Its logical place is as an augmentation to the tree UI.

Where the wild things are

We have our design, so let's step a little closer and examine the parts of the application where a little more detail may be required. For example, we have a controller method called `onAddClick` that will be handling the process of adding a new record, but what will this actually entail and are there any pain points hidden within? Here's what needs to happen when this handler is done with its job:

- Ask the user for a name for the new page
- Create a new blank record with default values and the page name
- Add the page as a child node of the current page
- Load the record in the detail panel
- Show the new record in the tree

That's a lot for a single controller action. Let's look at how we might code it to see whether we're trying to do too much. We'll write some pseudocode (fake code) to drill down into some detail:

```
newPageName = promptUser 'Please enter a page name'

newPageModel = new Page {
    text = newPagename
}


pageTree.addAndSelect newPageModel
```

There's no JavaScript here, no Ext JS classes in use. We're just writing the code we wish we could write if there weren't any language or framework constraints. Given that, this code looks good — it's clear what's happening and we're not doing too much.

One thing to notice is that `Ext.panel.Tree` doesn't have a native `addAndSelect` method. We'll need to write this, but if it makes our controller code cleaner and shorter, then that's a good thing.

Spiky and hairy

There's a truism in software development that code is harder to read than it's to write. Comprehending someone else's code without having the reasoning behind it can be difficult. Having said that, there's a difference between code that's a little hairy, a little scary — something that doesn't shout out its intent via comments, variable naming or method naming, and code that shows consideration for future maintainers.

In writing pseudocode, we're trying to ensure that the concepts behind our code are well fleshed out beforehand and that any difficulties are taken care of before we really start work on our application.

In complex cases, pseudocode won't go far enough. We'll have to write some real code in the form of a spike. In *Kent Beck's Guide to Better Smalltalk: A Sorted Collection, SIGS*, he talks a bit about this:

> *"Sometimes I call this a "spike", because we are driving a spike through the entire design. [...] Because people variously associate "spike" with volleyball, railroads, or dogs, I have begun using "architectural prototype" to describe this implementation."*

When creating a spike, we're pushing through any assumptions we have and testing our design decision on a tiny prototype (the smallest code snippet or application we can build to prove our idea).

This firms up our design by eliminating further unknowns. We can be sure that a UI component will support the feature we require because we've actually tested it in a practical example. If it's an architectural code spike, we can see whether the various elements of our design hang together in a way that "feels right", if it works within the framework being used, and the design patterns that have been chosen.

We can perform a spike on the `addAndSelect` method described previously, but we know that `Ext.tree.Panel` already has an `add` method and that the underlying `selectionModel` will allow us to mark a node as selected. Therefore, now that we have alleviated our concerns with pseudocode, there's no need to continue on to real code until we implement the real deal. As developers working under constraints of time and money, we need to be pragmatic, as long as we are certain that due diligence has been performed.

The real deal

We've designed the data layer and the UI layer, the glue that dictates how the two interact, and tackled the remaining bits of the client requirements that look like they may cause trouble. We're in good shape to start putting our fingers on the keyboard in our favorite text editor and show how the design can be implemented in Ext JS.

A short interlude on data binding

With the introduction of view models in Ext JS, the concept of data binding has also been brought to prominence. In short, data binding binds one value to another value. When the first changes, the second updates automatically. Two-way data binding means that when either value changes, the other updates accordingly.

On the whole, Ext JS has implemented this idea via view models. A UI component may have its title bound to a value and when this value is updated by another part of the application, the title automatically changes. This removes the need for the developer to wire up change events and ensures that data will be consistent across an application.

We're going to use data binding heavily in this example application and across all our practical chapters. In many cases, a little bit of binding configuration can remove a lot of boilerplate event wiring, so we're going to take advantage of it where we can.

Creating a structure

Using our knowledge from previous chapters, we'll create an application skeleton using Sencha Cmd and use it as a basis for our work. We're familiar with this by now:

```
sencha generate app -ext ArchitectureCms ./architecture-cms
```

With a simple command, we're up and running with a template. Let's fire up a web server and look for changes in our code:

```
cd architecture-cms
sencha app watch
```

We can now launch a web browser and navigate to `http://localhost:1841` to see the template in action. We don't want any of the example code that's been generated. So, we can remove it with the following command:

```
rm app/view/main/*
```

Now, we've got a clean directory structure on which we can build our content management system.

Data-driven design

In the same way that we designed our application by looking at the data layer first, we'll write the Ext JS model and store code first. Here's the model, which we'll build bit-by-bit to explain the thought process behind the code:

```
Ext.define('ArchitectureCms.model.Page', {
    extend: 'Ext.data.TreeModel',
fields: [
        { name: 'body' },
        { name: 'stub' },
        { name: 'text' },
        { name: 'published' }
    ]
});
```

Let's look back at our design for this class. We're defining the same fields we laid out there with the exception of the children field, which is a special case as we're using `Ext.data.TreeModel`.

Of course, this isn't enough to drive a real-world Ext JS model. This is where the design now differs from the implementation. Let's connect the model to the client's API:

```
Ext.define('ArchitectureCms.model.Page', {
    extend: 'Ext.data.TreeModel',

    fields: [
        { name: 'body' },
        { name: 'stub' },
        { name: 'text' },
        { name: 'published' }
    ]
});
```

Woah! The design is mostly language agnostic, but the implementation now shows off configuration options that are very Ext JS-specific. There are two ways of configuring a model. One way to configure is via its proxy and another is via its schema. The proxy configuration works just fine, but in larger applications, the schema can be shared between models and provides a central place to configure the base API URL and the path to fetch for a particular model.

Because of this, we're going to start off using schema even though we're only dealing with a single model in this application. Let's look at the various configuration options:

- namespace: This is the segment of the model's class name that represents the namespace. This means that Ext JS can remove the namespace part of the full class name and be left with nothing but the model, which it can then use to automatically build URLs. In this case, we set the namespace as ArchitectureCms.model, which allows Ext JS to work out that the model name is just Page. We'll use this later.

- urlPrefix: This is generally the hostname or the API endpoint to use in combination with the path to the specific resource being consumed.

- proxy.type: This is the type of proxy, which when dealing with the server will likely be ajax or rest. We know that our customer has a REST API, so it's set to rest.

- proxy.url: This uses all the preceding options to build a URL. The segments in curly brackets will be replaced in order to build a full URL to the resource being consumed. {prefix} is the urlPrefix from above, {entityName:uncapitalize} is the model's name parsed from the class name without the namespace in lower case.

Phew! At this point, we've done a pretty deep dive into Ext JS configuration options. This chapter, and indeed this book, is supposed to be about architecture. So from now on, there will be some cases where we'll skip over this kind of detail on the assumption that you've worked with Ext JS before and understand these configuration options.

We're trying to design this application; we're not trying to teach JavaScript or Ext JS. Although, we'll look at aspects of the Ext JS framework that contribute to a successful application, we're not going to regurgitate the Sencha documentation. With this in mind, let's add a little bit more to our model and talk about how it helps us meet the customer requirements:

```
Ext.define('ArchitectureCms.model.Page', {
    extend: 'Ext.data.TreeModel',
    clientIdProperty: 'clientId',
    identifier: {
        type: 'sequential',
        prefix: 'Unsaved-'
    },
    schema: {
        namespace: 'ArchitectureCms.model',
        urlPrefix: 'http://localhost:3000',
        proxy: {
```

```
            type: 'rest',
            url: '{prefix}/{entityName:uncapitalize}'
        }
    },
    fields: [
        { name: 'body' },
        { name: 'stub' },
        { name: 'text' },
        { name: 'published' }
    ]
});
```

This is the final iteration of the `Page` class, now with an identifier configured. We know that we need to differentiate between a saved and an unsaved model, and we know that the server will return `clientId` if it's supplied, so here we explicitly state that it's going to have the `Unsaved-` string in the ID until the server supplies an auto-incremented identifier to replaced it on save.

A model store

The store for this application is pretty simple:

```
Ext.define('ArchitectureCms.store.Pages', {
    extend: 'Ext.data.TreeStore',
    model: 'ArchitectureCms.model.Page',
    alias: 'store.pages',
    root: {} // set empty root as using bind doesn't do this
});
```

Everything here is self-explanatory, although there is a caveat. With the current version of Ext JS (5.0.1), we need to set an empty root node that allows you to use data binding to bind this store to a UI component. If we don't, an error will be thrown, so this is a simple workaround.

A room with a view

We mentioned that it was a good idea to design your application (starting with the data layer and then moving to the views) so that it's easier to understand the interactions that your controllers will have to deal with. When moving from the design to the code, the same applies, so we will write the user interface for this application and then later wire it up to the data via controllers.

First up, we need a viewport. We only have one page in the CMS, so the viewport is the container for all of the individual subviews (such as the tree and the detail panel). This application is fairly focused, so we're going to put all our views and associated classes under the `ArchitectureCms.view.main.*` namespace. Here's the code for our `ArchictureCms.view.main.Main` viewport:

```
// app/view/main/Main.js
Ext.define('ArchitectureCms.view.main.Main', {

    extend: 'Ext.panel.Panel',
  requires: [
        'ArchitectureCms.view.main.Detail',
        'ArchitectureCms.view.main.Tree'
    ],

    session: true,

    controller: 'main',
    viewModel: 'page',

    title: 'Architect CMS',
    bind: { title: 'Architect CMS - Currently Editing
"{currentPage.text}"' },

    layout: 'border',

    items: [
        { xtype: 'page-detail', region: 'center', reference:
'detail' },
        { xtype: 'page-tree', region: 'west', width: 300,
reference: 'tree', split: true }
    ]
});
```

This is mostly straightforward (we extend `Ext.Panel` rather than `Ext.Container` to give us support for a title bar). Next up, we require the view classes we're going to use in the viewport.

The `session` option is set to `true`. We'll discuss this in more detail shortly.

The view controller and view model are specified by their aliases; we'll create these classes later. Sencha Cmd knows that these are "auto-dependencies", so we will automatically require them without having to include them in the `requires` array.

We create a default title, namely, `Architect CMS`, but in the next line, we have our first use of the `bind` option. Let's break down what's happening here. We've already specified a view model for this class and always have to bind to a value in a view model. Not only this, the `bind` option is only triggered when the view model value changes, which is why we need to specify a default value via the title configuration. For the bind configuration, we specify the values we want to bind against (in this case title) and then provide a binding expression. Here, it's just a string. The segment in curly brackets determines the value on the view model to bind to. Later, we'll look at `currentPage.text` and see how this gets set, but it will suffice for now to realize that when this value changes; it gets incorporated into the value for title. We'll see something like this:

> **Architect CMS - Currently Editing "Our Work"**

Note that this will happen without having to wire up any event handlers. It's a little sprinkle of magic that reduces the boilerplate code we have to write.

Next up, we specify a border layout and then fill the items array with the tree and detail panel, referencing them by their `xtype`. Thanks to our configuration of the `requires` option, Ext JS is already aware of these classes, so we can use the aliases as shorthand.

Other than the binding configuration and a bit of auto-requiring magic, there's nothing special happening here. The key, in terms of application design, is the introduction of the binding concept in association with view models and view controllers. Hopefully, we've shown how these ideas can be introduced with barely any additional code.

The tree panel and searching

Now that we've got our viewport container, we can introduce the views themselves. First, we'll look at the code for the tree that shows the page hierarchy:

```
// app/view/main/Tree.js
Ext.define('ArchitectureCms.view.main.Tree', {
    extend: 'Ext.tree.Panel',
    xtype: 'page-tree',
    rootVisible: false,
     tbar: [
         { xtype: 'textfield', emptyText: 'Search...', width:
'100%', bind: { value: '{searchTerm}'}}
     ],
```

```
bind: { store: '{pages}', searchFor: '{searchTerm}' },

config: {
    searchFor: null
},

applySearchFor: Ext.emptyFn
});
```

More binding expressions! One important thing to realize is that a view model declared on a high-level component, in this case our `ArchitectureCms.view.main.Main` viewport, will cascade down and become available to child components. This means that our binding expressions in the tree will refer to the `Page` view model we assigned to the main viewport. What customer requirement are we trying to fulfill by using binding in the tree?

We want to be able to search for a page and have it highlighted in the tree. To do so, when we type in `textfield`, the value has to be passed to the tree. A traditional way of doing this would be to listen for a change event or `keypress` on `textfield`, then trigger a `search` method on the tree. Rather than doing this manually, we can use data binding via a view model to achieve the same effect:

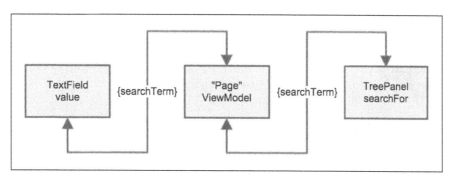

Data flows between UI components through the view model

The `searchTerm` value on the view model can flow back and forth between the `searchFor` config on the tree and the value on `textfield`. However, in this case, it's only one direction (from `textfield` down to the tree).

In addition, we tell the tree to bind to the pages value on the view model; we know we're going to need a list of pages from somewhere.

The missing piece in this puzzle is the part that actually does the searching on the tree. Thanks to the Ext JS configuration system, any `config` option that is specified also creates an `applyConfigName` method on the class instance and this is called every time the `config` option changes. This means that by creating `applySearchFor` on the tree, every time `searchFor` updates via its binding, we can run a piece of code to do something with the new value.

Note that we put a function placeholder in the last code snippet (the `Ext.emptyFn` part). Here's the actual code we're going to use here:

```
applySearchFor: function(text) {
    var root = this.getRootNode();
    var match = root.findChildBy(function(child) {
        var txt = child.get('text');

        if(txt.match(new RegExp(text, 'i'))) {
            this.expandNode(child, true, function() {
                var node = this.getView().getNode(child);
                Ext.get(node).highlight();
            }, this);
        }
    }, this, true);
}
```

In brief, use a regular expression to do a case-insensitive match on the search term against the text of each tree node. If a match is found, expand the tree to this point and call its `highlight` method to produce a visual cue.

Pages in detail

The tree is used to browse the hierarchy of trees in the CMS, so we now need a way to look at the detail of each page. The detail pane is a panel containing a number of form fields:

```
Ext.define('ArchitectureCms.view.main.Detail', {
    extend: 'Ext.form.Panel',
    xtype: 'page-detail',
    defaultType: 'textfield',
    bodyPadding: 10,
    hidden: true,
    bind: {
        hidden: '{!currentPage}'
    },
    items: [
```

```
        { xtype: 'container', cls: 'ct-alert', html: 'This record
is unsaved!', bind: { hidden: '{!isUnsavedPage}' } },
        { fieldLabel: 'Id', bind: '{currentPage.id}', xtype:
'displayfield'},
        { fieldLabel: 'Published', bind:
'{currentPage.published}', xtype: 'checkboxfield' },
        { fieldLabel: 'Label', bind: '{currentPage.text}' },
        { fieldLabel: 'URL Stub', bind: '{currentPage.stub}' },
        { fieldLabel: 'Body', bind: { value: '{currentPage.body}'
}, xtype: 'htmleditor' }
    ],
    bbar: [
        { text: 'Save', itemId: 'save' },
        { text: 'Add Child Page', itemId: 'addChild' },
        { text: 'Delete', itemId: 'delete' }
    ]
});
```

Each of the form fields has a binding expression, which ties the field value to a value on the `currentPage` object of the view model. When the user changes the field, the view model will automatically get updated. Note that we don't have to specifically state the property to bind to because form fields have their `defaultBindProperty` set to `value`.

The whole form panel has its hidden value bound to `currentPage`, so if this value is not set, the panel will be hidden. This allows you to hide the form when no page is selected. We've also got a warning message as the first item in the panel, which will be hidden when the view model's `isUnsavedPage` value changes to `false`.

We've only written a little bit of code outside the UI configuration, yet with the addition of the view model, we'll already have a populated tree panel with search tied to a detail panel. Next, we'll look at the view model code itself.

The magical page view model

This view model uses a simple formula to provide a calculated value to the view:

```
// app/view/main/PageModel.js
Ext.define('ArchitectureCms.view.main.PageModel', {
    extend: 'Ext.app.ViewModel',
    alias: 'viewmodel.page',

    requires: ['Architecture.store.Pages'],
```

```
        stores: {
            pages: {
                type: 'pages',
                session: true
            }
        },

        formulas: {
            isUnsavedPage: function(get) {
                return get('page.id').toString().indexOf('Unsaved-') >
    -1;
            }
        }
    });
```

Considering the functionality that this class enables, that's very little code. The store definition is fairly self-explanatory, just using the `ArchitectureCms.store.Pages` alias to specify that the view model has a page value powered by this store.

The formulas definition is a little more interesting. It's a way of declaring that a value will be returned based on other values in the view model. In this case, as we specified on our model that newly created records would use a prefix of `Unsaved-`, we can look for this to determine whether the record's been saved to the server or not. So, `isUnsavedPage` returns `true` or `false` depending on whether the record's ID contains this prefix or not.

The only missing thing here is the `currentPage` value. We can set arbitrary values on the view model. So, this gets set elsewhere in the controller. Before we talk about this, let's jump back to discuss a new concept in Ext JS 5: `Ext.data.Session`.

This data is now in session

An `Ext.data.Session` is a way of centralizing data in an application, ensuring that stores are working with the same set of data without having redundant reloading. It also allows much easier batched updates and deletions.

In our application, we set `session`, set to `true` on our top-level viewport, which tells Ext JS to automatically create a session and make it available to any other code that requests it. This is the simplest way of constructing a session, although there's a lot more customization that we can do if need be.

The reason we use a session in this application is to allow us to link the data that the tree and the detail panel uses. This helps with data binding too; we can use exactly the same model instance in the tree and the detail panel, which means that updates made in the detail panel will flow through the view model and into the correct page instance in the tree. In a moment, when we look at our view controller, we'll use the session a little more and get a glimpse of how it can help manage your data.

The glue controlling all

In previous chapters, we've looked at how the controller can use event domains to hook into anything interesting happening elsewhere in the application. Here, we use the same approach, which we discussed previously, and get the controller to hook up a bunch of event handlers to deal with user actions in the user interface:

```
// app/view/main/MainController.js
Ext.define('ArchitectureCms.view.main.MainController', {
    extend: 'Ext.app.ViewController',
    alias: 'controller.main',

    requires: ['ArchitectureCms.model.Page'],

    init: function() {
        this.listen({
            component: {
                'treepanel': {
                    'select': 'onPageSelect'
                },
                'page-detail #save': {
                    click: 'onSaveClick'
                },
                'page-detail #addChild': {
                    click: 'onAddClick'
                },
                'page-detail #delete': {
                    click: 'onDeleteClick'
                }
            }
        });
    },


    onPageSelect: function(tree, model) {
        this.getViewModel().setLinks({
```

```
                currentPage: {
                    type: 'Page',
                    id: model.getId()
                }
            });
        },


    onAddClick: function() {
        var me = this;

        Ext.Msg.prompt('Add Page', 'Page Label', function (action,
value) {
            if (action === 'ok') {
                var session = me.getSession(),
                    selectedPage = viewModel.get('currentPage'),
                    tree = me.lookupReference('tree');

                var newPage = session.createRecord('Page', {
                    label: value,
                    text: value,
                    leaf: true
                });

                selectedPage.insertChild(0, newPage);
                tree.setSelection(newPage);
                tree.expandNode(selectedPage);
            }
        });
    },


    onDeleteClick: function() {
        var me = this;

        Ext.Msg.confirm('Warning', 'Are you sure you'd like to
delete this record?', function(btn) {
            if(btn === 'yes') {
                me.getViewModel().get('currentPage').erase();
                me.getViewModel().set('currentPage', null);
                Ext.toast('Page deleted');
            }
        }, this)

    },
```

```
    onSaveClick: function() {
        this.getViewModel().get('currentPage').save();
        Ext.toast('Page saved');
    }
});
```

This view controller handles the following four events:

- The `select` event on the tree handled by the `onPageSelect` method
- The `click` event on the detail panel's save button handled by `onSaveClick`
- The `click` event on the detail panel's add child button handled by `onAddChildClick`
- The `click` event on the detail panel's delete button handled by `onDeleteClick`

Some of this will be self-explanatory, some relates to data binding, and some relates to the session. Let's break down the important parts.

Selecting a page

When the tree fires a `select` event, the view controller's `onPageSelect` method gets passed the model for the selected tree node. We mentioned earlier that we can set arbitrary values on the view model, specifically the `currentPage` value, and so this is what we do here, but with a twist.

Rather than just setting the data, we give Ext JS a hint that we want to set a model instance by using the links configuration. By supplying the name of the model class and its ID, Ext JS will use the matching instance if it's already available in the current `Ext.data.Session` or it'll automatically load it from the server. It's a handy shortcut for reducing the number of requests to the backend API and another example of how to use a session.

Adding a page

The view controller listens for events on a button with an item ID of #addChild. When it fires, we ask the user for the name of the new page, and the next step is to actually create a page record. Rather than using `Ext.create`, we call `createRecord` on the current `Ext.data.Session`, which allows you to continue to make Ext JS aware of the records we're managing. It also allows you to maintain a global understanding of the saved and unsaved records. This would be even more useful in an application where we need to do batch updates of records.

After creating a model instance, we follow the pseudocode we wrote earlier in the chapter, but tie it to actual Ext JS methods and add the page to the tree data structure before selecting it in the tree UI itself.

Deleting a page

This is fairly straightforward (handle the `click` event from the `#delete` button and then grab the `currentPage` from the view model). We also remove the leftover page from the view model so that the detail panel automatically clears itself, rather than leaving a dead record available to edit. We display a notification to the user with `Ext.toast`.

Saving a page

This is even simpler (handling a click on the #save button, grabbing the `currentPage` from the view model, and then calling its `save` method). There's nothing special happening here. The only thing to note is that if this is a new record, the server will respond with a new ID and replace the one that Ext JS automatically allocated. Thanks to the binding to `isUnsavedPage` on the view model, this will cause the "unsaved" message to disappear from the detail panel.

Summary

With our first practical application, we've taken the theoretical ideas discussed in previous chapters and shown how they apply to the creation of a useful code base. From analysis to what the customer really needs to see, whether we can fulfill their request to sketching out designs, and undertaking short code spikes down to applying the MVVM pattern via view models and their supporting infrastructure, we've built an application brain-first rather than code-first.

In the next chapter, we'll create a more complicated real-world application, but this time, we won't have to discuss the basics of data binding in so much detail. We'll apply our growing knowledge to build a more complex app, a log analyzer, which could be used by a system administrator to monitor their infrastructure. This will require more thought about how to design the various moving parts that will make up our second application.

6
Practical – Monitoring Dashboard

Now that we've started applying the things we've learned to a real-world application, we're going to gradually ramp up the complexity of the projects we build. By designing and creating a code base that imitates something an actual customer might pay money for, we're not coding abstract examples that exist in isolation. We're building something that showcases some of the design decisions you will likely face as a software architect.

In this chapter, we'll build a monitoring dashboard that can be used to view metrics from an application server. Developers and system administrators will use applications like this to visualize the performance of their servers and monitor load at any given time.

Such an application could be used for internal monitoring, or it could be deployed as a **Software as a Service** (**SaaS**) that could be resold to other users. Either way, it will serve as a great demonstration of the power of view models; we'll be expanding what we already know and will be using it in a more advanced way to shape the data we receive from the server. In this chapter, we'll cover:

- Designing the user interface
- Designing our data layer from the `Ext.data.Model` through to the view models needed to support our UI
- Using multiple view controllers
- Building components that are reused across views
- Adding routing to allow users to bookmark each screen of the application
- Using view model filters to focus our view of the underlying data

By the end of the chapter, we'll have fleshed out the concepts we've already begun to cover and introduced some new features (such as routing). These are important when designing the user experience for an application.

We're going to approach this as if we're designing an internal program, one that monitors another application in our theoretical software development shop. Although this means we're not bound by external customer requirements, it's still important that we follow all of the design guidelines we've already learned. This maybe an internal application, but it's still got to be robust, meet the expectations of stakeholders, and be maintained in the future.

Application design

This application will have several screens to view the various properties of the app being monitored. We'll have a dashboard screen that shows an overview of the important metrics being monitored. Then, for each of these metrics, we'll have individual screens that allow the user to drill down and filter the data. As each of these screens will be variations on a common theme, we'll only build-out a couple to demonstrate the concepts, but the framework we'll build with this application means it would be trivial to add more. The **Dashboard** tab can be seen in the following screenshot:

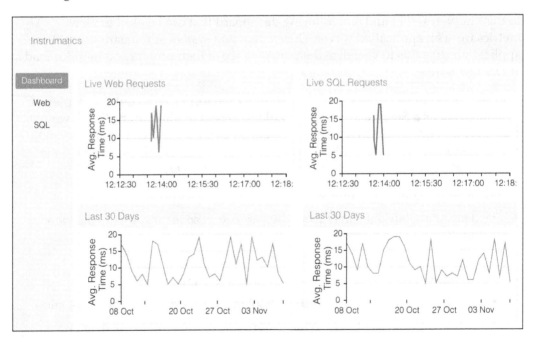

The **Web** tab is as follows:

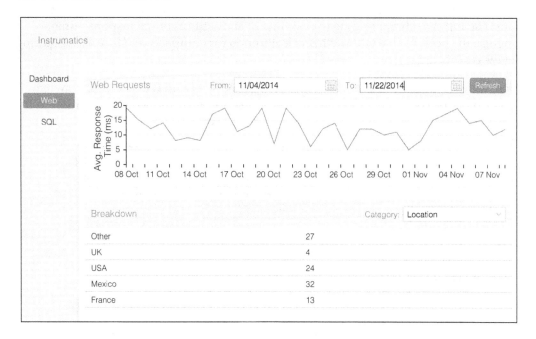

As users, what do we want to see in this monitoring application? We want information at a glance, but with the ability to easily get detailed information. Our primary concerns are the response times of web requests and queries to the database, so we want both these metrics available to us. Let's think about the user interface that supplies this information and what it might look like:

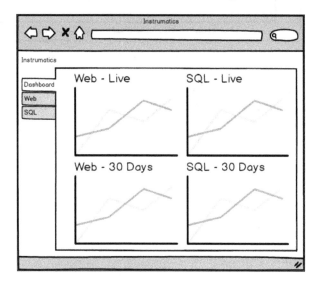

On the **Dashboard** tab, we're using charts to convey trend information—about both the short-term and the longer term—and this provides our at a glance view of the data. The top two charts update in real time to show the average response time, whereas the bottom charts show historical trends for comparison. How about getting details on this data?

Also, we've added tabs on the left-hand side of the screen that allow you to switch between log types. In this application, we've just got **SQL** and **Web** in addition to the initial **Dashboard** view, as shown in the following screenshot:

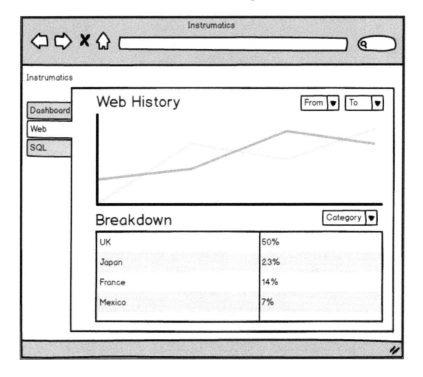

In the main part of the screen, we've got a set of controls to filter the data. The chart and grid underneath will update depending on the results of the filter. This gives the user the ability to view data within a particular date range. It also gives the user the ability to pick the category of detail to drill down.

What sort of categories? It could be extended in future, but here's our current list for the **Web** tab:

- Location
- Browser
- Type of device

We're displaying information on the web requests in our date range to provide more insight on who is visiting our application. Are we getting lots of visitors from Japan? Are they experiencing unacceptably high response times? Maybe we need to add a server somewhere in Asia to meet their requirements. Are we seeing a lot of tablet users? Do we need to improve our responsive design to better cope with a tablet screen size?

On the SQL front, we've got:

- Query type (select, insert, update, and so on)
- Slowest queries
- Query sources

The first is just general information; you could see whether your application was read-heavy or write-heavy here, which would inform how your technology stack changes over time. The other two go hand in hand, showing the slowest queries and which pages in the application issue most queries.

These metrics are useful to increase transparency in an application. In some cases, they won't be enough to diagnose subtle issues, but they will be invaluable in showing the trends of how your application and users are behaving.

Requirements

We've established the ideal UI for our application, but how does this translate into technical requirements?

- We want line charts to show trends
- We want these charts to be able to update when they receive new data
- We want to be able to choose a date range and update charts and grids accordingly
- We want to be able to choose a data category and have grids update accordingly

Let's look at each of these in the context of Ext JS:

- Ext JS charts have area, line, scatter series, and so on, so we can plot the data in a way that allows you to visualize a trend.
- The `load` method of `Ext.data.Store` can accept an `addRecords` parameter, which when set to `true` will cause newly loaded records to be appended to the store rather than overwriting the existing data. This will allow us to provide update data to a chart.

- Ext JS provides a date field component that can be linked to a view model to filter data based on a date range.

- Grids have a reconfigure method that allows you to change the columns of the grid on the fly if necessary.

Looks good!

Message received and understood

We've set out our own criteria for this project, but we're still being explicit at spelling out what we need before we start coding, and we're making sure that our technical framework will support what we need. Why not just get on with the job and put fingers to keyboards?

Although this isn't a job that has an explicit paying customer, it's still something that needs accountability. It's not enough as a professional developer to say that it'll be "done when it's done" because this attitude won't wash with the people who pay your salary. We must plan our projects in as much detail as to give us confidence in the delivery of our work—both from a time and quality perspective—as possible.

No matter who we are building software for, we must always strive to create something robust, something that meets or exceeds expectations.

Data structure

We will make an assumption in this chapter, that is, we have a friendly backend developer on our team who's able to provide us data in the format we need. Let's flesh out our requirements for the data that will power our application.

Another assumption is that we're looking for trends and statistics here, so we're going to be basically aggregating logs into something more suitable for user consumption.

Live charts

We planned to have two "live" charts on the dashboard (one to show SQL queries as they come in, and one to show web requests). In order for this to work, we need a URL we can poll every second or so. This will provide us with data on the last second of activity. Something like this:

```
GET /logStream
Accepts: n/a
Returns: [
```

```
{
    "type":"web",
    "subType":"request",
    "time":"2014-11-04T12:10:14.465Z",
    "ms":10,
    "count":5
},
{

    "type":"sql",
    "subType":"query",
    "time":"2014-11-04T12:10:14.466Z",
    "ms":17,
        "count":34

}
]
```

A GET request to /logs/all/live gives us an array of objects, one for each log type. As mentioned, we're restricting ourselves to SQL and the Web only. The ms property is the average response time of the operations that occurred in the past second. The count property is the number of operations that took place. We designed the API with a little bit of flexibility in mind, so it could be extended, for example, replace "all" in the URL with "sql" to filter on one log type.

Historical logs

On the dashboard and the subpages of our application, we also need to show graphs of historical data. On the dashboard, it'll be from the past 30 days, but on the subpages, it could be an arbitrary time frame. Here's our API:

```
GET /logEntry
Accepts:
filter=[{"property":"propertyName","operator":"=","value":"value"}
, ...]
Returns: [{
    "type":"sql",
    "subType":"query",
    "time":"2014-11-04T12:10:14.466Z",
    "ms":17,
    "count":34
}, ...]
```

We're going to rely on a feature of `Ext.data.Store: remoteFilter`. When this is set to `true`, Ext JS will defer filtering to the server and pass through the filter criteria as a JSON array. We can set an arbitrary number of filters, so in order to get SQL data within a date range, we'd be passing something like this:

```
[
    { property: 'type', operator: '=', value: 'sql' },
    { property: 'time', operator: '<=', value: '2014-01-01' },
    { property: 'time', operator: '>=', value: '2014-02-01' }
]
```

Our kind server-side developer will combine these filters into something that returns the correct response.

Log statistics

As well as general aggregated information about Web and SQL operations, we also want to display a grid of further detail on our tab pages. Again, these will be filterable based on the date range as well as the category of information we want to view:

```
GET /statistic
Accepts:
filter=[
    { property: 'type', operator: '=', value: 'web' },
    { property: 'category', operator: '=', value: 'location' },
    { property: 'time', operator: '<=', value: '2014-01-01' },
    { property: 'time', operator: '>=', value: '2014-02-01' }
]
Returns:
[{"category":"location","label":"Other","percentage":19.9}, ...]
```

We're using the `remoteFilter` feature again, meaning that Ext JS just passes the JSON filter straight through to the server as well as the `type` and `time` parameter from before. This time, we will add a `category` parameter to specify what subset of information—such as location for web logs or query source for SQL—we'd like to retrieve.

In response, we get an array of all of the items within the chosen category and the percentages allocated to each one over the specified time frame.

Model behavior

We've got our API. How does this translate into the JavaScript data models we'll need? Well, we only need two—look at the API responses we just documented—the `/logs` returns one type and `/statistics` returns another type. They'll look something like this:

```
Instrumatics.model.LogEntry: extends Instrumatics.model.BaseModel
- type
- subType
- time
- ms
- count
```

What's this `BaseModel` all about? In order to share schema configuration between models, we can use a base model from which all other models inherit. It looks like this:

```
Instrumatics.model.BaseModel: extends Ext.data.Model
- schema
```

Now, the model for statistics is as follows:

```
Instrumatics.model.Statistic: extends Instrumatics.model.BaseModel
- category
- label
- percentage
```

The `percentage` field represents the proportion of operations that are represented by this statistic. For example, if `category` is `location` and `label` is `Japan`, then the percentage could be something like `5 percent` (5 percent of our requests come from Japan). This is flexible enough to be used for all the data categories we'd like to view.

Finally, we need one for the live log stream:

```
Instrumatics.model.LogStream: extends Instrumatics.model.LogEntry
```

The log stream has the same fields as the `LogEntry` model, but we have it as a separate class, so its class name can affect the schema configuration. We'll go into more detail later.

> We're lucky with this theoretical API; in this, we are allowed to shape our requirements. In the real world, it might not be that simple, but having a friendly backend developer will always make our lives as frontend developers much easier.

Our API has strongly informed our data layer. While it's great to keep things simple—as we've been able to here—it's important not to mistake simplicity for naivety or inflexibility. In this case, our UI components will happily work with our data layer, which in turn works with our API without having to shoehorn any one piece into working with the others.

The view from the top

We have the fuel for our application; the data will bring life to the coding engine we're about to build. We now need to establish controllers that will constitute this engine and views that will give us a user interface to control and visualize it. Consider the following screenshot:

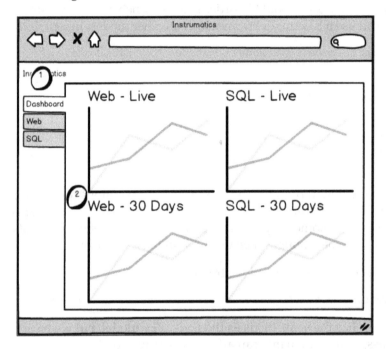

For the outer area marked as **1**, we have a main view that provides a container for other views. This will have a corresponding view controller that will manage any cross-application concerns from the main's subcomponents.

For the inner section marked as **2**, we have the dashboard view, a container for four charts. Its view controller will manage the live updates of the top two charts.

Each subpage will add an additional view (see **3**), for example, a **Web** view and an associated view controller. It will present and control the historical log chart, the statistics grid, and user input to the filtering date fields and button, as shown here:

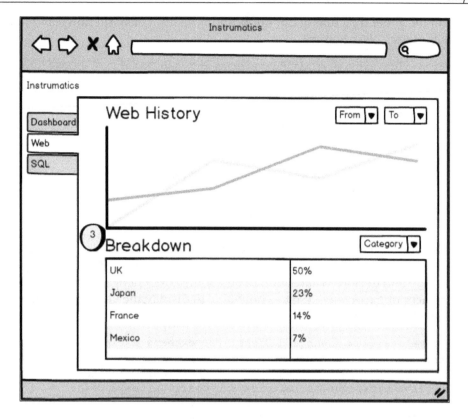

Here's how all our classes interact:

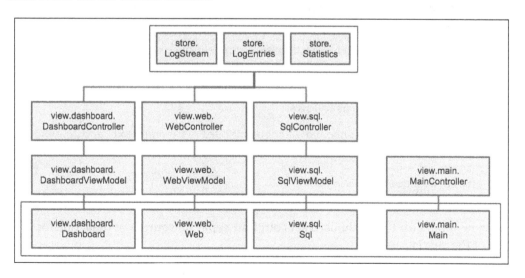

We've got the general picture of our application classes. Let's drill down and look at the details of each class in turn:

```
Instrumatics.view.main.Main: extends Ext.tab.Panel
- items[]
    - dashboard: extends Ext.panel.Panel
    - web: extends Instrumatics.view.web.Web
    - sql: extends Instrumatics.view.sql.Sql
```

The main view is a tab panel that contains all subpages:

```
Instrumatics.view.main.MainController: extends
Ext.app.ViewController
- onTabChange
- onNavigate
```

As we mentioned, the main controller deals with things that concern the whole application. It's responsible for swapping between the dashboard and subpages onTabChange and decides what action to take if the URL changes onNavigate. Four instances of Ext.chart.CartesianChart to display the various line charts that we need on the dashboard, as shown here:

```
Instrumatics.view.dashboard.Dashboard: extends Ext.panel.Panel
- items[]
    - live-sql-requests: extends Ext.chart.CartesianChart
    - live-web-requests: extends Ext.chart.CartesianChart
    - historical-sql-requests: extends Ext.chart.CartesianChart
    - historical-web-requests: extends Ext.chart.CartesianChart
```

We need some code to set up our live-updating charts, so we do this in initializeChartRefresh:

```
Instrumatics.view.dashboard.DashboardController: extends
Ext.app.ViewController
    - initializeChartRefresh
```

The Ext.app.ViewModel is as follows:

```
Instrumatics.view.dashboard.DashboardModel: extends Ext.app.ViewModel
- store.webLogs
- store.sqlLogs
- store.historicalWebLogs
- store.historicalSqlLogs
```

The view model for the dashboard sets out four separate sources of data, one for each of the charts:

```
Instrumatics.view.web.Web: extends Ext.panel.Panel
- filters: extends Ext.Container
```

```
- historical-web-requests: extends Ext.chart.CartesianChart
- statistics-grid: extends Ext.grid.Panel
```

The associated view controller is as follows:

```
Instrumatics.view.web.WebController: extends
Ext.app.ViewController
```

Ah! This is a pretty sparse view controller for a view, which is actually doing quite a lot. Let's look at the view model and things might become a bit clearer:

```
Instrumatics.view.web.WebModel: extends Ext.app.ViewModel
- stores
    - logData
    - logStatistics
    - categories
- data
    - currentCategory
    - currentStartDate
    - currentEndDate
```

The plan is to pull the historical log data and the statistics about this log data from a couple of stores. We'll have another that holds the categories that the user can use to filter the grid view.

 It's arguable that the categories could be held in the part of the user interface that filters the data in a completely separate store. However, it also makes sense to hold the data for a view in one place—the view model—and not over complicate things by adding another unnecessary store class.

The key part of this view model comes when we think about the current state of the application. For this subpage, it'll be stored in the `currentCategory`, `currentStartDate`, and `currentEndDate` variables.

As we're keeping all of the state in the view model, we can bind to the UI controls that set this state and in turn bind these values to a `store` filter. This means that changing the value using the UI will automatically change the filter value without requiring any glue code in the controller.

This implementation requires a strong understanding of the power of view models and a thoughtful eye for the design of the application. We'll go into detail on this later when we write the code for this section.

The last part of the application is the SQL subpage. This is essentially the same as the web subpage, but displaying a different set of information, so we won't go into detail about its design.

Flexibility and pragmatism

Something that we're yet to discuss in detail is how a design can change over time. We're setting out our thoughts on what we think our application should look like, but until we write it, we won't know all of the ins-and-outs of the exact implementation.

It's important to undertake a constant re-evaluation of the work that's taking place to ensure that the quality of what's being written remains high. We've documented our design earlier, but in one key place, we've also had the realization that subpages will be very similar to each other.

Depending on how these similarities are fleshed out in code, there could be scope for refactoring and reusing in a way that isn't immediately clear when drawing up the design document. However, if the implementation does turn out to be sufficiently similar with only minor variations between each subpage, then we need to look at extracting this code into a reusable class.

Code duplication—and even worse, copying and pasting code—is a very good way of ending up with a messy code base. In the event you need to change something, tweak behavior, add a feature, or fix a bug, you'll have to do the same thing in several places, increasing the overhead of the change and increasing the chance that more mistakes will creep into your code.

Copy and pasting is a blight on your code base. By blindly duplicating code, your developers are not applying any critical analysis. They are increasing the size of your code base unnecessarily and could well be introducing bugs.

Later in this chapter, we'll begin building out the code for this application. We'll also keep a close eye out for anything that looks like it might be duplicating what went before. In these cases, we'll take some time out to see whether there's functionality we can encapsulate and reuse.

Ext JS provides multiple methods to structure code—such as inheritance and mixins—and taking advantage of these methods will result in an application that is much easier to maintain and extend.

Does this hurt?

We've got our design in place, from top to bottom, so now it's time to cast a critical eye over it. Are there any unknown aspects of the design or are there any potential pain points? The live-updating chart is a little bit of a black box right now. While we know that charts support animation (via the `animate` **configuration** option), we want to be certain that the axis on the chart can update as the new data comes in. It's worth doing a very simple test to make certain this'll work. To do this, we're going to go a little bit retro.

Rather than using Sencha Cmd and the whole Bootstrap process, we're going to link directly to the files we need and use `Ext.onReady` to run our code. Here's the empty template:

```html
<!DOCTYPE HTML>
<html manifest="">
<head>
    <meta http-equiv="X-UA-Compatible" content="IE=edge">
    <meta charset="UTF-8">
    <title>Chart Test</title>
 <script type="text/javascript" src="ext/build/ext-all-debug.js"></script>
    <script type="text/javascript" src="ext/packages/sencha-charts/build/sencha-charts-debug.js"></script>
<link rel="stylesheet" type="text/css" href="ext/packages/ext-theme-neptune/build/resources/ext-theme-neptune-all-debug.css">
</head>
<body>
    <div id="chart"></div>

    <script type="text/javascript">
    Ext.onReady(function() {
        // Code goes here.
    });
    </script>
</body>
</html>
```

We've created an HTML page that links to the JS files for Ext JS and Sencha Charts as well as the CSS for one of the Ext JS Themes. In the body of the HTML, we will create a div with an ID of "chart" to render into and then an `Ext.onReady` block where we'll place the bulk of our code. First, let's set up a store in here:

```
var store = Ext.create('Ext.data.Store', {
    fields: [
            { name: 'value' },
            { name: 'time', type: 'date' }
    ]
});
```

Variables for the current time "from" and "to" times for the chart axis is shown here:

```
var now = new Date();
    fromDate = Ext.Date.subtract(now, Ext.Date.MINUTE, 1),
    toDate = Ext.Date.add(now, Ext.Date.MINUTE, 5);
```

And then the chart itself:

```
var chart = Ext.create('Ext.chart.Chart', {
    renderTo: 'chart',
    width: 500, height: 300,
    animate: true, store: store,
    axes: [
        { type: 'numeric', position: 'left', fields: 'value' },
        {
            type: 'time', fields: 'time', dateFormat: 'H:i:s',
            fromDate: fromDate.setSeconds(0),
            toDate: toDate.setSeconds(0)
        }
    ],
    series: [{ type: 'line', xField: 'time', yField: 'value' }]
});
```

Now, let's add some data to the store:

```
setInterval(function() {
    store.add({
        time: (new Date()).toISOString(),
        value: Ext.Number.randomInt(1, 30)
    });
}, 1000);
```

Every second, we add a new record to the store with the current time and a random value. After running this code, we get a line chart that updates every second, fantastic! However, while this is pretty close to what we need, there is a problem. As the line approaches the right-hand side of the chart, it just disappears off the canvas. We need to somehow update the bottom axis of the chart when we update its data.

The chart has a `redraw` event that we can use for just this purpose. What we'll try to do is move the `from` date and the `to` date located at the bottom axis forward by 15 seconds. As the `redraw` event will be triggered every second, thanks to our store updating via the `setInterval` call, every fifteenth time the `redraw` event is fired, we update the axes. This is how it looks in code:

```
var redrawCounter = 0;

chart.on('redraw', function() {
    redrawCounter++;

    if (redrawCounter > 15) {
        redrawCounter = 0;

        var timeAxis = this.getAxes()[1],
            oldFrom = new Date(timeAxis.getFromDate()),
            oldTo = new Date(timeAxis.getToDate()),
            newFrom = Ext.Date.add(oldFrom, Ext.Date.SECOND, 15),
            newTo = Ext.Date.add(oldTo, Ext.Date.SECOND, 15);

        timeAxis.setFromDate(newFrom);
        timeAxis.setToDate(newTo);
    }
});
```

We use a variable called `redrawCounter` to keep track of how many times the redraw event has fired since our last axis adjustment. The rest of the code should be fairly straightforward. Grab the bottom and set its dates 15 seconds ahead.

This was all fairly painless, although there were some unexpected hurdles in having to hook into the `redraw` event. Now that we've assured ourselves that this particular issue can be solved, we can move on to building the rest of the application.

Onwards and upwards

As with all of our example applications, we'll use Sencha Cmd and build an application template as follows:

```
sencha generate app -ext Instrumatics ./instrumatics
```

Remove all of the cruft and example files that the generator creates and use the `watch` command to fire up a web server. We can then proceed to create the first real code for our application: the data layer.

Data first

All our models will inherit from a base model, which will be used to specify the following command:

```javascript
// app/model/BaseModel.js
Ext.define('Instrumatics.model.BaseModel', {
    extend: 'Ext.data.Model',

    schema: {
        namespace: 'Instrumatics.model',
        urlPrefix: 'http://localhost:3000',
        proxy: {
            type: 'ajax',
            url: '{prefix}/{entityName:uncapitalize}'
        }
    },
});
```

 We've assumed that we have an API server running at localhost on port 3000 and supplied this information as the URL prefix.

We used the `schema` configuration in the last chapter, but now that we're about to use it with multiple models, it really comes into its own. In each of the models that inherit from `BaseModel`, the model's name will be inserting into the proxy URL in place of the `entityName` token. This avoids duplicating the URL configuration across multiple models. We can now create our `LogEntry` model as per our design:

```javascript
// app/model/LogEntry.js
Ext.define('Instrumatics.model.LogEntry', {
    extend: 'Instrumatics.model.BaseModel',

    fields: [
        { name: 'value' },
        { name: 'subType' },
        { name: 'type' },
        { name: 'time', type: 'date' }
    ]
});
```

Via the schema, this will result in the following URL:

```
http://localhost:3000/logEntry
```

Other than this, we're just implementing the fields, we specified in the design, on to the LogStream class:

```
// app/model/LogStream.js
Ext.define('Instrumatics.model.LogStream', {
    extend: 'Instrumatics.model.LogEntry',
});
```

This was simple. The LogStream class inherits all of the fields from the LogEntry class, but thanks to the use of the schema configuration in the BaseClass, LogStream will have a URL like this:

```
http://localhost:3000/logStream
```

Finally, here's the Statistics model:

```
// app/model/Statistic.js
Ext.define('Instrumatics.model.Statistic', {
    extend: 'Instrumatics.model.BaseModel',
    fields: [
        { name: 'category' },
        { name: 'label' },
        { name: 'percentage', type: 'number' }
    ]
});
```

Just the three fields from the design here and it gives us a model that produces this URL:

```
http://localhost:3000/statistic
```

Nothing in our data layer is particularly taxing, as we thought through the implementation during our design phase. By having an awareness of the features Ext JS provides before sitting down to write code, we were able to reduce code duplication by having the proxy configuration in a base class.

We should always look for places, either via refactoring or through the initial design, where we can reduce duplicated code. In this example, we could have had the same functionality by setting the proxy configuration on each of LogEntry, LogStream, and Statistic, but in the event where we want to change some part of the config, such as the hostname of the API, we'd have to change it in multiple locations. By centralizing in the way that we have, we will have less code to maintain and it's easier to work with.

One thing to note in the model classes earlier is the way we define the fields. There are two options in Ext JS, one option is to pass a field definition as an object literal as we have in our code, and the second option is to pass a string containing the field name. To use the `Statistic` class as an example, the field config will look like this:

```
'category',
'label',
{ name: 'percentage', type: 'number' }
```

Why choose one over the other? The answer is for consistency. This is a perfect example of something that could go in the programming style guide for your team, so rather than having one class declared using one method and a second class using another method, we have a unified approach. No alarms and no surprises for a new developer who opens up your model files and finds the field definitions well organized.

There is a third approach for field definitions; not bothering with them. Ext JS allows you to leave out the field definitions and will create them on the fly based on the data the model is consuming.

We're all for reducing the amount of code to maintain, but sometimes, it's better to be explicit. If we needed to use one of the other configuration options in a field, such as convert, then we'd have to manually define that field anyway, and so on, and then be left with some fields explicit in the model and some created on the fly.

This is a matter of preference, but for our purposes, we'll always define the full field definitions. It's consistent and self-documenting; we're always aware of the fields it's consuming when looking at a model file.

Storing the data

The stores in this project are as simple as it can be:

```
// app/store/LogEntries.js
Ext.define('Instrumatics.store.LogEntries', {
    extend: 'Ext.data.Store',
    alias: 'store.logentries',
    model: 'Instrumatics.model.LogEntry',
    autoLoad: true,
    remoteFilter: true
});

// app/store/LogStream.js
Ext.define('Instrumatics.store.LogStream', {
    extend: 'Ext.data.Store',
```

```
        alias: 'store.logstream',
        model: 'Instrumatics.model.LogStream',
        autoLoad: true,
        remoteFilter: true
    });

    // app/model/Statistics.js
    Ext.define('Instrumatics.store.Statistics', {
        extend: 'Ext.data.Store',
        alias: 'store.statistics',
        model: 'Instrumatics.model.Statistic'
    });
```

These classes are fairly boilerplate (define the model, define the alias, and that's it). There's an argument to be heard that these stores could actually be defined on individual view models, reducing the number of files in our code base. However, in this application, we'll reuse the stores in multiple view models, so it makes sense to keep their configuration in a centralized location.

Let's move on to the UI layer of our application.

With a view to a controller

In this application, we have a "main" view, which acts as the application's viewport, and an associated controller, which deals with user interactions with this viewport and handles routing. Let's look at the UI portion first: `view`:

```
    // app/view/main/Main.js
    Ext.define('Instrumatics.view.main.Main', {
        extend: 'Ext.tab.Panel',

        requires: [
            'Instrumatics.view.dashboard.Dashboard',
            'Instrumatics.view.web.Web',
            'Instrumatics.view.web.Sql',
        ],

        xtype: 'app-main',
        controller: 'main-main',

        header: {
            title: {
                text: 'Instrumatics', padding: 20
            }
```

```
        },

        tabPosition: 'left',
        tabRotation: 0,

        items: [
            { xtype: 'dashboard', title: 'Dashboard', reference:
    'dash' },
            { xtype: 'web-logs', title: 'Web', reference: 'web' },
            { xtype: 'sql-logs', title: 'SQL', reference: 'sql' }
        ]
    });
```

There are a few interesting bits in this code. We use the header config option to give us fine control over the panel's header, allowing us to add some formatting to the title.

We then change the default configuration of the panel's tabs to put them on the left-hand side of the screen (as opposed to the top of the screen). As tabs on the left-hand side default to displaying from top to bottom, we adjust tabRotation too, making them read from left to right. The tab selected by default is automatically the first component in the items array, so we can avoid setting any configuration to stipulate this.

Then, we set out the items that will be included in this tab panel, just the dashboard, the web logs subpage, and the SQL logs subpage, as dictated in our design. The only interesting part of this configuration is the addition of reference for each component and its utility will become clear when we look at the view controller.

The main view controller

There isn't a lot of code in this view controller, but the functionality it enables is very important. Let's take a look:

```
// app/view/main/MainController.js
Ext.define('Instrumatics.view.main.MainController', {
    extend: 'Ext.app.ViewController',
    alias: 'controller.main-main',

    routes: {
        ':controller': 'onNavigate'
    },

    listen: {
```

```
        component: {
            'tabpanel': {
                tabchange: 'onTabChange'
            }
        }
    },

    onTabChange: function(tab, newCmp, oldCmp) {
        this.redirectTo(newCmp.getReference());
    },

    onNavigate: function(controller) {
        var view = this.getView();

        view.setActiveTab(view.lookupReference(controller));
    }
});
```

Not much code, to be sure, but a lot going on. This is the part of the application that deals with routing, so let's take a bit of time out to discuss what routing actually is.

Rootin-Tootin

There's a pretty comprehensive description of routing in the Ext JS Guides, but let's cover it in brief here anyway. Routing allows you to keep the application's state in the page URL via the URL's hash (the hash is everything after the # symbol in a URL). For example:

```
http://localhost/#banana
```

This shows us we're on a page about bananas. Likewise, look at the following example:

```
http://localhost/#cars/56
```

This shows that we're on a page about car number 56. The beauty of using the hash is that it can be manipulated with JavaScript without reloading the page. Also, any change made to the hash symbol will be remembered by the browser's history. This means that we can navigate around our application and use the back button to retrace our steps. It also means that if we can bookmark a specific page in the application when it reloads the app, it will navigate to the state specified in the hash symbol.

Back to business

How do we implement routes in the `Instrumatics` app? The first step is to actually define a route as follows:

```
routes: { ':viewReference: 'onNavigate' }
```

The first part is the hash we're trying to match. Nothing's been specified apart from `:viewReference`, so in this case, everything in the hash symbol gets captured and passed on to a method called `onNavigate`. The name of the `:viewReference` token is arbitrary, in this it doesn't affect anything else, but in more complex routes, it's useful to name it in a descriptive way.

What are we trying to achieve here? When the hash symbol changes, we want to detect it and redirect the user to the correct page. The route definition does the detection part, so now let's look at how we move the user to the right page:

```
onNavigate: function(viewReference) {
    var view = this.getView();
    view.setActiveTab(view.lookupReference(viewReference));
}
```

The route definition means that all matching routes will be consumed by `onNavigate`. In this method, we can assume that the token passed in is a valid reference to a component on the view controller's view, so we just lookup the component using this reference and set it as the active tab on the "main" view.

We're missing something though, that is, how does the hash get set in the first place?

Route to nowhere

In the listen configuration for the view controller, we handle the "main" tab panel's `tabchange` event with the `onTabChange` method. This grabs the reference config from the tab the user is changing to and passes it to the view controller's `redirectTo` method:

```
onTabChange: function(tab, newCmp, oldCmp) {
    this.redirectTo(newCmp.getReference());
}
```

The `redirectTo` method simply changes the hash in the URL, in this case, to the reference of the new component. It's a simple approach that gives us a powerful way to improve the user experience.

The dashboard

We have the application infrastructure in place, so it's time to build out the components that are going to rest on this infrastructure. First up is the dashboard, something that requires us to carefully consider how to implement the rest of our application.

The dashboard consists of two live charts and two historical charts. The live charts are very similar to each other, as are the historical charts (just some minor formatting and binding configuration between them). However, in order to build a chart, you also have to build the axes and the series being drawn on it, which results in a fairly long-winded configuration object. Here's what the historical log chart from the dashboard will look like:

```
{
    xtype: 'cartesian',
    title: 'Last 30 Days',
    margin: 10, flex: 1
    bind: '{historicalWebLogs}'
    axes: [{
        type: 'numeric',
        position: 'left',
        fields: ['value'],
        title: {
            text: 'Avg. Response \nTime (ms)',
            fontSize: 15
        },
        grid: true,
        minimum: 0,
        maximum: 20
    }, {
        type: 'time',
        fields: 'time',
        dateFormat: 'd M'
    }],
    series: {
        type: 'line',
        xField: 'time',
        yField: 'value',
        style: { 'stroke': 'red' }
    }
}
```

Excellent! We have configured a chart with a line series that has a numeric left axis and a time-base bottom axis. This is exactly what we need for the dashboard, so where's the problem?

Duplication is the problem. The majority of this configuration object would be duplicated, one copy for the web logs and one copy for the SQL logs. We've mentioned before in this chapter that we'd like to battle duplication where possible, so in this case, we will create a new class that we can reuse in places where we need a chart to plot historical requests from the logs.

Here's the class:

```js
// app/ux/chart/HistoricalRequestChart.js
Ext.define('Instrumatics.ux.chart.HistoricalRequestChart', {
    extend: 'Ext.chart.CartesianChart',
    xtype: 'historical-request-chart',
    frame: true,
    axes: [{
        type: 'numeric',
        position: 'left',
        fields: ['value'],
        title: {
            text: 'Avg. Response \nTime (ms)',
            fontSize: 15
        },
        grid: true,
        minimum: 0,
        maximum: 20
    }, {
        type: 'time',
        position: 'bottom',
        fields: ['time'],
        dateFormat: 'd M'
        style: {
            axisLine: false
        }
    }],

    series: {
        type: 'line',
        xField: 'time',
        yField: 'value',
        style: { 'stroke': 'red' }
    }
});
```

It combines the basic definition of the chart, such as the axes and series, with things we know we'll reuse across the application, such as the title on the left axis.

Note that we're putting this class in a different location from anything we've seen so far in our example applications, but one that we discussed in *Chapter 3, Application Structure*. The ux namespace and corresponding directory is a fairly standard location for reusable classes in the Ext JS community, so we will follow this convention here.

We will create another reusable class, this time for the live request chart:

```
// app/ux/chart/LiveRequestChart.js
Ext.define('Instrumatics.ux.chart.LiveRequestChart', {
    extend: 'Ext.chart.CartesianChart',
    xtype: 'live-request-chart',
    redrawCounter: 0,
    frame: true,
    axes: [{
        type: 'numeric',
        position: 'left',
        fields: ['value'],
        title: {
            text: 'Avg. Response \nTime (ms)',
            fontSize: 15
        },
        grid: true,
        minimum: 0,
        maximum: 20
    }, {
        type: 'time',
        position: 'bottom',
        step: [Ext.Date.SECOND, 1],
        fields: ['time'],
        dateFormat: 'H:i:s',
        fromDate: new Date(new Date().setMinutes( new
Date().getMinutes() - 1)).setSeconds(0),
        toDate: new Date(new Date().setMinutes( new
Date().getMinutes() + 5)).setSeconds(0)
    }],
    series: {
        type: 'line',
        xField: 'time',
        yField: 'value',
        style: {
            'stroke-width': 2
```

```
            }
        },


        constructor: function() {
            this.callParent(arguments);

            this.on('redraw', this.onRedraw, this);
        },


        onRedraw: function() {
            this.redrawCounter++;

            if(this.redrawCounter > 15) {
                this.redrawCounter = 0;

                var timeAxis = this.getAxes()[1],
                    oldFrom = new Date(timeAxis.getFromDate()),
                    oldTo = new Date(timeAxis.getToDate()),
                    newFrom = Ext.Date.add(oldFrom, Ext.Date.SECOND,
    15),
                    newTo = Ext.Date.add(oldTo, Ext.Date.SECOND, 15);

                timeAxis.setFromDate(newFrom);
                timeAxis.setToDate(newTo);
            }
        }
    });
```

You'll notice that this code has a lot in common with the code from our code investigation earlier in the chapter. It's just that we've wrapped it up into a reusable class.

With these new classes ready to go, creating the dashboard is just a matter of piecing together what we've already written, as shown in the following code:

```
// app/view/dashboard/Dashboard.js
Ext.define("Instrumatics.view.dashboard.Dashboard", {
    extend: "Ext.panel.Panel",
    xtype: 'app-dashboard',
    title: 'hello',
    requires: [
        'Instrumatics.ux.chart.LiveRequestChart',
        'Instrumatics.ux.chart.HistoricalRequestChart'
```

```
        ],
        viewModel: {
            type: 'dashboard-dashboard'
        },
        controller: 'dashboard-dashboard',
        layout: {
            type: 'vbox',
            align: 'stretch'
        },
        items: [
            {
                xtype: 'container',
                flex: 1,
                layout: {
                    type: 'hbox',
                    align: 'stretch'
                },
                items: [
                    {
                        xtype: 'live-request-chart',
                        title: 'Live Web Requests', bind: '{webLogs}',
                        series: { style: { 'stroke': 'red' } },
                        margin: '10 5 0 10', flex: 1
                    },
                    {
                        xtype: 'live-request-chart',
                        title: 'Live SQL Requests', bind: '{sqlLogs}',
                        series: { style: { 'stroke': 'green' } },
                        margin: '10 10 0 5', flex: 1
                    }
                ]
            },
            {
                xtype: 'container',
                flex: 1,
                layout: {
                    type: 'hbox',
                    align: 'stretch'
                },
                items: [
                    {
                        xtype: 'historical-request-chart',
                        title: 'Last 30 Days', bind:
'{historicalWebLogs}',
```

```
                    series: { style: { 'stroke': 'red' } },
                    margin: '10 5 10 10', flex: 1
                },
                {
                    xtype: 'historical-request-chart',
                    title: 'Last 30 Days', bind:
    '{historicalSqlLogs}',
                    series: { style: { 'stroke': 'green' } },
                    margin: '10 10 10 5', flex: 1
                }
            ]
        }

    ]
});
```

Rather than duplication of the configuration that forms the charts, we'll just put together the containers — which use the vbox and hbox layouts — and set up titles, formatting, and bindings.

This is great. Rather than duplicating code and having lots of unnecessary configuration in the dashboard view itself, we've moved this code to a more logical location, promoting reuse and making for a tidier code base.

Constant evaluation

At this point, let's look at what we've built in comparison with our design. It matches our implementation so far, but there wasn't any mention of these reusable classes. There are two ways of looking at this:

- We didn't go far enough in our design and missed an opportunity to spell out exactly what we needed to build

- We saw an opportunity to refactor our code after we found ourselves duplicating something we'd already written

There's something to be said for both these viewpoints; however, in *Chapter 5, Practical – a CMS Application*, we discussed YAGNI — you aren't going to need it — which dictates that there's little point in planning for reuse if the component in question is never going to be reused.

In this case, the implementation process revealed that we'd have some duplication, so we refactored. While taking careful consideration at the design stage is important, re-evaluating our decisions and code should be an ongoing process, so it's critical to realize that even if there's a feeling that something should have been noticed in the design phase, nothing is set in stone. We can always change things as long as we understand why they need to change and use it as a learning experience.

The dashboard view model

Each of the four charts in the dashboard has its own data source and these are specified in the bind configuration for each. The definitions for these sources are in the dashboard view model:

```
// app/view/dashboard/DashboardModel.js
Ext.define('Instrumatics.view.dashboard.DashboardModel', {
    extend: 'Ext.app.ViewModel',
    alias: 'viewmodel.dashboard-dashboard',

    stores: {
        webLogs: {
            type: 'logstream',
            filters: [{
                property: 'type',
                value: 'web'
            }]
        },

        sqlLogs: {
            type: 'logstream',
            filters: [{
                property: 'type',
                value: 'sql'
            }]
        },

        historicalWebLogs: {
            type: 'logentries',
            filters: [{
                property: 'type',
                value: 'web'
            }]
        },
```

```
historicalSqlLogs: {
    type: 'logentries',
    filters: [{
        property: 'type',
        value: 'sql'
    }]
}
    }
});
```

We're setting up the data sources for the dashboard. If you look back at the associated store definitions, you'll see matching aliases and also the `remoteFilter` option set to `true`. This enables us to set the filter on the store definition in the view model and have these passed through to the server as JSON.

This makes for a very simple method to set up stores to retrieve filtered data from the server side (just pass over an array of filters and let the backend take care of it).

We've put together nearly all the pieces of the dashboard with one exception: the view controller. Let's look at this now.

The dashboard view controller

There isn't any interactivity on the dashboard, so there's not much for the view controller to do. We'll use it to control the live refresh aspect of the charts:

```
// app/view/dashboard/DashboardController.js
Ext.define('Instrumatics.view.dashboard.DashboardController', {
    extend: 'Ext.app.ViewController',
    alias: 'controller.dashboard-dashboard',

    init: function() {
        var data = this.getViewModel().getData(),
            me = this;

        setInterval(function() {
            data.webLogs.load({ addRecords: true });
            data.sqlLogs.load({ addRecords: true });
        }, 1000);
    }
});
```

It's as simple as this; every second, grab the store powering the live chart and call its load method with the `addRecords` option set to `true`. This will cause new records to be appended to the store rather than overwriting old records.

While there's not much code here, there are a couple of discussion points. We could have avoided using a view controller at all for the dashboard and baked this refresh behavior directly in the `LiveRequestChart` class, maybe setting the refresh rate via a configuration option.

By doing it in the controller, we get the chance to centralize the place in which the refresh rate is set. This isn't a massive win though. There's definitely a case to be made for moving this into the UI class. It's another situation where there's no right or wrong way of doing things; multiple options are available and it's better to pick one and move on than be paralyzed with the choices on offer.

We've got the first page of our application, so let's now move on to the subpages, starting with the web logs.

Web logs subpage

We've already built part of this screen already. We can reuse `Instrumatics.ux.chart.HistoricalRequestChart` we created earlier to display the trend for a specified date range. As this data's coming from the store, we can simply filter the store and don't have to do anything on the component itself. With this in mind, the **Web** view looks like this:

```
// app/view/web/Web.js
Ext.define('Instrumatics.view.web.Web',{
    extend: 'Ext.panel.Panel',
    xtype: 'web-logs',

    viewModel: {
        type: 'web-web'
    },

    layout: {
        type: 'vbox',
        align: 'stretch'
    },
    items: [
        {
            header: {
                title: 'Web Requests',
                items: [
                    { xtype: 'datefield', fieldLabel: 'From',
labelAlign: 'right', bind: '{currentStartDate}' },
                    { xtype: 'datefield', fieldLabel: 'To',
labelAlign: 'right', bind: '{currentEndDate}', labelWidth: 30 },
```

```
                        { xtype: 'button', text: 'Refresh', margin: '0
0 0 10' }
                ]
            },
            margin: 10, xtype: 'historical-request-chart', bind:
'{logData}', flex: 1
        },
        {
            xtype: 'grid',
            margin: 10,
            hideHeaders: true,
            viewConfig: {
              trackOver: false
            },
            disableSelection: true,
            header: {
                title: 'Breakdown',
                items: [
                    {
                        xtype: 'combo',
                        labelAlign: 'right', labelWidth: 60,
                        fieldLabel: 'Category',
                        bind: {
                            store: '{categories}',
                            value: '{currentCategory}'
                        },
                        queryMode: 'local',
                        editable: false,
                        forceSelection: true,
                        displayField: 'text',
                        valueField: 'value'
                    }
                ]
            },
            bind: '{logStatistics}',
            flex: 1,
            width: '100%',
            columns: [
                { name: 'Label', dataIndex: 'label', flex: 1 },
                { name: 'Percentage', dataIndex: 'percentage',
flex: 1 }
            ]
        }
    ]
});
```

It's a fair amount of code, but nothing other than component configuration is happening here. Let's break it down step-by-step.

Firstly, there's the configuration of the panel itself where we set up a vbox layout.

Then we add our first item, an instance of the HistoricalRequestChart we built earlier, and add To and From date fields to its header. The values of these are bound to values (currentStartDate and currentEndDate) in the view model, and the chart itself is bound to logData in the view model.

Finally, we have the configuration of the statistics grid. Its store is bound to logStatistics and in its header, we add a combo box that has its value bound to currentCategory in the view model and its store—to provide the combo box options—bound to categories. The combo box allows the user to choose which statistics category they'd like to view.

Onwards and upwards to the view model!

A view on the Web

Our Web view model follows our design and fleshes it out with some implementation details:

```
// app/view/web/WebModel.js
Ext.define('Instrumatics.view.web.WebModel', {
    extend: 'Ext.app.ViewModel',
    alias: 'viewmodel.web-web',
    stores: {
        logData: {
            type: 'logentries',
            filters: [
                { property: 'startDate', value:
'{currentStartDate}' },
                { property: 'endDate', value: '{currentEndDate}' }
            ]
        },

        logStatistics: {
            type: 'statistics',
            filters: [
                { property: 'category', value: '{currentCategory}'
},
                { property: 'startDate', value:
'{currentStartDate}' },
```

```
                    { property: 'endDate', value: '{currentEndDate}' }
                ]
            },


        categories: {
            fields: ['text', 'value'],
            data: [{
                text: 'Browser', value: 'browser'
            },{
                text: 'Location', value: 'location'
            },{
                text: 'Device Type', value: 'device'
            }]
        }
    },


    data: {
        currentCategory: '',
        currentStartDate: null,
        currentEndDate: null
    }
});
```

Note the bindings on the filters. This enables us to link the filters with a value on the view model, which in turn links through to values on the form controls in the view. This means that as soon as the user updates a form control, it'll update the filter on the store automatically, reloading the store, and redrawing the chart and grid.

We've also got a `categories` store, which is simply a way of holding data for the categories combo, nothing more.

Controlling the Web

Well here's a thing, this view has no corresponding view controller! In previous versions of Ext JS, we'd be listening for change events on the date fields and combo box, then grabbing the changed value and reloading the store with it.

In the brave new world of view models though, we don't need to do this. When a date field updates, it automatically updates the corresponding view model value, which in turn updates the store's filter.

We're already setting up the stores and the form components, so by adding an extra sprinkle of magic in the form of bind configurations, Ext JS will power all of this for us. This means less custom code for us to write, which can only be a good thing!

More and more subpages

We know that the other subpage in our application, the SQL log page, is going to be very similar to the web log page. This should be raising an eyebrow with regard to code duplication. We could pull out the grid and the chart header from the **Web** view into separate classes and turn them into reusable components, but is this the right thing to do? These components won't be reused! They have their place in only one location in the application to power the subpages. Unlike HistoricalRequestChart, which is used in both the dashboard and the subpages, these are only needed for one job.

Let's consider another approach: *subclassing*. We could create a new component that contains the chart, form fields, and grid from the **Web** view, and add some configuration options that give us the customization we need. This might look like the following command:

```
// app/view/SubPage.js
Ext.define('Instrumatics.view.SubPage', {
    extend: 'Ext.Container',

    requires: [
        'Instrumatics.ux.chart.HistoricalRequestChart'
    ],

    xtype: 'subpage',

    config: {

        layout: {
            type: 'vbox',
            align: 'stretch'
        },

        chartCfg: {
            header: {
                items: [
                    { xtype: 'datefield', fieldLabel: 'From',
    labelAlign: 'right', bind: '{currentStartDate}' },
```

```
                              { xtype: 'datefield', fieldLabel: 'To',
    labelAlign: 'right', bind: '{currentEndDate}', labelWidth: 30 },
                              { xtype: 'button', text: 'Refresh', margin: '0
    0 0 10' }
                    ]
            },
            margin: 10, xtype: 'historical-request-chart', bind:
    '{logData}', flex: 1
        },

        gridCfg: {
            xtype: 'grid',
            margin: 10,
            hideHeaders: true,
            viewConfig: {
              trackOver: false
            },
            disableSelection: true,
            header: {
                title: 'Breakdown',
                items: [
                    {
                        xtype: 'combo',
                        labelAlign: 'right', labelWidth: 60,
                        fieldLabel: 'Category',
                        bind: {
                            store: '{categories}',
                            value: '{currentCategory}'
                        },
                        queryMode: 'local',
                        editable: false,
                        forceSelection: true,
                        displayField: 'text',
                        valueField: 'value'
                    }
                ]
            },
            bind: '{logStatistics}',
            flex: 1,
            width: '100%',
            columns: [
                { name: 'Label', dataIndex: 'label', flex: 1 },
                { name: 'Percentage', dataIndex: 'percentage',
    flex: 1 }
            ]
```

```
            }
        },

        initComponent: function(arguments) {
            this.callParent(arguments);
            this.add(this.getChartCfg());
            this.add(this.getGridCfg());
        }
    });
```

We've pulled the entire configuration from the **Web** view into this base class called `SubPage` and separated out the key components, namely, the chart and the grid. We're also harnessing the power of the Ext JS class system by wrapping these in the config section, which not only generates get and set methods for `gridCfg` and `chartCfg`, but also provides us with a shortcut to override parts of these config objects. Let's demonstrate by showing the **SQL** view, which is powered by our new `SubPage` class:

```
// app/view/sql/Sql.js
Ext.define("Instrumatics.view.sql.Sql",{
    extend: "Instrumatics.view.SubPage",
    xtype: 'sql-logs',
    viewModel: {
        type: "sql-sql"
    },
    chartCfg: {
        title: 'SQL Requests'
    }
});
```

Yep, that's it! We've managed to get the same functionality that the **Web** view had, but reusing lots of the code. Note that `chartCfg` is exposed for us to configure, which means that all we have to do is set `viewModel` and the chart's title configuration and we're all set.

Turns out we can do the same for the view model too:

```
// app/view/SubPageModel.js
Ext.define('Instrumatics.view.SubPageModel', {
    extend: 'Ext.app.ViewModel',
    stores: {
        logData: {
            type: 'logentries',
            autoLoad: true,
            remoteFilter: true,
```

```
            filters: [
                    { property: 'startDate', value:
    '{currentStartDate}' },
                    { property: 'endDate', value: '{currentEndDate}' }
                ]
            },

        logStatistics: {
            type: 'statistics',
            autoLoad: true,
            remoteFilter: true,
            filters: [
                    { property: 'category', value: '{currentCategory}'
    },
                    { property: 'startDate', value:
    '{currentStartDate}' },
                    { property: 'endDate', value: '{currentEndDate}' }
                ]
            }
        },


        data: {
            currentStartDate: null,
            currentEndDate: null
        }
    });
```

And the following SQL view model:

```
    Ext.define('Instrumatics.view.sql.SqlModel', {
        extend: 'Instrumatics.view.SubPageModel',
        alias: 'viewmodel.sql-sql',

        stores: {
            categories: {
                fields: ['text', 'value'],
                data: [{
                    text: 'Query Source', value: 'source'
                },{
                    text: 'Query Type', value: 'type'
                }]
            }
        },
```

```
    data: {
        currentCategory: 'source'
    }
});
```

The **Web** and **SQL** views now share code in a logical way without polluting our UX namespace with classes that don't belong there. In future, we could easily add on more views like this, but for now, we've got a fantastic way to avoid code duplication and keep our application well structured.

Summary

In this chapter, we've built a second practical application and talked a lot about how a design can change as an application develops. While we produce an initial application architecture with the best of intentions and the knowledge we have hand as the application develops, it's important to be flexible in order to produce a successful final product. We also introduced routing, more on data binding, and showed how code can be reused in a variety of ways.

In the next chapter, we'll build an application that will be familiar to most readers: an e-mail client. It'll be a responsive app tailored for both desktop and tablet, and we'll once again take the ideas we've already discussed and develop them even further.

7
Practical – an E-mail Client

Our past two applications have been fairly straightforward examples, but ones that are useful to illustrate how to create a strong foundation for a future, more extensive product. In this chapter, we'll build a fully featured webmail client that will provide a tailored experience for users of both desktop browsers and smaller devices such as tablets.

Everyone knows the traditional e-mail interface, but we'll try and at the same time show how Ext JS technologies can be used to make short work of building such an application. Here's the breakdown of what we'll be doing in this chapter:

- Establishing essential requirements for the application
- Coming up with an ideal user interface for each form factor
- Analyzing the issues that may arise on a smaller screen
- Designing the view and controller structure to present and orchestrate it all
- Evaluating the design of our application

Along the way we'll reinforce our knowledge of routing and view models, as well as undertaking constant re-evaluation of our work to ensure the quality of the code.

We'll also take a little more time to finish the design of this application, dipping our toe in the water of Ext JS theming. While we won't be building a full replacement theme, we'll touch on some of the places where the theming system should be used in order to improve the maintainability of your application.

Form factors

This application will adapt to a variety of devices, from desktop browsers to tablets and mobile phones. The size of these devices is often called the "form factor" and Ext JS provides several mechanisms that allow you to customize the user experience depending on the form factor of the device being used.

In this chapter, we'll focus on `responsiveConfig`, an option available when you include the `Ext.mixin.Responsive` class in your views. In a standard desktop application, we might have two components side by side in the viewport, since desktop screen sizes are generally wider than they are tall. On a mobile phone, users will often be in portrait orientation, so this is no longer true; the screen is taller than it is wide. In this case, we can use `responsiveConfig` to override the original side-by-side configuration and use different layouts, items, and component widths—in fact any aspect of the original viewport configuration—and change the appearance and behavior of the application for a taller screen.

This one feature provides us with an exceptionally powerful means to deliver an experience that is tailored to a particular form factor. In this chapter, we'll see some practical examples of implementing `responsiveConfig`.

Application design

What features do we expect from an e-mail client? At a minimum:

- **Login**: This helps to gain access to your own account
- **Inbox**: This is a list of our e-mails
- **Sent**: This is a list of e-mails we've sent in the past
- **Archive**: This is a list of e-mails we've disposed of
- **Composer**: This helps to write e-mails
- **Search**: This helps to find archived e-mails

The final version of the app looks something like this:

The thread view on the left and messages from the selected thread on the right

What do we need to do to get to this point? Let's sketch out a design:

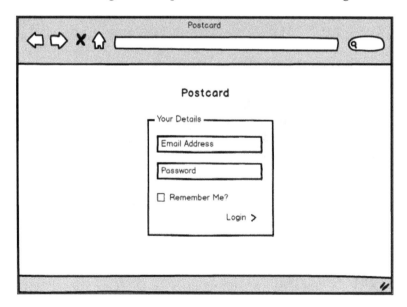

The login page is pretty standard. We'll want to validate user input, check the e-mail address, and ensure the password isn't blank, but there really isn't anything out of the ordinary here:

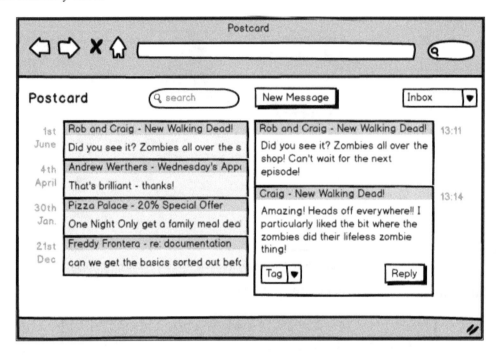

Here's the main interface for the application. We'll be implementing threaded e-mail; we have a list of threads on the left with an excerpt of the most recent message showing as the description of the thread. The date of the last message is shown on the left-hand side of each thread. On the right-hand side, we show the selected message thread, most recent message last. Each message has its received date on its left. The thread has a **Reply** button and a dropdown to allow the thread to be tagged, more on this shortly.

At the top of the screen we have a logo (from left to right), an icon for the **Contacts** section, a **search** bar, a button to create a new e-mail, and finally, a dropdown to filter threads by tag.

The **search** bar will cause matching message threads to appear below (in the same style as the **Inbox** view).

Rather than having separate screens for archived e-mail, sent e-mail, and so on, we make the assumption that **Inbox** threads are just untagged threads. When they are tagged — either automatically as "sent" or by some other arbitrary tag such as "home" or "work" — then they are removed from the **Inbox** view, as shown in the following screenshot. This concept is found in many e-mail clients, for example, Gmail.

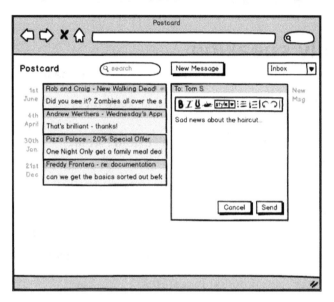

When composing new e-mails, it takes place in the right-hand position. As there is no selected thread at this time, the space is clear to be occupied by a panel that contains a combo box to choose a recipient for the e-mail, a basic HTML editor for the e-mail itself, and a **Send** button.

Replying to an e-mail works in a similar way; the composer panel appears under the messages and allows the user to write a response.

A couple more items to note are that the user will start off with a number of default tags:

- Draft
- Archive
- Spam
- Work
- Home

When selecting a tag for a thread, the user can easily add another by typing in the combo box.

I require to admire

As architects of a product, we always need to consider how to make our product exemplary, how to make sure the user experience is a good one, how to exceed the expectations of our stakeholders. The starting step is to work out in exacting detail the facets on the product we'd like to build.

Technically speaking

How do the requirements we've spelled out translate into the underlying tech?

- We want to display a login form with a "remember me" feature, so we need some kind of persistent storage
- We want to display thread data in a custom format
- We want to display full message threads in a custom format
- We want a basic HTML editor for message bodies
- We need an autocomplete box for recipients
- We need to display search results in the same format as message threads
- We need an autocomplete box for tags to be used in various locations

Let's translate each of these into Ext JS features:

- We can use cookies or local storage to hold login information between systems (either using native browser methods or an Ext JS-powered session class)
- We can use an Ext JS DataView to create a templated view of thread data
- We can use an Ext JS DataView to create a templated view of message data
- Ext JS provides an HTML editor widget
- The Ext JS combo box can be powered by a store that retrieves remote contact data
- We can reuse the message thread DataView with a different store
- We can use the `editable:true` option of the Ext JS combo box in cases where we need to add new tags

There are a couple of gray areas there that we'll review later, but it does look like Ext JS can provide all of the features we're going to need to build this application.

Responding to the situation

There's another requirement in this project: a responsive design that works on devices with smaller screens. Well, it turns out that the UI we've come up with already looks pretty good on a tablet, with one caveat. You have to be holding the device in landscape mode. This is a problem that you don't really have to consider on the desktop, but it becomes critical with mobile devices.

From an architectural standpoint, we need to understand how the layout of the application will differ between screen sizes in order to decide how to assemble the application. In the designs so far, there are two panes side by side; there simply won't be enough screen space to allow for this on a portrait phone or tablet.

Instead, we'll hide or show the "left" and "right" panes depending on user actions. If they click on a thread of messages or the **New Message** button, the threads will be hidden and the correct right-hand pane will appear.

The only other issue with a portrait screen is the application header; there are too many components in there to fit in the width of a smaller screen. Instead, we'll show a menu button when in portrait mode that hides some controls when toggled and shows others. This gives us a second level of menu that's only shown when the user needs it. Here's a mockup of some of these ideas:

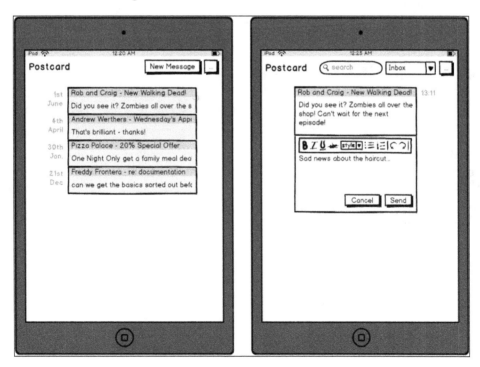

When clicking on one of the messages in the left screenshot, the list is replaced by the message thread seen in the right-hand side screenshot.

In an HTML-based responsive website, CSS media queries can be used to style the page in a fashion appropriate for any screen and orientation. While we can obviously still make use of CSS alongside Ext JS to do customization, our requirements are more complex; can Ext JS provide any extra features to assist?

The `responsive` plugin allows developers to tailor any component configuration based on a set of rules relating to the current device screen. Here are a few example scenarios in a theoretical responsive application:

- If the screen is less than 500 pixels wide, collapse the sidebar panel by default
- If the screen is in landscape mode, show a new column of data
- If the device is an iOS tablet, apply a different CSS class

In the webmail application, we've already mentioned showing and hiding header items. This can be done something like this:

```
{
    xtype: 'button', text: 'My Button',
    plugins: ['responsive'],
    responsiveConfig: {
        'portrait': { hidden: true }
    }
}
```

There's a built-in rule called "portrait" that allows you to specify a configuration object that will only be applied when the rule is in effect. As architects, we must carefully consider the best way of making use of this feature without ending up with lots of messy configuration.

In the desktop version of the application we have two panes side by side. For this, we can use the `hbox` layout. However, for the portrait orientation, we'd like to be able to switch between one pane and another. This seems like a good use of the card layout. We'll also have to consider how to trigger the switch of the panes and have this code run in portrait orientation only.

The important takeaway is that the responsive plugin—in a similar fashion to view models—allows you to avoid writing lots of glue code that responds to the state of the application environment, and instead lets us declare our intentions at configuration time. After this, Ext JS takes care of most of the rest.

This is another example in which analyzing the requirements with a strong understanding of the available technology can result in a simpler architecture and a clearer code base.

Input required

In previous chapters, we've gone into detail about the API we're going to be communicating with. There's no denying that it's one of the key parts of any application design; in fact many projects can live or die based on the quality of the API they're integrating with, but we've discussed this in the past two chapters and we've still got a lot to cover. From here on, we're generally going to assume that we're working with a well-designed RESTful API that works well with Ext JS. This'll give us some room to concentrate on some new ideas.

 That's not to say you can skip over the API when designing your application. It is very rare you'll be working with a perfect backend, so keep analyzing whether the server is providing the endpoints you need.

We'll move on to looking at the rest of the application, but in a different way to previous chapters; once the data's been pulled down from the server, we'll try and consider how it's going to move through our app. We'll also look at two other facets of the design in more detail: routing and events. Why this change in direction compared to previous chapters?

As our applications become more complicated, we have to continually think about how to keep that complexity under control. These three features: view models, events, and routing, all allow a "fire and forget" attitude, wire up some basic configuration, trigger an action at the source, and this bit of code is done. Somewhere else in the application will subscribe to this action—be it a view model binding, a routing change or the firing of an event—and consume it accordingly.

We'll first identify our views and controllers as we have in the past and look at how this will inform the routing, view models and events that will power the functionality of our application.

A view to a thrill

Let's break down the major views that will make up the main screen of the application:

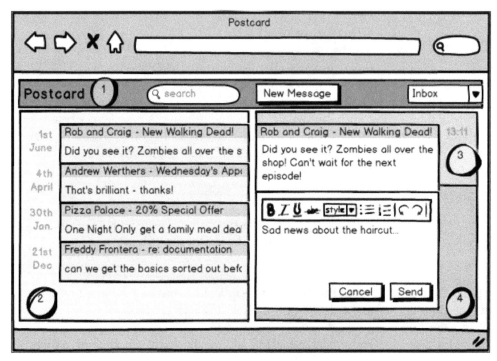

1: header view, 2: thread view, 3: message view, and 4: composer view; main view encompasses views 1 - 4

The login view is the simplest; a self-contained view, view controller, and a view model to bind with the values of the login form. It's not shown in the preceding mockup because it's the only one on the screen at the time, almost standalone.

There's a caveat to this. For the first time, we'll be using an over-arching controller to deal with the interactions between views. In the previous chapter, this was left to the "main" view controller, since the "main" view was the container for every part of our application. Here, the login view and the rest of the application are effectively independent from each other and so it makes sense to have a "third party" helping them to work together.

We'll call this top-level controller our "root" controller. It's not a view controller, but a completely self-contained class that is responsible for showing the login view and reacting to a successful login. To formalize this:

```
Postcard.controller.RootController: extends Ext.app.Controller
- onLaunch -> check for valid login
- onLoginSuccess -> show main view
```

The login view controller is responsible for processing a login attempt and after doing so, it will fire off the appropriate actions. Along with its view and view model, it looks like this:

```
Postcard.view.login.Login: extends Ext.window.Window
- items[]
    - e-mail: extends Ext.form.Text
    - password: extends Ext.form.Text
    - rememberMe: extends Ext.form.Checkbox
    - submit: extends Ext.Button

Postcard.view.login.LoginModel: extends Ext.app.ViewModel
- e-mail
- password
- rememberMe

Postcard.view.login.LoginController: extends
Ext.app.ViewController
- onLoginClick
```

Assuming the `onLoginClick` method is successful, we'll move on to the main screen of the application.

Mainly harmless

As in previous chapters, the main view is the viewport that contains the other views in the application, such as the application header and the list of threads. According to our design, the view should look like this:

```
Postcard.view.main.Main: extends Ext.Panel
- items[]
    - app-header: extends Ext.Container
    - threads: extends Ext.DataView
    - container: extends Ext.Container
        - items[]
            - messages: Ext.Container
            - composer: Ext.form.Panel
```

A couple of things to note here, the primary views that make up our application are mentioned here: header, threads, messages and, composer. We're also doing a bit of forward thinking regarding our design, in that the composer and messages views are enclosed in a separate container.

This will allow us to more easily work with the Ext JS layout system, having the threads view and this anonymous container in an `hbox` arrangement. The view model looks like this:

```
Postcard.view.main.MainModel: extends Ext.app.ViewModel
- currentTag
- searchTerm
```

It's just convenient for a few pieces of state that need to be shared between the views contained in the main view. The view controller looks like this:

```
Postcard.view.main.MainController: extends Ext.app.ViewController
- onLogout
- onHome
- onShowThread
- onNewThread
- onNewMessage
```

The first method (`onLogout`) will handle clicks on a logout button. The next four methods on the main view controller will be triggered by routing, and will be responsible for setting changes in the state of the application.

Remember that the main view and its associated classes don't really have any functionality of their own; they're responsible for orchestrating all of the other application parts contained within.

Full steam ahead

The first child view of the main viewport is the header view, containing a number of components that are available anywhere in the application as follows:

```
Postcard.view.header.Header: Ext.Toolbar
- items[]
    - homebutton: extends Ext.Button
    - searchfield: extends Ext.form.TextField
    - tagfilter: extends Ext.form.ComboBox
    - newmessagebutton: extends Ext.Button
    - menubutton: extends Ext.Button
```

There's actually a surprising amount happening here. We also have to bear in mind that this is the target for one of our portrait orientation pieces of functionality, so there will be some usage of the responsive plugin in our implementation, as shown in the following code:

```
Postcard.view.header.HeaderController: extends
Ext.app.ViewController
- onHomeClick
- onNewMessageClick
```

These methods are event listeners that will in turn trigger further functionality. You might wonder why we don't have handlers to toggle the menu open and closed or to choose an item from the combo box. Think about data binding. If we bind the state of the menu button and the combo box to a view model, other components can bind to the values in the view model and will receive updates without us having to write any glue code. To this end, the header view model will look like:

```
Postcard.view.header.HeaderModel: extends Ext.app.ViewModel
- tags
```

Nothing more than a store to populate the tag filter combo box. We'll talk about this use of data binding further when we come to implement the header.

Threading our way

A thread is just a fancy way of saying "a collection of e-mail messages". We're going to use Ext.DataView for this:

```
Postcard.view.threads.Threads: extends Ext.DataView
- stripHtml
```

We're going to support HTML e-mails in this application, but to prevent the thread view from looking messy, we'll strip out this HTML before presenting it to the user. Other than this, it's a normal implementation of DataView.

```
Postbox.view.threads.ThreadsModel: extends Ext.app.ViewModel
- threads
```

The view model contains the thread store that powers the view as follows:

```
Postcard.view.threads.ThreadsController: extends
Ext.app.ViewController
- onThreadClick
```

There's only a single method here, one that is triggered by the itemclick event on the thread DataView. It'll be responsible for redirecting the user to a list of messages in this thread.

Send me a message

The message view is responsible for showing the messages that make up a thread. As such, it's mainly based on DataView. It's a little more complicated than this though because DataView doesn't inherit from Ext.Panel; it can't have its own child items or docked toolbar.

In this case, we need to have some tools at the bottom of the message list in order to change the thread tag and send a reply. Therefore, we wrap the DataView in a panel:

```
Postcard.view.messages.Messages: extends Ext.Panel
- items[]
    - panel: extends Ext.Panel
        - items[]
            - messagelist: extends Ext.DataView
        - bbar[]
            - tagpicker: extends Ext.form.ComboBox
            - reply: extends Ext.Button
```

In the view model, we need two stores: one for the messages in the thread, and one for the tags that are available to choose from.

```
Postcode.view.messages.MessagesModel: extends Ext.app.ViewModel
- messages
- threads
```

The view controller has a couple of event handlers to manage the user's interactions with the message view:

```
Postcard.view.messages.MessagesController: extends
Ext.app.ViewController
- onReplyClick
- onNewThread
- onShwThread
- onTagChange
```

There's now only one missing piece to this application—how do we write new messages?

Stay composed

The composer view is responsible for writing new messages and writing replies. It needs several UI components to accomplish this:

```
Postcard.view.composer.Composer: extends Ext.form.Panel
- items[]
    - recipients: extends Ext.form.ComboBox
    - subject: extends Ext.form.TextField
    - message: extends Ext.form.HtmlEditor
```

Recipients and subject won't be used if the composer is replying to an existing thread. It will only be used when creating a new thread:

```
Postcard.view.Composer.ComposerModel: extends Ext.app.ViewModel
- items[]
    - contacts
    - newMessage
```

We have a store of contacts to power the recipients' field, and an object to store the form values as the user enters them:

```
Postcard.view.composer.ComposerController: extends
Ext.app.ViewController
- onSendClick
```

The view controller will be responsible for saving the message to the server, which in turn would send it to the designated recipients.

We don't exactly have an address book in this application; instead, any previously used e-mail addresses are just saved and are available to pick in future messages.

Design overview

We skipped over a lot of the data layer design this time around because it was very "boilerplate" in nature and we'd discussed such things in previous chapters. Why go through the class design process for the views and their associated view controllers and view models then? We've done this in previous chapters as well.

Clearly, every application is different. Breaking it down in this way helps us flesh out the code we're going to write without actually writing any code. This is important, because we'll avoid thinking too hard about the details of the implementation and have a better understanding of the shape of the larger pieces in the puzzle.

The next step is to revisit routes, events, and data flow and see how these large pieces will work together.

Application state

First up is routing. We said in *Chapter 6, Practical – Monitoring Dashboard,* that the route is a way of keeping part of the application's state in the URL. Another way of looking at this is that as the application changes through its various states, you are walking through the screens that the user would see as they interact with the interface.

By working out the various high-level states of our application, we can better visualize the user flow and establish the routes that we can employ in our code.

Home screen/initial load

This is displayed straight after login and represents the default state of the main screen of the application before the user interacts with it. It looks as follows:

```
Route: /#home
```

The views will have the following state:

```
view.threads.Main.activeItem = 'threads'
```

If we're in portrait view, we'll use a card layout.

 "Card" is one of the build-Ext JS layouts, which allows you to easily switch out one component for another. It's also the basis for the Ext.TabPanel component.

This means that the home state of the application needs to have the thread view as the active item:

```
view.main.Main.rightPane.hidden = true
```

In the initial state on a normal device, the user has neither selected a message nor has chosen to compose a new message. Therefore, there's nothing showing in the right-hand pane.

New thread

The route that handles requests for a new thread is displayed in the following command:

```
Route: thread/new
```

When the user presses the new message button, they are shown the composer view. The overall state changes as follows:

```
view.main.Main.activeItem = 'rightPane'
view.composer.Composer.hidden = false
view.messages.Messages.hidden = true
```

Remember that changing route doesn't mean that the state reverts to the initial state and then changes; we need to reset all things that could potentially have been shown by another route. In this case, if the user previously selected a thread, then the messages view would be showing, and we need to hide it when creating a new message.

Show thread

The route to handle requests for a specific message thread is as follows:

```
Route: thread/:id/messages
```

It's triggered when the user selects a thread as follows:

```
view.main.Main.activeItem = 'rightPane'
view.messages.Messages.hidden = false
view.composer.Composer.hidden = true
view.main.MainModel.currentThreadId = :id
```

Pretty much the opposite of a new message in which the messages are shown and the composer is hidden. The thread that was selected needs to be made available to the components that require it, in this case, the message view, so it can load the required messages.

New message/reply

The route to handle requests for a new message thread is as follows:

```
Route: thread/:id/messages/new
```

This is the final route in our application, and is used when a thread has been selected and then the user clicks on the "reply" button.

```
view.main.Main.activeItem = 'rightPane'
view.messages.Messages.hidden = false
view.composer.Composer.hidden = false
view.main.MainModel.currentThreadId = :id
```

Similar to the "show thread" route, except that the composer is shown as well as the messages view.

Routing overview

Examining the paths a user can take through your application can be a very valuable way of making sure nothing is missing from your design. It also gives the site the benefit of understanding the state of your application at various points on the path and allows you to translate this into routes to restore that state.

A binding agreement

Some of the state of the application is held in the URL, but other transient state is held in view models. We're going to look at an example of how data flows through this application in order to better understand how powerful data binding can be.

In portrait mode, our application has a menu button that toggles the visibility of various other components. The pseudocode for this could be:

```
if menu_button_is_pressed
    this.find('searchfield').show()
    this.find('newmessagebutton').hide()
    this.find('logo').hide()
else
    this.find('searchfield').hide()
    this.find('newmessagebutton').show()
    this.find('logo').show()
end
```

Code like this isn't complicated, but it's lengthy and error prone, a chore to write. Instead, we can use data binding to avoid this type of code and set up the behavior during configuration, something like this:

```
[
    {
        xtype: 'button', reference: 'menubutton',
        enableToggle: true
    },
    {
        xtype: 'searchfield',
        bind: {
            hidden: '{menubutton.pressed}'
        }
    }
]
```

There are a couple of things to understand here: firstly that a button will "publish" the state of its `pressed` value. Whenever `pressed` changes, either programmatically or because the user clicked on the button, the value will be pushed to the view model for this button. Secondly, if a component has its `reference` set, this will be available to access its published values in the view model.

Combine both of these and the bind configuration on the search field becomes clear; bind the value of `hidden` on the search field to the value of `pressed` on the menu button. If `pressed` is `true`, the search field will be hidden.

While we've covered data binding and view models in some detail in previous chapters, this is the first time we've looked at this particular approach. It's not even necessary to specify any configuration on the view model itself as long as one is available somewhere in the component hierarchy, this will work.

This is another weapon in the armory of tools that allow us to simplify our code. Using this kind of declarative approach, where we specify what we'd like to happen, but don't have to say how it happens, we can avoid writing methods like the pseudocode earlier and use a standardized approach that Ext JS provides.

The tricky part is fully embracing data binding and the view model concept. By thinking up-front about the dependencies between components and channeling data through view models, powerful interactions can be created with very little code.

An eventful application

An interesting observation about both routing and data binding is that they are built around events. When a route changes, an event is fired and a controller listens to it, setting the application's state accordingly. When a property is data bound, Ext JS publishes its changes and other properties listen for these changes.

We're also familiar with events, such as `click`, `select`, `show`, and so on, that are fired from the various Ext JS components. It would seem that as events are being used everywhere in an Ext JS application, we might as well make use of them ourselves!

We can use `fireEvent` from every `Observable` class in Ext JS. This allows you to fire a custom event from pretty much anywhere in our application. In previous versions of Ext JS, you needed to define events beforehand using an `addEvent` method, but this is no longer the case. However, what use is this? Does it offer a real-world advantage? Let's look at some bad code to demonstrate:

```
// Theoretical "messages" view controller
message.save({
    success: function(response) {
```

```
        var viewport = Ext.ComponentQuery.query('viewport')[0];

        // Refresh the list of records after adding this one.
        viewport.down('list').getStore().reload();

        viewport.showMessage(response.message);

        this.lookupReference('editor').hide();
    },
    scope: this
});
```

We save a message record. Then, in the callback, reload a list store, show a message in the viewport, and hide an editor component.

That's three separate things, only one of which—hiding the editor—is probably in the right place. The others should be handled by their own view controllers. This code would be much better:

```
message.save({
    success: function(response) {
        this.fireEvent('messagesaved', response.message.id);
    },
    scope: this
});
```

Now, any code anywhere in the application can listen for a `messagesaved` event and proceed accordingly. The key benefit this brings is that this example message view controller doesn't have to know anything about any other views, controllers, or even anything about the rest of the application.

This makes the messages view and view controller much more resistant to any changes in the rest of the system and much easier to test. In theory, it could be pulled out of the application and tested standalone.

Events and you

Let's go back to our webmail application. There's no point in adding events—or indeed anything—to our code base unless we're going to use them. A lot of places where we could use custom events will be rendered unnecessary by data binding and rendered unnecessary by routing.

There is one place that a custom event will be useful: when creating a reply. The composer controller is responsible for this, but when the reply's been saved we also need to refresh the messages view so that we can see the reply. This is a perfect place to make use of a custom event. We'll see how this is implemented shortly.

Coding – it's been a long time

We've spent a lot of time examining this proposed application and thinking about the techniques we can use to create it in an elegant way. Now, it's time to start building it.

We mentioned that the data layer for this application is very straightforward with lots of boilerplate code and nothing that is unexpected based on the knowledge we've gained in previous chapters. Let's jump straight in:

```
// app/model/BaseModel.js
Ext.define('Postcard.model.BaseModel', {
    extend: 'Ext.data.Model',
    schema: {
        namespace: 'Postcard.model',
        urlPrefix: 'http://localhost:3000',
        proxy: {
            type: 'rest',
            url: '{prefix}/{entityName:uncapitalize}'
        }
    },
});

// app/model/Contact.js
Ext.define('Postcard.model.Contact', {
    extend: 'Postcard.model.BaseModel',
    fields: [
        { name: 'e-mail' }
    ]
});

// app/model/Message.js
Ext.define('Postcard.model.Message', {
    extend: 'Postcard.model.BaseModel',
    fields: [
        { name: 'id' },
        { name: 'people' },
        { name: 'subject' },
        { name: 'body' },
        { name: 'date', type: 'date' },
        { name: 'tag' }
    ]
});

// app/model/Tag.js
```

```
Ext.define('Postcard.model.Tag', {
    extend: 'Postcard.model.BaseModel',
    fields: [
        { name: 'name' }
    ]
});

// app/model/Thread.js
Ext.define('Postcard.model.Thread', {
    extend: 'Postcard.model.BaseModel',
    fields: [
        { name: 'id' },
        { name: 'people' },
        { name: 'subject' },
        { name: 'lastMessageOn', type: 'date' },
        { name: 'lastMessageSnippet' }
    ]
});
```

Four models: `Contact`, `Tag`, `Message`, and `Thread`, all extend a `BaseModel` class that contains our data schema. Note that the `BaseModel` class specifies a rest proxy, so we know what to expect from the load and save behavior on our models. This is completely standard and very familiar from our previous example applications. The stores are correspondingly straightforward:

```
// app/store/Contacts.js
Ext.define('Postcard.store.Contacts', {
    extend: 'Ext.data.Store',
    model: 'Postcard.model.Contact',
    alias: 'store.contacts',
    autoLoad: true
});

// app/store/Tags.js
Ext.define('Postcard.store.Tags', {
    extend: 'Ext.data.Store',
    model: 'Postcard.model.Tag',
    alias: 'store.tags',
    autoLoad: true
});

// app/store/Messages.js
Ext.define('Postcard.store.Messages', {
    extend: 'Ext.data.Store',
    model: 'Postcard.model.Message',
```

```
        alias: 'store.messages'
});

// app/store/Threads.js
Ext.define('Postcard.store.Threads', {
    extend: 'Ext.data.Store',
    autoLoad: true,
    model: 'Postcard.model.Thread',
    alias: 'store.threads'
});
```

There is one store for each model class; everything apart from messages will load automatically because we need them across the application and they don't require any parameters to be passed to them.

It's under control

The data fundamentals are in place, so let's look at a feature we'll be using for the first time in this application: the `Controller`. Not a view controller this time, but the over-arching application controller we talked about in our design:

```
// app/controller/Root.js
Ext.define('Postcard.controller.Root', {
    extend: 'Ext.app.Controller',

    routes: {
        'home': 'onHome',
        '': 'checkLogin'
    },

    onLaunch: function() {
        this.checkLogin();
    },

    checkLogin: function() {
        if(!window.localStorage.getItem('loggedin')) {
            this.loginWindow =
Ext.create('Postcard.view.login.Login');
        } else {
            Ext.create('Postcard.view.main.Main');
        }
    },

    onHome: function() {
```

```
        if(this.loginWindow) {
            this.loginWindow.destroy();
        }

        this.checkLogin();
    }
});
```

In previous examples, app/Application.js has been responsible for creating the viewport that represents the main view of the application. In this case, the root controller takes on this role. We override its onLaunch method to detect whether the user is logged in, regardless of the route they are on. It also specifies the default URL for the application (just an empty string) and again checks for a valid login.

When a valid login is detected, the main view is shown, otherwise the login is shown. This is a super-simple mechanism to create a crude login system.

Login view

The login view is a window centered in the screen that contains a number of fields. Their values are bound to a login object on the view model, as shown in the following code:

```
Ext.define('Postcard.view.login.Login', {
    extend: 'Ext.window.Window',
    xtype: 'login-window',

    title: 'Login to Postcard',
    closable: false,
    autoShow: true,

    controller: 'login',
    viewModel: 'login',
    items: [{
        xtype: 'textfield',
        name: 'e-mail',
        bind: '{login.e-mail}',
        fieldLabel: 'E-mail',
        allowBlank: false
    }, {
        xtype: 'textfield',
        bind: '{login.password}',
        inputType: 'password',
        fieldLabel: 'Password',
```

```
            allowBlank: false
    }, {
        xtype: 'checkbox',
        bind: '{login.rememberMe}',
        fieldLabel: 'Remember Me?'
    }],

    buttons: [{ text: 'Login' }]
});
```

Note the `controller` and `ViewModel` configuration options and the prefix of the bind values that links to the login object on the view model. Speaking of which:

```
Ext.define('Postcard.view.login.LoginModel', {
    extend: 'Ext.app.ViewModel',
    alias: 'viewmodel.login',
    data: {
        login: {}
    }
});
```

Nothing is happening here other than defining this login object. Let's move on to the view controller:

```
Ext.define('Postcard.view.login.LoginController', {
    extend: 'Ext.app.ViewController',
    alias: 'controller.login',

    listen: {
        component: {
            'button': {
                click: function() {
                    window.localStorage.setItem('loggedin', true);
                    this.redirectTo('home');
                }
            }
        }
    }
});
```

The view controller does nothing more than listen for the `click` event on the login form's button and then fake a successful login. For simplicity, this application doesn't do any validation of user details, so we just instantly fire a redirect to the home route.

We saw earlier that the root controller handles the home token, which removes the login view and creates the main view. Let's move on and take a look at that now.

Main force

Looking back at our design, the main view is the container for the rest of the UI in our application. It looks like this:

```
// app/view/main/Main.js
Ext.define('Postcard.view.main.Main', {
    extend: 'Ext.Panel',
    xtype: 'app-main',
    plugins: ['viewport', 'responsive'],
    controller: 'main',
    viewModel: 'main',
    session: true,

    responsiveConfig: {
        'tall': {
            layout: {
                type: 'card'
            }
        },

        'wide': {
            layout: {
                type: 'hbox',
                align: 'stretch'
            }
        }
    },

    dockedItems: [
        { xtype: 'app-header' },
        {
            dock: 'bottom', xtype: 'button', cls: 'logout',
            overCls: '', focusCls: '', text: 'Logout'
        }
    ],

    items: [
        { xtype: 'threads', flex: 1 },
        {
            xtype: 'container',
```

```
                flex: 1,
                defaults: { hidden: true },
                items: [
                        { xtype: 'messages' },
                        { xtype: 'composer' }
                ]
            }
        ],

        isCard: function() {
            return this.getLayout().type === 'card';
        }
    });
```

There's a lot going on here, but only a couple of new concepts. Note that we have added a couple of plugins to this class: viewport and responsive. As we didn't let our application auto create a view as a viewport, adding the viewport plugin will do just that. The responsive plugin allows you to use the responsiveConfig option, which we discussed earlier in the chapter.

In this instance, on screens that are tall, that is, higher than they are wide, such as portrait screens, we use a card layout. On screens that are wide, that is, wider than they are high, we use an hbox layout because there's a lot more horizontal space. This simple declarative way of setting up a responsive view has allowed us to make very distinct changes to our application with only a few lines of configuration.

We've added a utility method to this view to help with manipulating our responsive setup; the isCard view will let us neatly determine whether this view is using a card layout or hbox layout.

 Syntactic sugar is an alternative way of writing something that makes it easier to read or allows it to better express its intent. The isCard method is an example of this, not strictly necessary, but it makes the calling code shorter and easier to understand.

The rest of this configuration should be very familiar: two dockedItems, one is the application header view and another supplying a logout button, and the three other views of this application in the items array.

Main ViewModel

On first glance, the code for this will look pretty standard, but when you look back at the code for the main view itself, you notice that currentTag or searchTerm is not going to be used anywhere. So, why define them if they're not going to be used? Refer to ViewModel in the following code:

```
// app/view/main/MainModel.js
Ext.define('Postcard.view.main.MainModel', {
    extend: 'Ext.app.ViewModel',
    alias: 'viewmodel.main',

    data: {
        currentTag: 'Inbox',
        searchTerm: null
    }
});
```

In Ext JS, we have the concept of parent and child view models. The main view model, configured on the main view, will become available to all child components of the main view. This means that subviews can get data on the main view and also pass information back up to it. This is a fantastic way of passing data between two child components.

Main ViewController

Refer to ViewController in the following code:

```
// app/view/main/MainController.js
Ext.define('Postcard.view.main.MainController', {
    extend: 'Ext.app.ViewController',
    alias: 'controller.main',

    routes: {
        'thread/new': 'showRightPane',
        'thread/:id/messages': 'showRightPane',
        'thread/:id/messages/new': 'showRightPane'
    },

    listen: {
        component: {
            'button[cls="logout"]': {
                click: function() {
                    window.localStorage.removeItem('loggedin');
                    window.location = '/';
```

```
                }
            }
        }
    },

    showRightPane: function(id) {
        if(this.getView().isCard()) {
            this.getView().setActiveItem(1);
        }
    }
});
```

The most interesting thing happening in here is the route handlers; we're giving several routes to the `showRightPane` handler. Looking back at our examination of user flow and routes in our application, many of the routes need us to ensure that the right-hand panel is in view. This only applies to the responsive portrait view, so we only change the active panel if the portrait view's card layout is available.

The interesting part is that we've got route handlers that only do part of what we'd expect. Where are the bits that pass IDs and show subviews? Don't worry, we'll revisit this shortly.

The head of the family

Refer to the `Header.js` file:

```
// app/view/header/Header.js
Ext.define('Postcard.view.header.Header', {
    extend: 'Ext.Toolbar',
    requires: ['Postcard.view.header.HomeButton'],
    xtype: 'app-header',
    height: 60,
    controller: 'header',
    viewModel: 'header',
    session: true,
    items: [
        {
            xtype: 'home-button', cls: 'title', html: 'Postcard',
            bind: { hidden: '{menuButton.pressed}' }
        },
        {
            xtype: 'tbspacer',
            bind: { hidden: '{menuButton.pressed}' } },
        {
```

```
                    xtype: 'textfield', flex: 1,
                    cls: 'search-box', emptyText: 'Search',
                    bind: '{searchTerm}',
                    plugins: ['responsive'],
                    responsiveConfig: {
                        'tall': {
                            hidden: true,
                            bind: { hidden: '{!menuButton.pressed}' }
                        },
                        'wide': { hidden: false }
                    }
                },
                {

                    xtype: 'tbfill',
                    bind: { hidden: '{menuButton.pressed}' }
                },
                {

                    xtype: 'combobox', flex: 1, editable: false,
                    displayField: 'name', idField: 'name',
                    queryMode: 'local', forceSelection: true,
                    bind: {
                        store: '{tags}', value: '{currentTag}'
                    },
                    plugins: ['responsive'],
                    responsiveConfig: {
                        'tall': {
                            hidden: true,
                            bind: { hidden: '{!menuButton.pressed}' }
                        },
                        'wide': { hidden: false }
                    }
                },
                {

                    xtype: 'button', cls: 'new-message',
                    text: 'New Message',
                    bind: {
                        hidden: '{menuButton.pressed}'
                    }
                },
                {

                    text: 'Menu', reference: 'menuButton',
                    width: 30, enableToggle: true,
                    plugins: ['responsive'],
```

```
                responsiveConfig: {
                    'tall': { hidden: false },
                    'wide': { hidden: true }
                }
            }
        ]
    });
```

Wow! That's actually a lot of code for a header bar! Look back at our original class design for this view and we did say there was "a surprising amount happening", so we weren't wrong.

In the section, *A binding agreement* we discussed a cut-down example of what is happening in this class. The `reference` option on the menu button is used to allow the other header components to bind to the menu's pressed value; look at the previous code and you'll see this approach used in various places to show or hide components when the menu button is toggled.

We're not only using the responsive plugin again mostly to set the initial hidden state of the header components, but also using it to make sure the hidden config is only bound when the viewport is tall. This avoids issues with initial visibility of other components when the menu button isn't even in use. This kind of conditional binding opens up some exciting possibilities.

A couple more things of note: we mentioned the main view model had some values that seemed unused. Well, here they are, bound to the values of the tag filter combo and the search text field. When these values change, they'll be passed up to the main view model and available for use by other components.

There's a final item of note: a mysterious home-button component. The code for this looks like this:

```
Ext.define('Postcard.view.header.HomeButton', {
    extend: 'Ext.Container',
    xtype: 'home-button',

    afterRender: function() {
        this.callParent(arguments);
        this.getEl().on('click', function() {
            this.fireEvent('click');
        }, this);
    }
});
```

We're using this as a fake button, extending the simple container to fire a `click` event. This allows you to get a lightweight, unstyled, and clickable component to use as a home button.

Header ViewModel

Refer to `ViewModel` in the following code:

```
Ext.define('Postcard.view.header.HeaderModel', {
    extend: 'Ext.app.ViewModel',
    alias: 'viewmodel.header',
    stores: {
        tags: {
            type: 'tags',
            session: true
        }
    }
});
```

This `ViewModel` class supplies the tags to populate the tag filter combo. We use a session to make sure that we're using the same tag instances across the application.

Header ViewController

Refer to `ViewController` in the following code:

```
// app/view/header/HeaderController.js
Ext.define('Postcard.view.header.HeaderController', {
    extend: 'Ext.app.ViewController',
    alias: 'controller.header',
    listen: {
        component: {
            'button[cls="new-message"]': {
                click: function() {
                    this.redirectTo('thread/new');
                }
            },

            'home-button': {
                click: function() {
                    this.redirectTo('home');
                }
            }
        },
```

```
controller: {
    '*': {
        tagadded: function() {
            this.getViewModel().get('tags').reload();
        }
    }
}
});
```

There are two component event listeners, one on the new message button and one on the home button. Both redirect to routes that will be consumed by other controllers.

There's also a controller listener that waits for a `tagadded` event and refreshes the tag store on `ViewModel`. This is great because we don't have to worry about where this event comes from or which component issued it; we just consume it in isolation and perform the action we're interested in.

The reverse applies too, meaning the issuer of the `tagadded` event doesn't need to work out how to refresh the tag filter combo; instead, it can just declare that a tag was added and rest easy.

Unravel the thread

A thread is a collection of e-mail messages, and the thread view makes up the left-hand pane of our application. It looks something like this:

```
// app/view/threads/Threads.js
Ext.define('Postcard.view.threads.Threads', {
    extend: 'Ext.DataView',
    xtype: 'threads',
    cls: 'thread-view',
    viewModel: 'threads',
    controller: 'threads',
    border: true,
    deferEmptyText: false,
    emptyText: 'No messages',
    autoScroll: true,
    itemSelector: '.thread',
    bind: '{threads}'
    tpl: new Ext.XTemplate('<tpl for=".">',
        '<div class="thread">',
            '<div class="date">{lastMessageOn:date("H:m")}</div>',
```

```
        '<div class="details">',
            '<div class="header">{people} - {subject}</div>',
            '<div class="body">{[this.stripHtml(values.
lastMessageSnippet)]}</div>',
        '</div>',
    '</div>',
    '</tpl>', {
        stripHtml: function(html) {
            var div = document.createElement('div');
            div.innerHTML = html;
            return div.textContent || div.innerText || '';
        }
    })
});
```

We knew from our design work that we would use a DataView for this class and its implementation turns out to be fairly straightforward. We're binding its store to the threads store on the view model itself also called as threads.

Look back at the design and you'll see that we anticipated a method to strip HTML from the message body and here it is; a little bit of trickery that uses a temporary DOM element to let the browser do the work for us.

Thread ViewModel

Refer to ViewModel in the following code:

```
// app/view/threads/ThreadsModel.js
Ext.define('Postbox.view.threads.ThreadsModel', {
    extend: 'Ext.app.ViewModel',
    alias: 'viewmodel.threads',
    stores: {
        threads: {
            type: 'threads',
            remoteFilter: true,
            filters: [
                {
                    property: 'tag',
                    value: '{currentTag}'
                },
                {
                    property: 'searchTerm',
                    value: '%{searchTerm}%'
                }
            ]
        }
    }
});
```

This is actually the most complicated view model in the whole application and most of this complexity should be familiar from *Chapter 6, Practical – Monitoring Dashboard*. The filter array, along with the `remoteFilter` setting, will be responsible for sending a JSON object containing a filter definition through to the server. In this case, we see that we are consuming values from the main view model as broadcast up by the tag picker combo and search field in the header.

We talked about this before, but it's worth highlighting again. The data flows from the header view to the main view model and then into the thread view. This is an incredibly simple way of communicating between parts of an application without these parts needing to be aware of each other.

Thread ViewController

Refer to `ViewController` in the following code:

```
// app/view/threads/ThreadController.js
Ext.define('Postcard.view.threads.ThreadsController', {
    extend: 'Ext.app.ViewController',
    alias: 'controller.threads',

    listen: {
        component: {
            'threads': {
                itemclick: function(dataview, record) {
                    this.redirectTo('thread/' + record.getId() +
'/' + 'messages');
                }
            }
        },

        controller: {
            '*': {
                threadschanged: function() {
                    this.getViewModel().get('threads').reload();
                }
            }
        }
    }
});
```

More of these event listeners, and so on. We knew they'd come in handy, but they're everywhere! In the thread view controller, we listen for the DataView's `itemclick` event and simply redirect the application off so that another controller's route can take care of it. Fire and forget.

In turn, we listen for a `threadschanged` event, which is issued when a thread is added. This allows you to refresh the DataView's store in the view model to see the effects of the added thread. We don't know or care where `threadschanged` came from.

I am the best message

Refer to the `Messages.js` file in the following code:

```
// app/view/messages/Messages.js
Ext.define('Postcard.view.messages.Messages', {
    extend: 'Ext.Panel',
    xtype: 'messages',
    controller: 'messages',
    viewModel: 'messages',
    autoScroll: true,
    session: true,
    bbar: [
        {
            xtype: 'combobox', displayField: 'name',
            idField: 'name',
            reference: 'tagPicker',
            queryMode: 'local', value: 'Inbox',
            bind: { store: '{tags}' }
        },
        {
            text: 'Set Tag',
            itemId: 'setTag'
        },
        '->',
        {
            text: 'Reply',
            itemId: 'reply',
            reference: 'replyButton'
        }
    ],
    items: [{
        xtype: 'dataview',
        bind: '{messages}',
        flex: 1,
```

```
        cls: 'message-view',
        tpl: new Ext.XTemplate('<tpl for=".">',
            '<div class="message">',
                '<div class="date">{date:date("H:m")}</div>',
                '<div class="details">',
                    '<tpl if="xindex == 1">',
                    '<div class="header">{people} -
{subject}</div>',
                    '</tpl>',
                    '<div class="body">{body}</div>',
                '</div>',
            '</div>',
        '</tpl>'),
        itemSelector: '.message'

    });
```

In an ideal situation, the code should flow out of your team as the culmination of the design process. Any difficult classes or methods should have been part of a code spike. Your data layer would have been designed on top of your backend API. User interface has been described in wireframes, user stories provide routing, and so on.

This is what we're seeing now. As seasoned Ext JS developers, we know how to configure a combo box and a store. This book is not here to help with that. We're going to continue to focus on the design and the decisions that make your code simple.

Look at the previous class. The design of the messages view with its DataView nested inside a panel allows you to use a `bbar`; we knew about this before we even wrote a line of code. This is the crux of a good design. With developers who understand the technology they are working with, implementations become easy and predictable because it's all been thought about in advance.

Messages ViewModel

Refer to `ViewModel` in the following code:

```
// app/view/messages/MessagesModel.js
Ext.define('Postcode.view.messages.MessagesModel', {
    extend: 'Ext.app.ViewModel',
    alias: 'viewmodel.messages',
    stores: {
        messages: {
            type: 'messages'
        },
```

```
        tags: {
            type: 'tags',
            session: true
        }
    }
});
```

See! With an up-front design, you can pass the documentation over to a developer and have them create the messages view model. There's little scope for error because the shape of the class has already been decided.

Messages ViewController

Having said that, there are times when the code is lengthy, so a breakdown of what's happening really helps as shown here:

```
// app/view/messages/MessagesController.js
Ext.define('Postcard.view.messages.MessagesController', {
    extend: 'Ext.app.ViewController',
    alias: 'controller.messages',

    listen: {
        component: {
            '#reply': {
                click: 'onReplyClick'
            },

            '#setTag': {
                click: 'onTagChange'
            }
        }
    },

    routes: {
        'thread/:id/messages': 'onShowThread',
        'thread/new': 'onNewThread'
    },

    onShowThread:function(id) {
        this.getViewModel().get('messages').load({
            params: {
                parentId: id
            },
```

```
            callback: function(records) {
                this.getView().show();
            },
            scope: this
        });
    },

    onNewThread: function() {
        this.getView().hide();
    },

    onReplyClick: function() {
        this.redirectTo(window.location.hash + '/new');
    },

    onTagChange: function() {
        var tagPicker = this.lookupReference('tagPicker'),
            newTag = tagPicker.getValue(),
            viewModel = this.getViewModel(),
            threadParent = viewModel.get('messages').getAt(0);

        threadParent.set('tag', newTag);
        threadParent.save({
            callback: function() {
                this.getViewModel().get('tags').reload();
                this.fireEvent('tagadded');
                this.fireEvent('threadschanged');
            },
            scope: this
        });
    }
});
```

As usual, we have our event listeners. Let's look at the component ones; firstly the one that handles the reply button's `click` event as it's straightforward. It just redirects to a route that will take care of setting up the application to reply to a thread.

Next, there's the `onTagChange` method that handles a click on the "set tag" button. This will get the selected value from the tag combo box and set it as the tag for the first message in the thread. Then, it saves that message to the server.

Note the callback for this save request (it fires off two events that we've seen before). One (`threadschanged`) notifies the application that threads have changed in some way; in this case, it's a thread's tag that has changed, so a thread list may need to be refreshed. The other (`tagadded`) signifies that there may be a new tag and any interested classes should refresh their tag data accordingly.

The next two handlers are for routes, but there's something to note here. These routes have already been handled by the main view controller! This is a powerful feature; we can handle routes in multiple locations so that the classes that are interested in this route can do their own thing. This avoids us having to do all of the work in the main view controller, for example, the messages view controller can take care of loading the messages rather than doing so in the main view controller.

Compare using routes in this way to using events. They're very similar; we can redirect to a route, fire this redirect and forget about it, or else, where in the application a controller will handle this route. With routes, you get the added benefit of keeping state in the URL, thus enabling bookmark support. With events, you can send complex data in the event arguments. Both have their strengths.

A composed finish

Now, we come to the view that allows you to actually send e-mails, a pretty important part of this application!

```
// app/view/composer/Composer.js
Ext.define('Postcard.view.composer.Composer', {
    extend: 'Ext.form.Panel',
    xtype: 'composer',
    cls: 'composer',
    viewModel: 'composer',
    controller: 'composer',
    session: true,
    items: [
        { xtype: 'hiddenfield', bind: '{newMessage.parentId}' },
        {
            fieldLabel: 'To', xtype: 'combo', width: '100%',
            valueField: 'e-mail',
            displayField: 'e-mail',
            queryMode: 'local',
            bind: {
                hidden: '{newMessage.parentId}',
                store: '{contacts}',
                value: '{newMessage.people}'
            }
        }
```

```
        },
        {
            xtype: 'textfield', fieldLabel: 'Subject',
            cls: 'subject', emptyText: 'Subject',
            bind: {
                value: '{newMessage.subject}',
                hidden: '{newMessage.parentId}'
            },
            width: '100%'
        },
        {
            xtype: 'htmleditor',
            bind: { value: '{newMessage.body}' }
        }
    ],
    bbar: [
        '->',
        { xtype: 'button', text: 'Send' }
    ]
});
```

Another straightforward component definition, with the values of the form fields being bound to the newMessage object in the view model for later use. There's another view model trick here, that is, if this newMessage object has a parentId value, we know that we're replying to an existing thread. This means that we can hide the subject and recipient form fields, so we bind the parentId to their hidden value, making this step automatic as follows:

```
// app/view/composer/ComposerModel.js
Ext.define('Postcard.view.Composer.ComposerModel', {
    extend: 'Ext.app.ViewModel',
    alias: 'viewmodel.composer',
    stores: {
        contacts: {
            type: 'contacts'
        }
    },

    data: {
        newMessage: {}
    }
});
```

We have the contacts store that corresponds to the one in the view that was bound to the recipient's combo and then an empty definition for the newMessage object discussed previously.

```javascript
// app/view/composer/ComposerController.js
Ext.define('Postcard.view.composer.ComposerController', {
    extend: 'Ext.app.ViewController',
    alias: 'controller.composer',
    listen: {
        component: {
            'button': {
                click: 'onSendClick'
            }
        }
    },

    routes: {
        'thread/:id/messages': 'hideComposer',
        'thread/:id/messages/new': 'showComposer',
        'thread/new': 'showComposer'
    },

    hideComposer: function() {
        this.getView().hide();
    },

    showComposer: function(parentId) {
        this.getViewModel().set('newMessage.parentId', parentId);
        this.getView().show();
    },

    onSendClick: function() {
        var session = this.getSession(),
            data = this.getViewModel().get('newMessage');

        session.createRecord('Postcard.model.Message', {
            people: data.people,
            subject: data.subject,
            body: data.body,
            parentId: data.parentId
        });

        var batch = session.getSaveBatch().start();

        batch.on('complete', this.onSaveComplete, this);
    },

    onSaveComplete: function(batch, operation) {
        var record = operation.getRecords()[0],
            id = record.getId(),
```

```
        parentId = record.get('parentId');

        this.redirectTo('thread/' + (parentId || id) +
    '/messages');
        }
    });
```

In component listeners, we handle the `click` event of the send button with the `onSendClick` method. This creates a new record on the current session and saves it to the server. In the `callback` method, we dispatch the application to the route that shows thread messages, but note that we'll use the ID of the new message in the event of it being a brand new thread and the `parentID` of the new message if it's a reply.

In terms of handling routes, there's one (`hideComposer`) that hides the composer when viewing the messages in a thread because there's no need for it to be visible at that point. Then, there's a second (`showComposer`) that sets the `parentId` on the `newMessage` and shows the composer. For new threads, there's no ID captured by the route, so the `parentId` argument will be undefined and `newMessage.parentId` will be set as such. This enables the automatic viewing and hiding of the recipient and subject back in the composer view itself. Back when designing the app, we referred to this as `currentThreadId`, but we can see now that it makes sense to incorporate it in the `newMessage` object and pass this to the server when we save the new record.

Deciding on a theme

We've covered all of the parts of this application apart from one: the way it looks. Cast your mind back to the screenshot of the app in action earlier in the chapter. In fact, have a look at the login screen to see how it differs from a standard Ext JS app:

We've changed key things such as the font and color of the window frame, but take a look at the code to perform this:

```scss
// sass/etc/all.scss
$body-font-family: 'Roboto', sans-serif;
$window-base-color: #fff;
$window-header-color: #000;
$window-padding: 20px;
$window-header-font-family: $body-font-family;
$toolbar-footer-background-color: #fff;
$form-label-font-family: $body-font-family;
```

Ext JS themes provide an extensive range of variables designated by the dollar sign in front of them. By defining our own, such as `$body-font-family`, and overriding existing ones, we can easily shape the look of our application to suit different requirements.

Not only this, but from a maintenance point of view, it's far preferable to set a few variables than it's to write a swathe of CSS rules to override theme style sheets. We can avoid problems like CSS precedence and finding the correct selectors to use and get on with making our app stand out. However, if we need to, we can drop down to use SASS, the CSS-like compiler that Ext JS uses for theming. Take a look at the styling for the thread view:

```scss
// sass/src/view/threads/Threads.scss
.thread-view {
    font-family: $body-font-family;
    margin: $gutters;

    .x-view-item-focused {
        outline: 0 !important;

        .header {
            color: rgb(255, 20, 108);
        }
    }

    .header {
        font-size: 125%;
    }

    .body {
        font-size: 105%;
        color: #666;
        padding: 10px 0;
```

```
            line-height: 160%;
    }

    .date {
            color: $subdued-grey;
            font-size: 150%;
            padding: 0 15px;
            font-weight: bold
    }
}

.thread {
    display: flex;
    padding: 50px;

    &:hover {
            cursor: pointer;
    }

    .details {
            border-bottom: 1px solid $subdued-grey;
    }

    &:last-child .details {
            border-bottom: 0 !important;
    }

    .date {
            width: 80px;
            text-align: right;
    }
     .details {
            flex: 1;
    }
}
```

The thread view is a DataView, meaning its template can contain any custom HTML. Writing new SASS rules makes sense here, but Ext JS allows you to do this in a modular and reusable way, similar to the features it provides to write JavaScript classes. In the next few chapters, we'll discuss this and other features of theming in more depth.

Summary

We've taken a different approach to designing and implementing this application. Rather than discussing the same details we have in previous chapters, we've avoided retreading old ground and talked about a higher level of architecture.

By implementing routes, view model bindings, and events more extensively than ever before, we've shown how a declarative approach to Ext JS can simplify our code and make it incredibly easy to understand. At the same time, components that issue and listen to events are more decoupled, leading to fewer bugs and increased testability.

We also touched on theming, showing how a few lines of code can dramatically affect the look of an app and how we can write custom style rules to create brand new components.

In the next chapter, we'll continue to explore the architectural ideas we've used already, but expanding them to look at how to make best use of them in the design phase. We'll look at how Ext JS architecture applies to theming and how we can continue to improve our code reuse all across our application.

Practical – Questionnaire Component

8

We now have three practical applications under our belt. The objective has been to show the process of designing an application and think it through in a series of careful steps to create a clear picture of the project that's we're going to build. This time around, there's going to be a change of pace and rather than looking at how "we" would design and build an application, I'll be guiding you through my own process of creating a multiple-step, dynamic questionnaire component.

Here are the features of the application that will be the subject of this chapter:

- A reusable package that can be included in any application
- Theme variables and mixins to allow visual integration in other apps
- Splitting a questionnaire into multiple steps, each with multiple questions
- Construct the UI dynamically from incoming server data
- A JSON object produced by the questionnaire, representing the steps, questions, and the answers that the user has provided
- Use Ext JS Associations to help structure application data

Why the step back from the all-inclusive "we" to a look at my own architecture process? I hope that it'll give you a more practical look at the thought processes that go into an application design. You can also see how there are always multiple correct paths that an architect can pursue. Sketching out these paths and investigating them before writing any code will avoid the "analysis paralysis" that hits many projects and causes them to grind to a halt when difficult questions need answers.

Application design – my way

My first port of call when thinking about an application doesn't involve fancy tools or an IDE. Once the customer requirements are established, I take myself as far away from a computer as possible, wash all thoughts of JavaScript and Ext JS from my head, and remove as many distractions as possible.

With that done, I grab a large notebook and a pencil and get scribbling. I've never found a better way to quickly draft ideas than a bit of manual labor, so while I'm designing in the same way as we've seen in the previous few chapters, I can avoid getting bogged down with drawing tools and UML diagrams.

[All of this needs to be formalized in documented design decisions later. The purpose is to quickly test out ideas and avoid dead ends.]

How did I start?

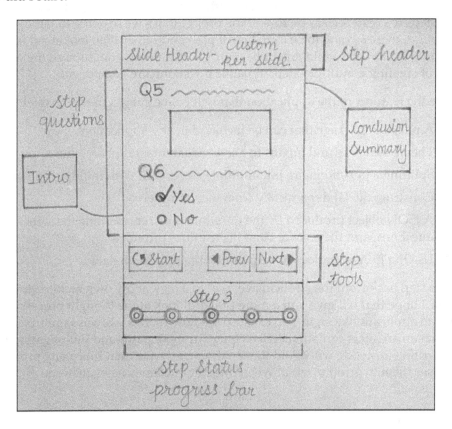

Well, it's not pretty, but you can see the relationship between this and the diagrams of UI views we saw in previous chapters. Note that the intention with these images is not to spell out the design in exacting detail, but simply to give an insight into the process I went through, warts and all! Eventually, I'll use these sketches to build something like this:

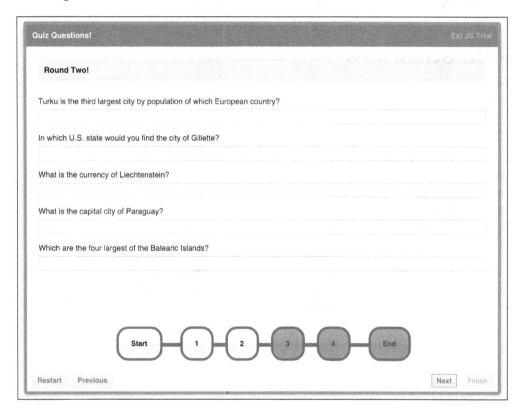

What are the features I picked out from this original sketch?

- Questionnaire header, changing per step
- Panes containing an introduction and a conclusion to the questionnaire
- Panes for each of the steps making up the application
- A step can have introduction text
- A question needs explanation text
- Navigation buttons to move between steps
- A progress bar to show the number of steps completed and numbers until the end

In addition, this component needs to be able to validate the mandatory questions in a step that have been completed before the user can move to the next step.

Rather than spending lots of time in front of a computer creating the perfect UI design, I was able to quickly flesh out an idea to see how it looked and this informed me about my design requirements.

Data structure

These initial sketches enabled me to quickly think about the underlying data powering the component. In previous chapters, we've stopped here to discuss whether the design requirements can be fulfilled by Ext JS. Instead, we're going to push ahead, put technology to one side, and just focus purely on architecture.

In some ways—as we're going with MVVM—the architecture is technology agnostic. We can create the kind of application that we want to build without feeling constrained by the framework we're using. This can be dangerous; in that, we might lose sight of particular client requirements or start drafting something that might turn out to be impossible. To this end, we introduce new checks and balances that we'll discuss in a little while.

For now, I continued with my pencil and paper to work out a data structure. As in previous cases, the UI design informs the underlying data requirements. Here's a quick insight into my design doodles:

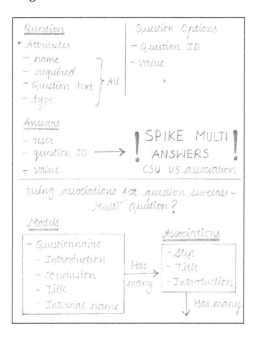

It's the same as in previous chapters, just a bit messier! Again, don't worry about the detail. Look at the rough notes and the scribbles and realize that the initial stages of an application design are an organic process and things can (and will) take a meandering path. Here's what my doodles led to in terms of data structure:

- Questionnaire
    - Title
    - Introduction
    - Conclusion
    - Steps[]
        Title

        Introduction

        Questions[]
            Name

            Required?

            Question text
- Field type

I'm not yet worrying about what inherits from what at this stage. I just know that I'd like to have a single questionnaire that has many steps and these steps will each have many questions. From here, I just fleshed out the fields each class needs.

Consider carefully

It's at this point I have to tell you that I lied to you. In the purest sense, it would be fantastic to think that you can sketch out the full application architecture on paper, but in reality, you will always do so with an eye on the real world. Look back to my last page of pencil doodles and you'll see a few notes like "associations" with a giant underline. That's there because I knew that the data structure I've described previously will be implemented using Ext JS associations, a feature we haven't yet used in this book, but one that can be very powerful.

As much as possible though, I've tried to push past any thoughts of detail, but trusted my knowledge of Ext JS to pop to the fore without any warning signs.

Data flow

With the previous data structure in mind, I started to think more about how the information supplied from an API would flow through view models and allow me to build the user interface.

I had a feeling that validation was going to complicate the application, so I started sketching out some ideas for the parts of the UI that would be affected. The user can't proceed to the next step until the current step is valid. In this, its mandatory questions have been answered so the "next" button needs to be disabled until this happens. I started drawing again, but quickly a degree of "analysis paralysis" kicked in. How should this work? There are several Ext JS features that could help; will model validation binding work here or will it have to be manual handling of validation events. Earlier, I mentioned "checks and balances" to avoid building something that Ext JS won't support; I decided to take some time out and investigate the best way to implement this in Ext JS.

Call this a "spike" as we did in *Chapter 5, Practical – a CMS Application,* or call it a prototype. It doesn't really matter whether we write this code and then throw it away; if it helps the process, then it's a valuable exercise. I built it standalone (outside of an MVC or MVVM structure) and it's horrible. Look at this code snippet:

```
s.questions().each(function(q) {
    var input = stepForm.add({
            xtype: 'textfield', modelValidation: true,
            viewModel: {
                data: { question: q },
                formulas: {
                    isValid: {
                        bind: {
                                bindTo: '{question}',
                                deep: true
                        },
                        get: function() {
                            return
this.get('step').isValid();
                        }
                    }
                }
            },
            bind: '{question.answer}',
            fieldLabel: q.get('text')
    });
});
```

I don't wish this code to be my worst enemy. Shouldn't every piece of code we write be pristine and well considered? In the real world, almost no one can see this code. It's to test out my ideas and find out what feels right and it doesn't have to be tidy or maintainable. It's a one-off. Here's what I wanted to test out:

- Will the `modelValidation` feature be useful with auto-generated form fields?
- Will I be able to bind to questions to get the validation state of the current step?
- Will it feel natural to use these features or is there an easier way?

We've seen how view models can be used to create simple declarative applications and they can be extremely powerful when used correctly. In this application, fields are being generated from API data and each field had its own question model. Propagating the validity of this model up to the relevant parts of the user interface via view models seemed like it might be difficult. What did I discover?

- A view model binding trick
- A slight difference of opinion with the team at Sencha regarding the way `modelValidation` behaves
- A way of binding a button state to the state of an association

This seems like a great result for this grubby code. Let's look at each point in turn.

A binding trick

This snippet of code is from the view model of a question's form field:

```
formulas: {
    isValid: {
        bind: {
            bindTo: '{question}',
            deep: true
        },
        get: function() {
            return this.get('step').isValid();
        }
    }
}
```

The view model has a question model and inherits the step model from its parent view model. We tell Ext JS that we'd like to bind to changes in the question model, deep changes, so any of its property changes and then trigger the isValid method on the parent step. This is great because the isValid method can in turn trigger changes on the parent step, propagating the state of the questions up to the step. Here's the isValid code:

```
isValid: function() {
    var valid = true;
    this.questions().each(function(q) {
            if(q.isValid() === false) {
                valid = false;
            }
    });
    this.set('valid', valid);
    return valid;
}
```

It checks the validity of all the child questions and sets the valid property of the step accordingly. We can then bind to this valid value and have it affect other things (such as the disabled state of the "next" button in the UI).

This is slightly counterintuitive because we're not binding directly to the isValid formula. Instead, we're using it to watch for changes on the question and then trigger changes on the step model.

A difference of opinion

There was a change in the behavior between Ext JS 5.0 and 5.0.1. The modelValidation feature matches validation in the model with validation in the form, reducing duplication of code. In Ext JS 5, when the form values change, these changes will be synchronized to the model via binding. In Ext JS 5.0.1, this synchronization will only happen when the form field is valid. The idea is that the model should never be left in an invalid state based on form changes, but the problem occurs like this:

- User completes the form field and it becomes valid
- The form value is passed to the model's field, which in turn becomes valid
- User changes the form field to make it invalid again
- The change is not passed to the model, which remains valid

This means that when binding to model value, you'll get something that doesn't reflect the real state of the UI. The model will say everything is valid when in fact the UI says differently. In the case of this application, the plan is to bind the "next" button to the model state, which will enable the button incorrectly in the preceding situation. My solution was to override this and return to the Ext JS 5.0 behavior as follows:

```
Ext.form.field.Text.prototype.publishValue = function () {
    var me = this;

    // Don't check for errors when publishing the field value
    //if (me.rendered && !me.getErrors().length) {
    if (me.rendered) {
        me.publishState('value', me.getValue());
    }
}
```

An alternative workaround would be to bind the "next" button to the value of the form field rather than the model value, but in our case, we need to do further work on the model value, so it's not a great solution.

A means to an end

All of this allows you to have a chain of configuration that goes all the way from each individual question field to the question model, then to the step model, and to higher-level places in the user interface that depend on it.

When I was writing this chapter, there were other ideas kicking around in my head as to how to implement it. A solution that handles validation events and uses listeners to propagate state through the application was another approach, but it ended up being less elegant despite the final idea being a little more complicated than our previous binding code.

Ext JS allows you to watch for deep changes in associations en-masse that would help, but at the time of writing this book, this change is not documented. Hopefully, it's coming in a post-5.0.1 version!

 You can see this change documented in the 5.0.1 release notes as EXTJS-13933 at http://dev.sencha.com/extjs/5.0.1/release-notes.html.

Sketchy sketching

My biggest concern of the application has been solved to my satisfaction; I won't go into any more detail on my code spike because I'll reuse some of this code later once it's been tidied up.

I moved on to working out the role of controllers in this application. What user-initiated events will we need to handle?

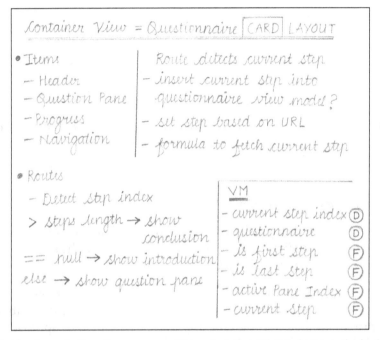

Initial sketches for controllers; there are several things here that didn't make it into the final version

The user can perform two main actions: completing the questionnaire itself and navigating between pages. It's the navigation that the controller will concern itself with.

At this point, I felt fairly confident that I'd fleshed out most of the tricky parts of the application. In the role of an architect, each of the diagrams and interactions that I sketched need to be turned into formal documentation in order to provide a point of reference for developers. Here's what I came up with for the UI:

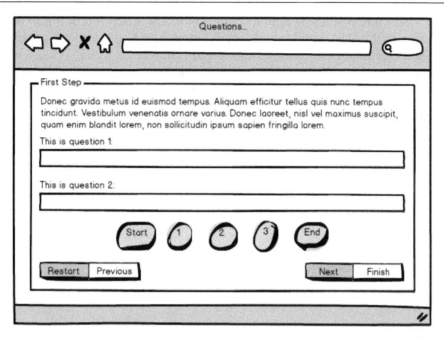

There's no point in duplicating the work I've already shown you, so I won't go through each of these formalized diagrams, but it should be stressed that this isn't a step that can be skipped. As a developer, it's essential that there's a solid design document to refer back to when writing code and also to keep the architect accountable. The next step in the process is to move from pencil and paper back to the computer and start to write the code for our questionnaire component.

Get set

The questionnaire component that we'll build in this chapter will be reusable in any application. To that end, we can use an Ext JS package to create a bundle of code that can be built in the same way as a normal Ext JS application, but it can be incorporated as a component in our future applications. We discussed packages in *Chapter 3, Application Structure*, but now we'll see how they can be used in practice.

Here's how I started up the project that I used as a basis for this component and its test application:

```
sencha generate workspace ./questionnaire-space
cd questionnaire-space
sencha generate package wizard
sencha -sdk ~/Downloads/ext-5.0.1 generate app Questions ./questions
```

Building a package requires us to first create a workspace, so after doing so using the latest version of the SDK that I downloaded, I moved on to the workspace directory and issued the command to create the package itself, which I called wizard. Then, I created a test application that would host the package during development; I called this questions.

I then get the test application up and running with:

```
cd questions-space/questions
sencha app watch
```

The web server is now up and running at http://localhost:1841/. The final step is telling the test application to include the new package. I edited questions-package/questions/app.json and amended the requires member:

```
// was "requires": []
"requires": ["wizard"]
```

As we gave the package the name wizard, just add this in the array and we're good to go.

The package we're going to build is contained at questions-space/packages/wizard and will start off containing most of the same directories as an Ext JS application. We can now move to this directory and start building it in just the same way as we have in the past few chapters.

The data layer

When writing the prototype, I did partially build the data classes that were required, so now let's fully flesh them out:

```
// packages/wizard/src/model/Questionnaire.js
Ext.define('Wizard.model.Questionnaire', {
    extend: 'Ext.data.Model',
    fields: [
        { name: 'title' },
        { name: 'introduction' },
        { name: 'conclusion' }
    ],
    proxy: {
        type: 'rest',
        url: 'http://localhost:3000/questionnaire'
    },

    toJSON: function() {
```

```
        return this.getData(true);
    }
});
```

Standard stuff here with one exception is that a toJSON method that consumes applications can override in order to obtain JSON in a format they can use for further processing. The default implementation returns the data of the questionnaire object along with its association data. Alternatively, they can override the proxy configuration to save the questionnaire data to their own server.

Let's take a look at the model I used to represent a step in the questionnaire:

```
// packages/wizard/src/model/Step.js
Ext.define('Wizard.model.Step', {
    extend: 'Ext.data.Model',
    fields: [
        { name: 'title' },
        { name: 'introduction' },
        {
            name: 'questionnaireId',
            reference: {
                type: 'Wizard.model.Questionnaire',
                inverse: 'steps'
            }
        }
    ],

    isValid: function() {
        var valid = true;

        this.questions().each(function(q) {
            if(q.isValid() === false) {
                valid = false;
            }
        });

        this.set('valid', valid);

        return valid;
    }
});
```

There are a couple of things to note on the Step model; firstly, the use of associations, which I realized would provide a really easy way to load the nested data for the whole questionnaire in a single action.

 The association is created using the reference option on the field with the type option specifying the full class name of the parent model and the inverse is the name of the association store that will be created on this parent Questionnaire. Ext JS 5 associations are a little confusing at first as they're always defined on the child, not the parent.

Secondly, the isValid method enumerates the questions belonging to this step and sets the step's own valid field according to the validity of its questions.

Finally, here's the Question model I built:

```
// packages/wizard/src/model/Question.js
Ext.define('Wizard.model.Question', {
    extend: 'Ext.data.Model',
    fields: [
        { name: 'name' },
        { name: 'required', type: 'boolean' },
        { name: 'questionText' },
        { name: 'type' },
        { name: 'answer' },
        {
            name: 'stepId',
            reference: {
                type: 'Wizard.model.Step',
                inverse: 'questions'
            }
        }
    ],

    validators: { answer: 'presence' },

    getValidation: function() {
        if(this.get('required')) {
            return this.callParent();
        } else {
            return new Ext.data.Validation();
        }
    }
});
```

Again, I have `child-side` of the `Step -> Questions` association defined in the same way as `Questionnaire -> Steps`. Using the `validators` config, I specify that answer should always be present, but I stumbled on a catch here that I could never have known about when just sitting down with a pencil and paper.

I really wanted to be able to add validators at runtime so that I could check the required field of the `Step` model and add the `presence` check to the answer. This enables the end user to toggle whether a particular question is required or not.

Unfortunately, after some intimate time with the Ext JS source code, it turns out that validators can only be defined on model class instances when they're defined and not on each instance of that class. Hopefully, this will be allowed in a later version—which at time of writing this book was 5.0.1—but I managed to come up with workarounds that enable this functionality.

We need to override the `Question` class's `getValidation` method. In the event that required is `true`, I call the `getValidation` on the superclass to proceed with validation normally. However, if it's `false`, I return a new `Ext.data.Validation` instance, but don't actually run its validation in effect, providing the same result as if the validation had passed.

While this works, and it's simple, it's one of these things that should be revisited with each new Ext JS version to see whether there's a more elegant way of solving the issue. I recommend code like this should be commented to let others know exactly why the workaround is needed and which version it applies to.

The payload

An interesting feature of associations is that it allows for the use of nested data. By loading data for the questionnaire and its steps and questions as a single JSON object, the child's steps and questions association will be populated too. For example, take a look at this JSON:

```json
{
    "id": 1,
    "title": "Quiz Questions!"
    "introduction": "Welcome!",
    "conclusion": "Thanks!",
    "steps": [
        {
            "id": 1,
            "title": "Round 1"
            "introduction": "Welcome to Round One!",
            "questionnaireId": 1,
```

```
            "questions": [{
                "id": 1,
                "questionText": "Turku is the third largest city
by population of which European country?",
                "required": true,
                "stepId": 1,
                "type": "textfield"
            }],
        }
    ]
}
```

This object includes data for the questionnaire with an array of child steps. The steps have their own array of questions, as shown here:

```
Questionnaire.load(1, {
    success: function(q) {
        console.log(q.steps().first().get('title'));
    }
});
```

If we load this, we would see "round 1" logged to the console. Some might question why we bother using models at all; we could use `Ext.Ajax` to load the JSON object directly into a view model. Models allow us to use validation and let us augment each `Model` instance with utility methods. The stores that are auto created on parent models give us shortcut methods to enumerate the records within and find individual child records.

There's a little bit of overhead in setting up and working with models here, but it's worth it in the long run.

The wizard component

I felt pretty good about the data layer I'd built. It was frustrating to have spent time trying to work around this limitation to validators that I found, but the final result works well. It was time to move on to the user interface, starting with the main container for the questionnaire wizard:

```
// packages/wizard/src/view/Wizard.js
Ext.define('Wizard.view.wizard.Wizard', {
    extend: 'Ext.Panel',
    xtype: 'wizard',
    requires: [
        'Wizard.model.Questionnaire',
        'Wizard.model.Step',
```

```
            'Wizard.model.Question'
    ],
    ui: 'wizard',
    bodyCls: 'wizard-body',

    viewModel: 'wizard',
    controller: 'wizard',

    layout: 'card',

    config: {
        questionnaire: null
    },
    bind: {
        questionnaire: '{questionnaire}',
        activeItem: '{currentPosition}',
        title: '{questionnaire.title}'
    },

    applyQuestionnaire: function(questionnaire) {
        if(!questionnaire) {
            return;
        }

        var intro = questionnaire.get('introduction'),
            conclusion = questionnaire.get('conclusion');

        this.add({ html: intro });

        questionnaire.steps().each(this.addStepPane, this);

        this.add({ html: conclusion });

        return questionnaire;
    },

    setActiveItem: function() {
        if(this.items.length > 0) {
            this.callParent(arguments);
        }
    },

    addStepPane: function(step, i) {
        this.add({
```

```
            xtype: 'wizard-step',
            viewModel: {
                data: { step: step }
            },
            bind: { step: '{step}' }
        });
    },

    load: function(id) {
        this.getViewModel().setLinks({
            questionnaire: {
                type: 'Wizard.model.Questionnaire',
                id: 1
            }
        });
    },

    dockedItems: [
        { xtype: 'wizard-navigation', dock: 'bottom' },
        {
            xtype: 'wizard-progress', dock: 'bottom',
            bind: '{questionnaire.steps}'
        }
    ]
});
```

I'll break down each of the important parts of this code and try and explain the design decisions behind them.

The `ui` and `bodyCls` options are set as a way of hooking into this component via theming and CSS later. In particular, the `ui` option is a great way of reusing parts of the Ext JS theming system with your own components. We'll revisit this towards the end of the chapter.

After configuring the `viewModel`, `controller`, and `layout` options, I use a tactic that we've seen before, which is to create a new custom configuration option that will be used to bind to. I created a `questionnaire` config for me to bind a view model value to and you can see that bound value is also called `questionnaire`.

The final piece of the configuration puzzle is to bind the title of the questionnaire to the title of the wizard panel itself.

Do it yourself

One of my favorite things about creating custom configuration options is that you get an extra hook in the form of an `applyOptionName` method. It's created automatically for each config option and is called by Ext JS before setting the value. It lets us customize or validate the configuration option and if we've bound a view model value to it, it lets us perform actions when the bound value updates.

I used this with `applyQuestionnaire`, which is used to build the items for the wizard panel when the questionnaire is bound. It performs the following three actions:

1. Adds a container for the questionnaire introduction.

2. Adds a container for the questionnaire conclusion.

3. Adds a `wizard-step` component for each step in the questionnaire using the `addStepPane` method.

Within `addStepPane`, the new `wizard-step` component is supplied with a view model that contains the `Step` model itself and immediately binds this to a step config option. It will be simpler to just pass in the `Step` model as a configuration option rather than using view models, but this would mean that we can't use this step in further binding formulas and it will be more awkward to react to changes in `Step`, such as validation.

The second use of apply is via `applyActiveItem`, which will be triggered every time the `currentPosition` value on the view model changes. It's used to update the panel's `currentPosition` to switch from card to card as the user progresses through questionnaire, but I added in a check to ensure the wizard's items have been initialized before doing this. Without this check, setting `currentPosition` can raise an error if `currentPosition` is changed before the items have been set up.

Wizardly tools

The last piece of configuration for the main wizard panel is to create the navigation buttons and the progress indicator. I added these as `dockedItems` with the dock set at the "bottom" in order to have them in the footer of the panel. The progress bar is bound to the questionnaire's steps from the view model in order to build its step icons.

One step forward

The navigation bar allows the user not only to proceed through the questionnaire, but also return to previous steps to review them. There's a "restart" button that takes the user back to the introduction. The "finish" button will be the one we'll use to communicate back to the host application when all questions are complete.

Each of these buttons is enabled or disabled depending on the validation state of each step (and therefore each question) and the user's position in the questionnaire. Here's the code:

```
// packages/wizard/src/view/Navigation.js
Ext.define('Wizard.view.wizard.Navigation', {
    extend: 'Ext.Toolbar',
    xtype: 'wizard-navigation',
    items: [
        {
            text: 'Restart', itemId: 'restart',
            bind: { disabled: '{isIntroduction}' }
        },
        {
            text: 'Previous', itemId: 'prev',
            bind: { disabled: '{isIntroduction}' }
        },
        '->',
        {
            text: 'Next', itemId: 'next',
            bind: { disabled: '{!isNextEnabled}' }
        },
        {
            text: 'Finish', itemId: 'finish',
            bind: { disabled: '{isNotLastStep}' }
        }
    ]
});
```

I've delegated the responsibility for enabling and disabling these buttons to a view model. As there are other components that will be interested in these values, they're going to rest at the top-level view model of the wizard. We'll take a look at this code later.

Making progress

The progress bar is a series of buttons that allows the user to determine how far they are along the questionnaire process and skip back to an earlier step. Each button needs to be aware of the user's position in the questionnaire in order to determine whether it should be enabled or disabled. The "start" and "end" buttons are fixed, wherein they are available on every questionnaire, but the numbered step buttons need to be automatically generated and bound to the steps for currently loaded questionnaire. Let's take a look at the code:

```
// packages/wizard/src/view/Progress.js
Ext.define('Wizard.view.wizard.Progress', {
    extend: 'Ext.Container',
    xtype: 'wizard-progress',

    config: {
        steps: null
    },
    defaultBindProperty: 'steps',
    defaultType: 'button',
    baseCls: 'wizard-progress',
    layout: {
        type: 'hbox',
        pack: 'center'
    },

    applySteps: function(steps) {

        var lineHtml = '<div class="wizard-progress-bar"></div>',
            stepArr = steps.getData().items,
            items = this.buildProgressIcons(stepArr),
            container;

        this.removeAll();

        items.unshift({ text: 'Start', stepIndex: 0 });
        items.push({
            text: 'End', bind: {
                disabled: '{isNotLastStep}'
            }
        });

        container = this.add({
            xtype: 'container', cls: 'wizard-progress-inner',
            defaultType: 'button', items: items
        });

        container.getEl().insertHtml('afterBegin',  lineHtml);

        return steps;
    },


    buildProgressIcons: function(steps) {
```

```
                return Ext.Array.map(steps, function(step, i){
            return {
                text: i + 1, stepIndex: i + 1,
                bind: { disabled: '{!isEnabled}' },
                viewModel: {
                    formulas: {
                        isEnabled: function(get) {
                            return get('currentPosition') > i;
                        }
                    }
                }
            };
        });
    }
});
```

There's a surprising amount going on in this component. Remember that in the wizard panel, I set the bind config on this progress component to the questionnaire steps, and in the preceding code, you can see the custom steps configuration option — as long with the defaultBindProperty — that enables this.

 Remember that defaultBindProperty allows you to avoid explicitly setting the property to bind to, and Ext JS will automatically use the default.

I'll skip over the layout, cls, and defaultType options and move on to the way I implemented applySteps. It builds an array of the following buttons:

- The start button, which is always enabled
- The number buttons for each step, which are only enabled if the user has advanced to that step
- The end button, which is only enabled when the user is on the questionnaire conclusion

The end button's disabled state is deferred to a binding on the parent view model. For the individual step icons, a simple view model with the isEnabled formula is used to toggle the disabled state based on the current active step pane.

When I was researching *Chapter 2, MVC and MVVM*, I found a little snippet describing MVC in Smalltalk and the way that individual UI components would have their own controller right down to text fields and the like. While it's rare that we'd go that far in our Ext JS applications, the use of a small, one formula view model for the step icons reminded me of this concept.

My only gripe as I was writing it was that while the functionality was great, the syntax to just bind one property like this felt a little verbose. On the other hand, introducing another shorthand syntax would mean a new feature for Ext JS developers to learn; I think we have enough already!

A final point regarding this component is that I append `lineHtml` to the container and configure a couple of styling hooks. This allows for a thin line connecting the progress buttons; it's a minor visual element, but has a nice effect.

Step by step

The next component to examine is the one that represents a step in the questionnaire and shows the associated questions:

```
// packages/wizard/src/view/Step.js
Ext.define('Wizard.view.wizard.Step', {
    extend: 'Ext.form.Panel',
    xtype: 'wizard-step',
    cls: 'wizard-step',


    defaults: {
        labelSeparator: '', labelAlign: 'top',
        labelWidth: 250, msgTarget: 'side',
        width: '100%'
    },

    config: {
        step: null
    },

    modelValidation: true,

    applyStep: function(step) {

        this.add({
            xtype: 'container',
            cls: 'wizard-step-introduction',
            html: step.get('introduction')
        });

        step.questions().each(function(question) {
            this.add({
                xtype: question.get('type'),
```

```
                    fieldLabel: question.get('questionText'),
                    required: question.get('required'),
                    bind: '{question.answer}',
                    viewModel: 'progress-step'
                }).getViewModel().set('question', question);
            }, this);

            step.isValid();
        }
    });
```

There's the standard setup for `Ext.form.Panel` here, configuring labels, and so on. Once again, I created a custom step config that we bound to in the parent `Wizard` panel's `addStepPane` method and use the matching apply method to build out the contents of the form.

Note how I have set the `modelValidation` config to `true`. As a result of my prototype earlier in the chapter, I know that this is great way to avoid code duplication by creating validation on a model and have it take effect in the form UI. When building the questions for the step in `applyStep`, I make sure and bind `question.answer` to the form field value. This means that any validation on the question model's answer field will be applied to the form field UI automatically.

All of the other attributes of the form field are built dynamically from the question data, such as the label and the field type. The final thing to note here is that I use a separate view model and immediately populate it with the question. Look at the code for this view model:

```
// packages/wizard/src/view/ProgressStepModel.js
Ext.define('Wizard.view.wizard.ProgressStepModel', {
    extend: 'Ext.app.ViewModel',
    alias: 'viewmodel.progress-step',

    data: {
        question: null
    },

    formulas: {
        isValid: {
            bind: {
                bindTo: '{question}',
                deep: true
            },
            get: function() {
                return this.get('step').isValid();
```

```
            }
        }
    }
});
```

It's nothing complicated; it's just a little bit long to define inline and so I moved it to a separate file. The code here should also look very familiar because it's the same as the code from my prototype that I showed earlier in the chapter under the heading "A Binding Trick". I knew this would come in useful!

Questionnaire command and control

Nearly all of the pieces are in place. Note that I used a lot of binding expressions in the Wizard component so far, but I haven't shown either the top-level view model or how the wizard deals with user interactions. I always like to keep controllers slim and the view controller here is no exception:

```
// packages/wizard/src/view/WizardController.js
Ext.define('Wizard.view.wizard.WizardController', {
    extend: 'Ext.app.ViewController',
    alias: 'controller.wizard',
    listen: {
        component: {
            '#next': { click: 'onNextClick' },
            '#prev': { click: 'onPrevClick' },
            '#restart': { click: 'onRestartClick' },
            '#finish': { click: 'onFinishClick' },
            'wizard-progress button': { click: 'onStepClick' }
        }
    },

    onNextClick: function() {
        var current = this.getViewModel().get('currentPosition');
        this.getViewModel().set('currentPosition', current + 1);
    },

    onPrevClick: function() {
        var current = this.getViewModel().get('currentPosition');
        this.getViewModel().set('currentPosition', current - 1);
    },

    onRestartClick: function() {
        this.getViewModel().set('currentPosition', 0);
    },
```

```
onFinishClick: function() {
    var q = this.getViewModel().get('questionnaire');
    this.fireEvent('wizardcomplete', q);
},

onStepClick: function(btn) {
    this.getViewModel().set('currentPosition', btn.stepIndex);
}
});
```

The view controller listens for clicks on the navigation buttons and any enabled buttons on the progress bar, and in every case apart from onFinishClick, it manipulates the value of currentStepIndex on the view model. It doesn't have to speak to any other components, just this one value. I really like the elegance of this solution. We'll see how currentStepIndex influences the application when we review the wizard's view model.

The onFinishClick method is called when the user clicks on the finish button and raises a controller-level event called wizardcomplete with the completed questionnaire as its only argument. The host application can handle this event and retrieve the completed question data and dispose of the wizard component as it sees fit.

This is another good example of decoupling this component from its host; the wizard needs to know nothing about the application it's embedded inside. It just fires the event and forgets about it.

The wizard model

The final, and in my opinion most important, part of the puzzle is the top-level view model. This is the one that the wizard panel uses directly and is available to all child components of the panel thanks to the view model inheritance. Here's the code:

```
// packages/wizard/src/view/WizardModel.js
Ext.define('Wizard.view.wizard.WizardModel', {
    extend: 'Ext.app.ViewModel',
    alias: 'viewmodel.wizard',

    data: {
        currentPosition: 0
    },

    formulas: {
```

```
currentStep: function(get) {
    var pos = get('currentPosition') - 1;
    return get('questionnaire').steps().getAt(pos);
},

stepCount: function(get) {
    return get('questionnaire').steps().count();
},

isIntroduction: function(get) {
    return get('currentPosition') === 0;
},

isNotLastStep: function(get) {
    return get('currentPosition') < get('stepCount') + 1;
},

isNextEnabled: function(get) {
    // when current step is valid
    var stiv = get('currentStep') ? get('currentStep.valid') :
true;

    // when not last step
    var last = get('isNotLastStep');

    return stiv && last;
}
    }
});
```

Note that currentPosition is initialized at 0, which represents the questionnaire introduction page in the UI and the first card in the wizard panel.

This one value is probably the most important in the whole application because it not only drives what is displayed on the UI through its binding to activeItem on the wizard panel, but also the state of the navigation and progress buttons. This is both direct—the progress component inherits and consumes currentPosition to set the disabled state of its buttons—and indirect, as in the way isNextEnabled uses it to get the currentStep model's validity and in turn is bound to the "next" navigation button.

Building up a couple of dependent formulae and allowing them to cascade down to child components gives a clear picture of how data flows from a single source (questionnaire and currentPosition on the wizard view model).

A delightful host

The wizard is functionally complete and it's time to show how we can embed it in an application. Look back and you'll see that the main wizard component had the following `load` method:

```
load: function(id) {
    this.getViewModel().setLinks({
        questionnaire: {
            type: 'Wizard.model.Questionnaire',
            id: id
        }
    });
}
```

This uses the `links` feature of the view model to trigger the loading of a questionnaire using its preconfigured proxy. With this in mind, the calling code could look like this:

```
Ext.define('Questions.view.main.MainController', {
    extend: 'Ext.app.ViewController',
    requires: [
        'Wizard.view.wizard.Wizard'
    ],

    alias: 'controller.main',

    listen: {
        controller: {
            'wizard': {
                'wizardcomplete': function(q) {
                    console.log(q);
                }
            }
        }
    },

    onClickButton: function () {
        this.wizard = Ext.create('Ext.Window', {
            header: false, modal: true, layout: 'fit',
            autoShow: true, resizable: false,
            width: 800, height: 600,
            items: [{ xtype: 'wizard' }],
        });
```

```
        this.wizard.down('wizard').load(1);
    }
});
```

When `onClickButton` handler fires, `Ext.Window` is created containing our wizard component, and we then call the `load` method on the wizard itself, passing the ID of the questionnaire to load.

> Remember to include the wizard package in your application's `app.json`, as discussed earlier in the chapter.

The view controller also listens for the `wizardcomplete` event and can use this to get the completed questionnaire instance for further processing and could also close the wizard window. These two integration points are all that a developer needs to use the wizard in their own application, but there's one last thing that I wanted to explore when building this component: `theming`.

Mixin the night away

I wanted consumers of the wizard component to be able to customize it, but this turned out to be very simple in most cases. As the main container for the wizard is a subclass of `Ext.Panel`, all of the relevant SCSS variables for this class can be overridden and it'll take effect for the wizard's container too.

However, I wanted to create a custom look for the progress bar and in turn allow end users to customize it. To this end, I wrote a custom mixin:

```
// packages/wizard/sass/src/Wizard/view/wizard/Progress.scss
@mixin wizard-progress-ui(
    $ui: null,
    $ui-border-color: #2163A3,
    $ui-background-color: #ffffff,
    $ui-button-border-width: 4px,
    $ui-button-border-radius: 20px
) {
    .wizard-progress-#{$ui} {
        padding: 10px 0;

        .#{$prefix}btn:last-child {
            margin-left: 20px;
            margin-right: 0px;
        }
```

```
        .#{$prefix}btn {
            margin: 0 10px;
        }

        .#{$prefix}btn:first-child {
            margin-right: 20px;
            margin-left: 0px;
        }

        @include extjs-button-small-ui(
            $ui: 'default',
            $border-radius: $ui-button-border-radius,
            $border-width: $ui-button-border-width,
            $background-color: $ui-background-color,
            $background-color-disabled: mix($ui-border-color, $ui-
background-color, 50%),
            $border-color: $ui-border-color,
            $color: black,
            $color-disabled: shade($ui-border-color, 50%),
            $opacity-disabled: 0.9999,
            $inner-opacity-disabled: 0.9999
        );

        .wizard-progress-bar {
            width: 100%;
            background: $ui-border-color;
            height: $ui-button-border-width * 1.5;
            position: absolute;
            top: 50%;
            margin-top: -(($ui-button-border-width * 1.5) / 2);
        }
    }
}

@include wizard-progress-ui(
    $ui: 'default'
);
```

The mixin accepts four variables, each with a default value:

- $ui-border-color: #2163A3

- $ui-background-color: #ffffff

- $ui-button-border-width: 4px

- $ui-button-border-radius: 20px

With this, not only can I style the component, but developers can also call this mixin from their own code and override colors and borders. As the mixin bases a lot of its other styles on values calculated from these variables, the various colors and sizes should always stay in keeping with these variables. For example, the following customization would result in a progress bar with thinner and less round borders with a pink coloring:

```
@include wizard-progress-ui(
    $ui: 'default',
    $ui-border-color: #ff69b4,
    $ui-background-color: #ffffff,
    $ui-button-border-width: 1px,
    $ui-button-border-radius: 4px
);
```

Summary

In previous chapters, we walked through the design and creation of a series of applications in a formal manner, using a series of diagrams to illustrate the process. This time, I tried to give a glimpse of some of the ways I would build the system architecture and some of the techniques I use day-to-day.

In addition, we saw how a view model can become the primary point from which data flows through an application, cascading through child view models and child components, and triggering multiple UI updates via binding.

We revisited styling and showed how the Ext JS theming system allows you to build reusable mixins that give us the same modularity in our SASS code as we have in our JavaScript classes.

In the next chapter, we'll be writing a shopping application for tablet device that allows users to browse and buy items from an online store. It'll be our most complicated application yet, which marries all of the different ideas and techniques we've discussed so far.

9
A Shopping Application

In this chapter, we'll design one last application from start to finish. Rather than continuing to introduce new ideas or techniques to visualize and construct an application architecture, we'll double up on the work we've done so far. We'll incorporate routes, view models, and events in order to consolidate everything that's been discussed, and we'll create design documentation to inform the application's structure.

In each chapter of this book so far, I've tried to stress that there's no "one true way" to application architecture. Every application is different; there is plenty of room for interpretation. At the beginning of the book, we discussed the MVC and MVVM design patterns and what an architect must find is their own pattern (a way of working that feels natural). More than this, a pattern is something that emerges because of a regularity in our work, that is, repeating the same thing again and again. While different architects will have different ways of working and can use different methods in different ways, in the practical chapters, we've completed there is a logical development path that it's easy to fall into.

"Falling into the pit of success" is a phrase used to describe a methodology that works well without users having to try hard to follow it. That's what we've been working towards. Showing you the choices Ext JS provides, not only giving you options, but also trying to illustrate why they're good options to use. By now, you should have a picture of the design of an Ext JS application and the features you can use to fulfill this design.

In this final practical chapter, we'll once again see how, despite having a choice in how to implement this application, we'll end up selecting a a path that's similar to the one we took before, a path that feels logical and that makes development easy.

About the app

The application we'll build is designed to shop on a tablet-sized screen. We'll be taking advantage of the burgeoning "craft beer" scene and creating an application that allows customers to select from categorized beers in the store. Here's the full feature list:

- Login and register
- Category list
- Product list with sorting
- Shopping cart
- Touch-friendly

In other words, the standard set of features you'd see on a straightforward e-commerce website. The final product looks like this:

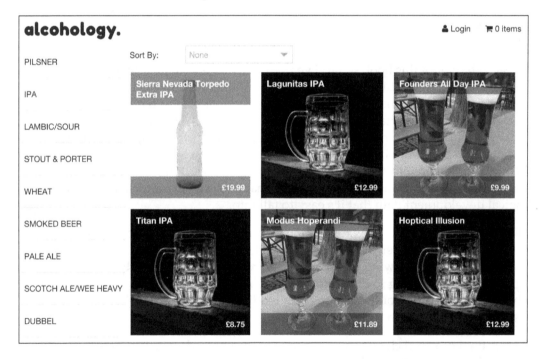

We have a simple interface that provides large tappable areas for tablet users. There are more screens in this application than any other we've worked on so far, so let's sketch these out and see what the full app will look like:

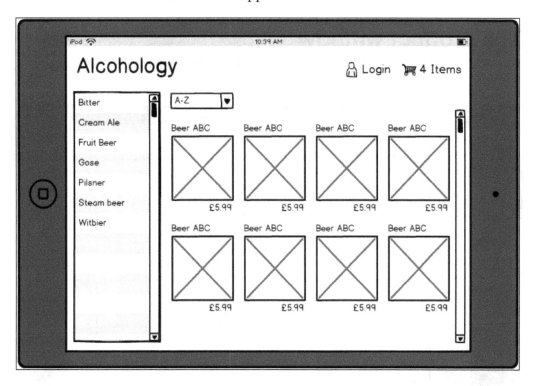

Here, we have the wireframe of the first screen that the user sees when opening the site. As you can see, it maps out the features and layout, as shown in the previous screenshot.

This mockup mentions all of the main features of the application. Note that, unlike in our earlier e-mail application, the user doesn't have to log in to start browsing. This only happens when they want to place an order.

The categories of beer are listed on the left-hand side in alphabetical order; the user can scroll through the list when it extends past the bottom of their screen. In the main part of the screen, the beers in the selected category are listed with the sort order determined by a combo box above the list. Each beer on sale is represented by its name, an image, and its price.

Finally, at the top-right corner of the screen, we have the "login" and "cart buttons" that will change to reflect the application state and are both clickable, revealing further windows.

The product window

This next screen shows the product detail page when the user selects a product to view:

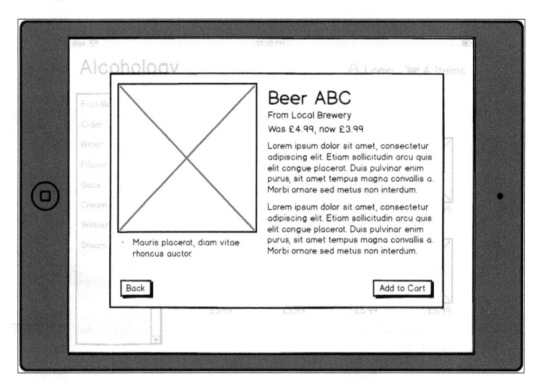

This screen fleshes out more of our requirements and the way they'll be implemented. When the user clicks on a product from the list, a modal window pops up showing more information about the product in question, such as a discount message showing price reduction, a full description, the brewery that made the beer, and a tagline that sells beer to the customer. This is all accompanied by a larger image of the product as well as buttons to add the beer to the shopping cart and to close the product window.

The shopping cart

At the top-right corner of the main app screen, we can see a shopping cart icon and a label that changes to reflect the number of items in the cart. When the user clicks on the icon or label, the cart window is shown:

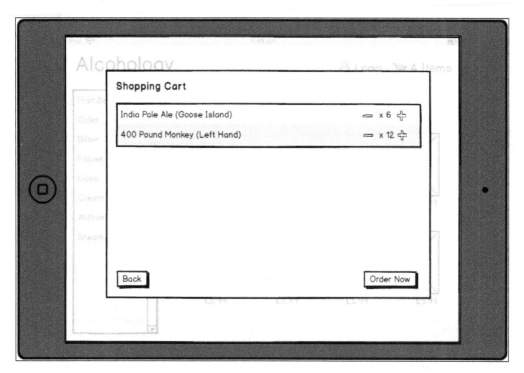

This modal window contains a list of products in the cart and the quantity of each item. The user can adjust the quantities of each item here as well by clicking on or tapping the plus or minus icons. The other key feature of this window is the **Order Now** button, which processes the current cart into an order.

If the user hasn't already logged in, clicking on this button will show the login and registration screen, which we'll look at next.

Login and registration

The **Login** and **Register** options are shown in the following screenshot:

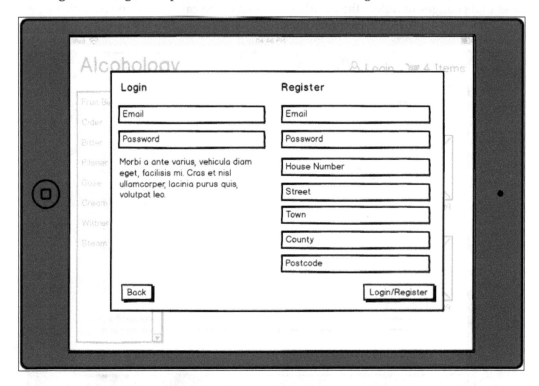

The login and registration forms are shown side-by-side because they're simple enough to fit in the same window. The fields will have validation in order to ensure e-mails are correctly formatted and required fields are completed. When the registration or login process is completed, the **Login** icon on the main screen will be replaced by the user's e-mail address; clicking on this link will show an account screen.

User account

The user account page allows the user to edit their details and view their past orders:

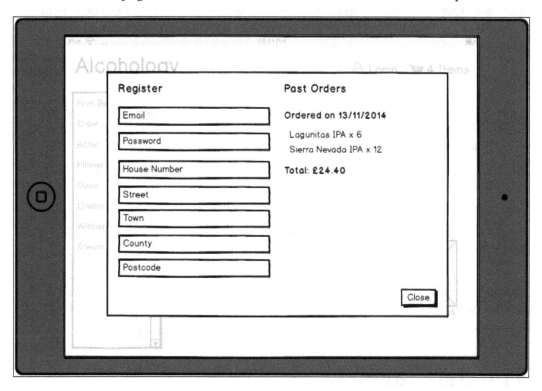

The text fields on the left-hand side allow the user to amend their address and user credentials, and the pane on the right-hand side is a list of previous orders, showing the items that were ordered, the date, and the total amount.

Design overview

We've looked at all of the main application views in turn; for simplicity, we've excluded an actual payment process to avoid integrating with a third-party service. When the user proceeds with an order, it will immediately be processed and added as a past order in their account.

One great thing about Ext JS 5 is that it adds support for touch devices and includes a touch-friendly theme. This should make it super simple to achieve our goal of presenting this app to tablet users; however, we'll include some theming tweaks to create a custom look and improve the experience for users on tablet devices.

Back to Ext JS

While we now know that Ext JS can help with the creation of a touch-friendly interface, does our design suggest any other ideas that Ext JS might not be able to cope with? Remember that the design phase is an exploration of what works for the user and what is possible with the technology at hand. Let's break it down:

- The scrolling product category list can be a `Ext.grid.Panel` class with most features, such as headers, disabled
- The scrolling product list can be an `Ext.view.View` class (also known as a DataView), as we need to include custom HTML for each product to display an image and other details
- Product list sorting will be achieved via a combo box containing the sort criteria

Other than this, we just need modal windows (which Ext JS supports), another grid for the shopping cart, a few form fields for the login and registration. We're pretty much there.

In addition to this, we'll use routing to provide the ability to bookmark categories or products, which allows the user to share links. We'll also use view models and events to wire everything together. The data will again be drawn from a server-side API, so let's look at this next.

The data layer

The shopping application needs to be supplied with the following data:

- A list of categories
- A list of products, filtered by category and sorted by the selected criteria
- Details of a single product

This makes things pretty straightforward. So, in a moment, we'll break down exactly what sort of data responses we'll see when we make a server request.

Before this, you might notice that we're skipping over the part of the application that will integrate with the server-side. The key reason for this is that it will add complexity to our example application without adding much more value; we want to highlight the decisions that we made in order to piece together this application and do it in a concise and understandable way. While there are many features we can add to this application and indeed our previous examples, we want to make sure that the really important aspects of building an application can shine through.

Let's go back to the data that we'd like our backend to supply. Firstly, retrieving a list of categories:

```
GET: /category
Accepts: N/A
Returns: [{"id":1,"name":"Pilsner"},{"id":2,"name":"IPA"}]
```

It accepts no parameters and returns a JSON array containing the ID and name of each available category. To see the products in a category, we talk to the products API:

```
GET: /product
Accepts:
sort = [{"property":"id","direction":"ASC"}]
filter = [{"property":"categoryId","value":2}]
Returns: [{"id":1,"name":"Sierra Nevada Torpedo Extra
IPA","price":"19.99", "imagePath":"snte1.jpg"}]
```

It returns an array of objects, each containing the properties needed to render a product list item. The array can be filtered by passing a sort query parameter with a JSON array of fields to sort against, and we fetch only the category of products we need by passing a `filter` query parameter with a JSON array. This array contains one object to filter the `categoryId` property. This JSON filter and sort approach is one we've used in the past and it fits well with the way Ext JS works on the client side.

Finally, we have the request for the details of a single product as follows.

```
GET: /product/:id
Accepts: N/A
Returns: { "id": 1, <all product fields omitted> }
```

It does not accept any query parameters per se. Instead, the ID is passed as part of the URL path, as it's more often seen in a RESTful API. The full JSON response is omitted for brevity, but it returns the full set of fields required to populate the product window.

Now that we've gathered this information, we can start to think about how it will shape our data classes.

Information contemplation

Based on the API we've just described, we have two main models and their associated stores:

```
Alcohology.model.Product: extends Alcohology.model.BaseModel
- id
- name
- imagePath
- description
- price
- previousPrice
- brewery
- features
- categoryId

Alcohology.model.Category: extends Alcohology.model.BaseModel
- id
- name
```

These will have accompanying stores that do nothing more than wrap their model. In addition to the classes that interact with the API, we'll have a couple more to deal with some other moving parts in the application. Firstly, we'll look at the various items in the cart:

```
Alcohology.model.CartItem: extends Alcohology.model.BaseModel
- productId
- productName
- price
- quantity
```

An alternative to this design will be to hold only `productId` and `quantity` and look up the product details from the product store at render time. However, the method we've chosen makes the resulting code simpler and it also allows you to store data such as the price at the time the user adds it to the cart. This can be handy in complex or busy sites if the product price changes after the user adds it to the cart.

Secondly, we have a model to hold an order:

```
Alcohology.model.Order: extends Alcohology.model.BaseModel
- date
- totalCost
- items[]
    - productId
    - productName
    - price
    - quantity
```

This will be used to represent a shopping cart that has been converted to an order. While this class will be consumed by a simple wrapper store, `CartItem` will have a store that does a little bit more:

```
Alcohology.store.Cart: extends Ext.data.Store
 - addProduct
 - toOrder
```

The `addProduct` method can be passed to a product model that is to be added to the cart. It adds a bit of logic to detect whether a matching product already exists in the cart; if it does, it increments the quantity rather than creating a new cart item.

The `toOrder` method converts the cart and all its items to an `Order` model, which can then be saved to the server.

The API for this project is simple, but we'll also use models and stores to organize our data and application state in memory, favoring the `Ext.data` classes over standard JavaScript objects in order to leverage their powerful features. With the data design pretty much complete, we can move on to see how this data will interact with the rest of the application.

Component interaction

In Ext JS 4, we have the MVC pattern to build and clean well-structured applications. Looking back at our past few practical chapters, though, it seems difficult to imagine going back to MVC from the MVVM architecture that Ext JS gives us because, in each example, we've used view models to great effect to provide a logical way for data to flow through our application.

The interesting thing about these examples is how little code we write in many situations. Analyzing the application requirements and spiking a few tricky areas leads to writing a small amount of configuration of UI, controllers, view models, and so on. Ext JS automatically builds the plumbing through which our data can flow.

It's another example of why application architecture is so important, particularly when combined with a strong understanding of the tools at hand. It would be very easy for a naïve developer to jump in and start writing code to manually handle movement of data from an API through to the user interface using `Ext.Ajax` rather than models and proxies and manually loading data into components. However, by taking a patient and methodical approach, we can build a conceptual overview of the application that easily slots into the framework provided by Ext JS. By thinking about things upfront, we're making our lives much simpler for later use.

To this end, let's think about the controllers and views we'll need in this application.

In control

What's the purpose of a controller? As you learned in *Chapter 2*, *MVC and MVVM*, it's to act as the glue between other parts of the application, and in the majority of cases, this is manifested in code that handles events. From UI clicks to routing events, the controller consumes them and passes off the real work to another class.

What does this mean for the way we think about architecture? It means that any action or event in the application will likely need an associated controller. If these actions can be bundled into a distinct grouping, then this could be an indication they warrant their own controller. With this in mind, let's look at our shopping application again:

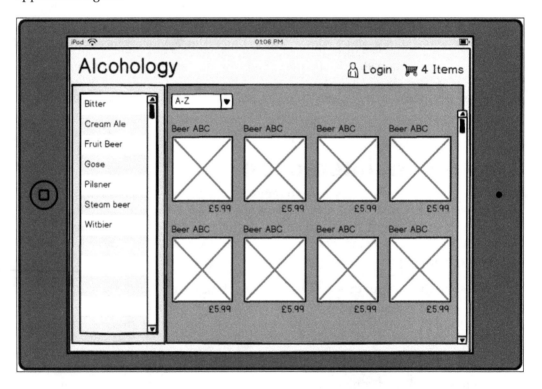

What elements of the page could raise an event? A click on a category in the blue left-hand pane, so alongside the category list view, we'll have a category view controller as follows:

```
Alcohology.view.categories.CategoriesController: extends
Ext.app.ViewController
- onItemClick
```

Clicking on a product in the product list is an action we need to handle, so we'll have a product list view and a product view controller as follows:

```
Alcohology.view.product.ProductController: extends
Ext.app.ViewController
- onSortSelect
- onCategoryRoute
- onProductRoute
- onProductClick
- onProductClose
- onAddToCart
```

Next up, the two icons at the top-right corner of the window need to trigger UI changes, so they need a view controller. Do we want a "header" controller to handle the events from the cart and account icons or can we use a "main" controller? It's one of these things that can boil down to a matter of preference; here, we'll use the main controller just to keep the number of classes from getting out of hand:

```
Alcohology.view.main.MainController: extends
Ext.app.ViewController
- onLoginRequired
- onCartClick
- onAccountClick
- onAccountRoute
- onCartRoute
```

Let's look back at our other UI wireframes. There are three remaining UI components and they're all modal windows. Firstly, the product detail window (interactions with this will be handled by the product controller that we've already identified).

Next is the shopping cart window, which will be paired with a controller that handles the user's interactions with the various buttons on the cart:

```
Alcohology.view.cart.CartController: extends
Ext.app.ViewController
- onCartClose
- onOrderNow
```

Finally, the account window with its account view controller to handle login and registration is shown in the following code:

```
Alcohology.view.account.AccountController: extends
Ext.app.ViewController
- onAccountClose
- onLoginRegister
```

There's a final place that will raise events that our application will need to handle. The requirements for this project stipulate that we implement routing to allow product pages to be shared via e-mail or social media. To meet this need, we'll have a controller specify the routes' definitions and matching handlers. The exact controller to take this role will depend on the nature of the route definitions, for example, if it's a route related to products, then the product controller will handle it. You can see a few of these route handling methods dotted around the controller designs in the preceding section.

Grouping actions and events in this way will often make the choice of which controllers to build an easy one, particularly when used in association with wireframes that allow you to look at the corresponding UI views.

The simplicity of view models

We've discussed view models and application architecture using the word "flow" several times. As the user manipulates various parts of the user interface, data flows through controllers and view models to represent the current state of the application. Rather than writing out a list of all of the junctions through which data can flow in this application, let's try and picture it instead as follows:

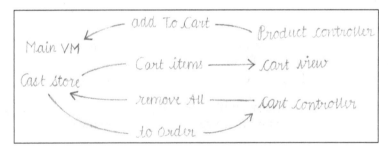

Interactions between the cart store on the main view model and its dependents

Being able to conceptualize your application at this level is a good sign that it is well-understood and well-conceived. In larger applications, it will be hard to visualize every part of the application in this way, so it will often be broken into multiple smaller visualizations. Either way, building a top-level mapping of data and user flow is a fantastic way to confirm the logic and simplicity of a design.

Code, code, and more code

It's time to get our hands dirty and put fingers to keyboards. As always, we generated a new base application using Sencha Cmd and will use the resulting "main" view as a starting point for our user interface. First though, let's flesh out the data layer that we designed earlier:

```
// app/model/BaseModel.js
Ext.define('Alcohology.model.BaseModel', {
    extend: 'Ext.data.Model',

    schema: {
        namespace: 'Alcohology.model',
        urlPrefix: 'http://localhost:3000',
        proxy: {
            type: 'rest',
            url: '{prefix}/{entityName:uncapitalize}'
        }
    }
});
```

We've used a base model in previous chapters because it gives us a good way of centralizing proxy configuration. The models that inherit from it are all straightforward, as shown in the following code:

```
// app/model/CartItem.js
Ext.define('Alcohology.model.CartItem', {
    extend: 'Alcohology.model.BaseModel',
    fields: [
        { name: 'productId' },
        { name: 'productName' },
        { name: 'price' },
        { name: 'quantity' }
    ]
});

// app/model/Category.js
Ext.define('Alcohology.model.Category', {
    extend: 'Alcohology.model.BaseModel',
    fields: [
        { name: 'id', type: 'integer'}
    ]
});

// app/model/Order.js
```

```
Ext.define('Alcohology.model.Order', {
    extend: 'Alcohology.model.BaseModel',
    fields: [
        { name: 'date', type: 'date' },
        { name: 'items', type: 'auto' }
    ]
});

// app/model/Product.js
Ext.define('Alcohology.model.Product', {
    extend: 'Alcohology.model.BaseModel',
 fields: [
        { name: 'id', type: 'integer'},
        { name: 'name', type: 'string' },
        { name: 'imagePath', type: 'string' }
    ]
});
```

Looking back at our design, these models exactly follow the specification we laid out. All we've really done is add the Ext JS implementation on top of the original field definitions.

What's in store?

As we know, stores are often just wrappers to give us a few more helpful methods to work with a collection of models. Looking back at our design documents, this is the case for three of the stores in this application:

```
// app/store/Categories.js
Ext.define('Alcohology.store.Categories', {
    extend: 'Ext.data.Store',
    model: 'Alcohology.model.Category',
    alias: 'store.categories'
});

// app/store/PastOrders.js
Ext.define('Alcohology.store.PastOrders', {
    extend: 'Ext.data.Store',
    model: 'Alcohology.model.Order',
    alias: 'store.pastorders'
});

// app/store/Products.js
Ext.define('Alcohology.store.Products', {
```

```
    extend: 'Ext.data.Store',
    model: 'Alcohology.model.Product',
    alias: 'store.products'
});
```

All very straightforward. The cart store is a bit more interesting, as shown in the following code:

```
// app/store/Cart.js
Ext.define('Alcohology.store.Cart', {
    extend: 'Ext.data.Store',
    model: 'Alcohology.model.CartItem',
    alias: 'store.cart',

    addProduct: function(product) {
        // find a product with a matching ID
        var item = this.findRecord('productId', product.getId());

        if(item) {
            item.set('quantity', item.get('quantity') + 1);
            item.commit();
        } else {
            item = this.add({
                productName: product.get('name'),
                price: product.get('price'),
                productId: product.getId(),
                quantity: 1
            });
        }

        return item;
    },

    toOrder: function() {
        var items = [], total = 0;

        this.each(function(item) {
            items.push({
                name: item.get('productName'),
                quantity: item.get('quantity')
            });

            total += item.get('price') * item.get('quantity');
        });
```

```
        return Ext.create('Alcohology.model.Order', {
            date: new Date(), items: items, total: total
        });
    }
});
```

Many of the stores we've built in past chapters have been used to store information that has been fetched from the server. Here, we're using the store as an in-memory representation of the shopping cart itself; we're adding a couple of custom methods to help with this function.

The addProduct method will add the specified product to the store by converting it to a CartItem model. If a product with the same ID already exists as an item in the cart, it will have its quantity increased by one rather than being duplicated.

The toOrder method converts the whole cart to an Order model, which is used later in the application to show past orders in the user's account.

These methods are interesting because they demonstrate a place where we're not writing glue code or code that handles events. It's the code that deals with the really interesting parts of an application, sometimes called "business logic". One of the benefits of developing a strong architecture with strong development practices is that you will have less boilerplate code and more time to work on the business logic that's important to your client.

In *Chapter 11, Application Testing*, we'll look at ways to isolate this business logic and create automated tests that give you confidence in your code base.

That's our data layer in place, so we can move on to building the user interface.

Interface in your face

An Ext JS application created with Sencha Cmd will set up the main view as a viewport filling the entire browser window. We'll use this view and adapt it to our needs, as shown in the following code:

```
// app/view/main/Main.js
Ext.define('Alcohology.view.main.Main', {
    extend: 'Ext.Panel',
    xtype: 'app-main',

    controller: 'main',
    viewModel: 'main',
```

```
    layout: 'border',

    header: { xtype: 'app-header' },
    items: [
        { xtype: 'categories', width: 200, region: 'west' },
        { xtype: 'product-list', region: 'center' }
    ],

    initComponent: function() {
        this.callParent(arguments);

        this.add(Ext.create('Alcohology.view.cart.Cart', {
            reference: 'cartWindow'
        }));

        this.add(Ext.create('Alcohology.view.account.Account', {
            reference: 'accountWindow'
        }));
    }
});
```

Here we are! Our first view component, the panel that will contain everything else in the application. The `header` config is set to a custom `xtype` that we'll build later. The items in the panel are configured to use a border layout and consist of the category list and the product list.

There is one oddity here: adding windows to a panel within the `initComponent` method. This provides two benefits:

- The main view controller can refer to the windows using `lookupReference`
- The windows will have access to the main view model via the view model inheritance

This is a simple approach that solves an obvious sounding issue, that is, where do I create my windows? It doesn't feel "right" to put them in the `items` config with the product and category list, although we certainly can without any ill effect. Another common solution is to instantiate the window in the view controller itself, but as the window then isn't a child of the main view, this leads to issue with the view model inheritance. Creating the windows in the `initComponent` method feels like a natural way to bypass this problem.

One step ahead

We decided earlier that the main view controller will also handle events from the header, so let's look at the header view next:

```
// app/view/header/Header.js
Ext.define('Alcohology.view.header.Header', {
    extend: 'Ext.panel.Header',
    xtype: 'app-header',
    cls: 'app-header',
    layout: 'hbox',
    title: 'alcohology.',
    items: [
        { xtype: 'account-indicator', width: 80, bind:
'{currentUser}' },
        bind: { data: { count: '{cartCount}' } }}
    ]
});
```

Our custom header component inherits from `Ext.panel.Header` and implements an `hbox` layout. The two items contained within are also custom classes, one for the cart icon and one for the account icon. These are configured to bind to `currentUser` and `cartCount` respectively, which are values in the main view model that we'll look at later.

The cart icon is called `MiniCart` and it looks like this:

```
// app/view/header/MiniCart.js
Ext.define('Alcohology.view.header.MiniCart', {
    extend: 'Alcohology.ux.ClickContainer',
    xtype: 'minicart',
    cls: 'mini-cart',
    tpl: new Ext.Template('<span style="font-
family:FontAwesome;">',
        '&#xf07a;</span> {count} items')
});
```

In the `header` component, we specified that the `data` config for `MiniCart` should be an object with a `count` value. This `count` value will be bound to a `cartCount` value in the view model. In turn, we now use this `count` value in the template, which allows you to have an icon that updates with the count of items in the cart.

There are a couple of other things to note here. We're using the `FontAwesome` icon set to add a bit of graphical flair to the cart; you can see it being used in a `span` tag in the `tpl` configuration.

FontAwesome can be found at `http://fortawesome.github.io/Font-Awesome/`.

The second point to note is that this class inherits from `Alcohology.ux.ClickContainer`. What's this? Take a look at the following code:

```
// app/ux/ClickContainer.js
Ext.define('Alcohology.ux.ClickContainer', {
    extend: 'Ext.Container',
    xtype: 'clickcontainer',
    listeners: {
        'afterrender': function(me) {
            me.getEl().on('click', function() {
                me.fireEvent('click');
            });
        }
    }
});
```

A normal container doesn't have a `click` event, so this `ClickContainer` hooks into the underlying element that allows you to handle user interaction with the container. This is handy if you don't need button styling and would like a bare-bones clickable component.

 This feature can also be implemented as a mixin rather than a base class.

The account indicator also extends `ClickContainer` as follows:

```
// app/view/header/AccountIndicator.js
Ext.define('Alcohology.view.header.AccountIndicator', {
    extend: 'Alcohology.ux.ClickContainer',
    xtype: 'account-indicator',
    cls: 'account-indicator',
    config: {
        user: null
    },
    defaultBindProperty: 'user',
    data: {
        label: 'Login'
    },
```

```
        tpl: '<span style="font-family:FontAwesome;">&#xf007;</span>
    {label}',

    applyUser: function(user) {
        if(user) {
            this.setData({ label: user.email });
        }
    }
});
```

Our favorite trick of binding to a custom configuration option is again used here with a little twist. If the value of a user being bound is `null`, that is, if the user has yet to log in, we use the default value of the `data` config to set a label on this component. If they have logged in, we set the label to their e-mail address.

You can see in the `tpl` configuration that we're using `FontAwesome` again. It's also the place we use the label that has a default value of `login`.

Let's get back to the code that handles the user's interactions with these components.

Under the main control

The main controller is not only the place that handles user clicks and taps, but the place that defines some relevant routes. It even handles a custom event. Let's take a look:

```
// app/view/main/MainController.js
Ext.define('Alcohology.view.main.MainController', {
    extend: 'Ext.app.ViewController',
    alias: 'controller.main',

    listen: {
        component: {
            'component[cls="mini-cart"]': { click: 'onCartClick'
},
            'component[cls="account-indicator"]': { click:
'onAccountClick' },
        },

        controller: { '*': { loginrequired: 'onLoginRequired' } }
    },

    routes: {
        'account': 'onAccountRoute',
        'cart': 'onCartRoute'
```

```
        },

        onLoginRequired: function() {
            Ext.toast('Please login or register.');
            this.redirectTo('account', true);
        },

        onCartClick: function() {
            this.redirectTo('cart', true);
        },

        onAccountClick: function() {
            this.redirectTo('account', true);
        },

        onAccountRoute: function() {
            this.lookupReference('accountWindow').show();
        },

        onCartRoute: function() {
            this.lookupReference('cartWindow').show();
        }
    });
```

There's a very handy technique demonstrated here: the click handlers for account-indicator and minicart both simply redirect to their relevant routes. This means that we can put the logic to show the account and cart windows in onAccountRoute and onCartRoute route handlers.

The other piece of functionality implemented in this view controller is the listener on the controller domain. It listens for any controller firing the loginrequired event and handles it with the onLoginRequired method. Within onLoginRequired, we pop up a brief note to the user via the Ext.toast feature and simply redirect them to the login/registration page.

This enables any controller or view controller to request the user to log in without having to be explicitly aware of the implementation of the account system. Let's take a look at the view model for the main viewport:

```
// app/view/main/MainModel.js
Ext.define('Alcohology.view.main.MainModel', {
    extend: 'Ext.app.ViewModel',
    alias: 'viewmodel.main',

    stores: {
```

```
            cart: { type: 'cart' },
            orders: { type: 'pastorders'}
        },

        data: {
            cartCount: 0
        },

        constructor: function() {
            var me = this;

            me.callParent(arguments);

            me.get('cart').on('datachanged', function(store) {
                me.set('cartCount', store.count());
            });
        }
    });
```

This top-level view model provides the stores for past orders and the shopping cart as well as a property giving us the number of items in the shopping cart.

Due to the default in Ext JS, we have to manually listen to the `datachanged` event on the cart store in order to get a "live" count of items because a change in the size of the store won't trigger a databind.

We've covered the "main" view and associated classes, so let's move on to the view that will list product categories.

Categorically speaking

We're going to use a simplified grid to build this view:

```
// app/view/categories/Categories.js
Ext.define('Alcohology.view.categories.Categories', {
    extend: 'Ext.grid.Panel',
    xtype: 'categories',
    controller: 'categories',
    viewModel: 'categories',
    bodyCls: 'categories-body',
    requires: [
        'Alcohology.view.categories.CategoriesModel',
        'Alcohology.view.categories.CategoriesController'
    ],
```

```
        bind: {
            store: '{categories}'
        },
    hideHeaders: true,
        viewConfig: {
            trackOver: false
        },
        columns: [
            { text: 'Name',  dataIndex: 'name', flex: 1 }
        ]
});
```

We've hidden the `grid` headers and used the `flex` configuration option to tell the single column to fill all of the available space. This gives us the functionality we need for a simple scrolling list.

The list's store is then bound to the `categories` that's defined on the category view model that we'll look at shortly. First, let's take a look at the categories view controller:

```
// app/view/categories/CategoriesController.js
Ext.define('Alcohology.view.categories.CategoriesController', {
    extend: 'Ext.app.ViewController',
    alias: 'controller.categories',
    listen: {
      component: {
        'categories': { 'itemclick': 'onItemClick' }
      }
    },

    onItemClick: function(view, record) {
      this.redirectTo('category/' + record.getId());
    }
});
```

This really couldn't be much simpler; just catch the `itemclick` event, grab the ID of the selected category, and pass it off to the routing system so that another controller can take care of it. The final part of the category puzzle is the view model and it's even more straightforward, as shown in the following code:

```
// app/view/categories/CategoriesModel.js
Ext.define('Alcohology.view.categories.CategoriesModel', {
    extend: 'Ext.app.ViewModel',
    requires: ['Alcohology.store.Categories'],
    alias: 'viewmodel.categories',
    stores: {
```

```
        categories: {
            type: 'categories',
            autoLoad: true
        }
    }
});
```

This is the MVVM pattern in action, each of the three classes shown here are doing its own thing and nothing more. The view class is describing the presentation, the view model provides the data behind this presentation, and the view controller deals with user interaction.

Product placement

Here's the code for the list of products:

```
// app/view/product/List.js
Ext.define('Alcohology.view.product.List', {
    extend: 'Ext.Panel',
    controller: 'product',
    xtype: 'product-list',
    cls: 'product-list',
    viewModel: 'product',
    tbar: [
        {
            xtype: 'combo',
            store: Ext.create('Ext.data.Store', {
                fields: ['text', 'field', 'direction'],
                data : [
                    { text: 'Date Added', property: 'id',
direction: 'DESC' },
                    { text: 'Name A-Z', property: 'name',
direction: 'ASC' },
                    { text: 'Name Z-A', property: 'name',
direction: 'DESC' },
                    { text: 'Price ASC', property: 'price',
direction: 'ASC' }
                ]
            }),
            displayField: 'text',
            queryMode: 'local',
            fieldLabel: 'Sort By',
            emptyText: 'None',
            editable: false
```

```
        }
    ],
    items: [
        {
            xtype: 'dataview', itemId: 'productListView',
            emptyText: '<span class="empty">No Products
Found.</span>',
            itemSelector: '.product', bind: '{products}',
            tpl: '<tpl for="."><div class="product"><h2>{name}</
h2><img src="/resources/product-
images/{imagePath}-thumb.jpg" /><p>&pound;{price}</p></div></tpl>',
        }
    ],

    constructor: function() {
        this.callParent(arguments);

        this.add(Ext.create('Alcohology.view.product.Detail', {
            reference: 'productWindow'
        }));
    }
});
```

The top toolbar for the product list contains a combo box with an inline store containing available sort options. Note that we include the property to sort against and the direction of the sort so that we can pass these straight through to the server later.

There's a case to be made for this combo to be extracted into a separate class or the store to be set up on the view model; it might make this class a bit clearer. On the other hand, the proliferation of files and classes for their own sake will make things less clear too, so we'll keep it inline.

The real work in this class is performed by the `dataview` bound to a products store on the view model. Note how again that we're creating a window in the constructor of this class too, which will enable it to use the same view controller as the product list `dataview`.

Here's the code for this window (it's the one that shows details of a product):

```
// app/view/product/Detail.js
Ext.define('Alcohology.view.product.Detail', {
    extend: 'Ext.Window',
    modal: true,
    header: false,
    resizable: false,
    autoScroll: true,
```

```
        height: 600,
        width: 800,
        layout: 'column',
        cls: 'product-detail',
        items: [
            {
                xtype: 'container',
                columnWidth: 0.5,
                defaults: {
                    xtype: 'component',
                    bind: { data: '{currentProduct}' }
                },
                items: [
                    {
                        xtype: 'container',
                        tpl: '<img src="/resources/product-
images/{imagePath}-thumb.jpg" />'
                    },
                    { tpl: '<ul><li>{features}</li></ul>' }
                ]
            },
            {
                xtype: 'container',
                columnWidth: 0.5,
                defaults: {
                    xtype: 'component',
                    bind: { data: '{currentProduct}' }
                },
                items: [
                    { tpl: new Ext.Template('<h1>{name}</h1>',
                        '<h2 class="brewery">{brewery}</h2>',
                        '<h2><p class="price">&pound;{price}</p>',
                        '<p class="previousPrice">Was:
&pound;{previousPrice}</p>',
                        '</h2>') },
                    { tpl: '<div class="description">{description}</div>'
}
                ]
            }
        ],

        bbar: [
            { text: 'Back', itemId: 'close', glyph: 0xf190 },
            '->',
```

```
        { text: 'Add to Cart', itemId: 'addToCart', glyph: 0xf07a
    }
    ]
});
```

There's a neat little trick used in this class. The window is split into two using a column layout and filled with a number of components that have their `data` config bound to the `currentProduct` on the view model. By using the `tpl` config on these components to set up an HTML template, each pane in the window can pull properties from the `currentProduct` and they'll be incorporated in the template. This gives us a hybrid approach that leverages the Ext JS column layout and standard HTML/CSS for customization.

 In `bbar` for this window, we use the `glyph` property to set `FontAwesome` icons on the buttons using the `unicode` character code of the icon in question.

The view controller that works with the product list and detail has a couple of interesting features as follows:

```
// app/view/product/ProductController.js
Ext.define('Alcohology.view.product.ProductController', {
    extend: 'Ext.app.ViewController',
    alias: 'controller.product',
    listen: {
        component: {
            '#productListView': { 'itemclick': 'onProductClick' },
            '#close': { 'click': 'onProductClose' },
            '#addToCart': { 'click': 'onAddToCart' },
            'combo': { 'select': 'onSortSelect' }
        }
    },

    routes : {
        'product/:id': 'onProductRoute',
        'category/:id': 'onCategoryRoute'
    },

    onSortSelect: function(combo, records) {
        if(records.length > 0) {
            var prop = records[0].get('property'),
                dir = records[0].get('direction');

            this.getViewModel().set('sortProperty', prop);
```

```
                this.getViewModel().set('sortDirection', dir);
            }
        },

    onCategoryRoute: function(id) {
        var cfg = { reference: 'Alcohology.model.Category', id: id
    };
        this.getViewModel().linkTo('currentCategory', cfg);
        this.lookupReference('productWindow').hide();
    },

    onProductRoute: function(id) {
        var cfg = { reference: 'Alcohology.model.Product', id: id
    };
        this.getViewModel().linkTo('currentProduct',  cfg);
        this.lookupReference('productWindow').show();
    },

    onProductClick: function(view, record, el) {
        this.redirectTo('product/' + record.getId());
    },

    onProductClose: function() {
        var id =
    this.getViewModel().get('currentCategory').getId();
        this.redirectTo('category/' + id);
    },

    onAddToCart: function() {
        var product = this.getViewModel().get('currentProduct');

        this.getViewModel().get('cart').addProduct(product);

        Ext.toast('Product Added');
    }
});
```

After wiring up event listeners and routes, we have the onSortSelect method that handles the user's selection of a sort option. We pick out the values we need and send them to the view model.

The routing handles on this view controller: onCategoryRoute and onProductRoute deal with the selection of a category (which shows a list of products) and the selection of a product (which shows a single product), and do so using a technique (which is new to us).

By using the `linkTo` method, we tell Ext JS to load the record with the specified ID if it's not already loaded it before. By doing this, we save the manual labor of loading the record ourselves. It's a neat shortcut that lets us set `currentProduct` and `currentCategory` on the view model with minimal code.

The `onProductClick` and `onProductClose` methods use `redirectTo` and hand off the real behavior to the relevant routes. The `onAddToCart` method grabs the cart store from the view model and uses the `addProduct` method that we created back in our data layer to push the current product into the cart.

Finally, we have the product view model:

```
// app/view/product/ProductModel.js
Ext.define('Alcohology.view.product.ProductModel', {
    extend: 'Ext.app.ViewModel',
    alias: 'viewmodel.product',
    links: {
        currentCategory: {
            type: 'Alcohology.model.Category',
            id: 1
        }
    },
    data: {
        sortProperty: 'id',
        sortDirection: 'ASC'
    },
    stores: {
        products: {
            type: 'products',
            autoLoad: true,
            remoteFilter: true,
            remoteSort: true,
            sorters: [{
                property: '{sortProperty}',
                direction: '{sortDirection}'
            }],
            filters: [{
                property: 'categoryId',
                value: '{currentCategory.id}'
            }]
        }
    }
});
```

The `links` configuration sets up the initial category to be loaded; Ext JS will do this automatically and anything that's been bound to it will be able to make use of it as soon as the load is complete. No manual intervention here is required; just wire up the configuration and go.

The `data` object contains the default values for product sorting and you can see that these are used by the `products` store and sent off to the server thanks to `remoteSort`. The product store is used to power the list of products in a category, and to this end it has a filter that's bound to the ID of `currentCategory`. This gets sent along with the sort options as JSON.

Categories and products are taken care of. It's time to move on to the shopping cart UI.

A basket case

The cart itself is a grid showing the products in the cart and the quantity of each. It's enclosed in a window with a couple of action buttons at the bottom as follows:

```
// app/view/cart/Cart.js
Ext.define('Alcohology.view.cart.Cart', {
    extend: 'Ext.Window',
    requires: ['Alcohology.view.cart.CartController'],
    controller: 'cart',
    width: 500,
    height: 350,
    modal: true,
    resizable: false,
    header: false,
    onEsc: Ext.emptyFn,
    layout: 'fit',
    items: [
        {
            xtype: 'grid',
            bind: '{cart}',
            plugins: {
                ptype: 'cellediting',
                clicksToEdit: 1
            },
            listeners: {
                edit: function(editor, e) {
                    e.record.commit();
                }
            },
```

```
                hideHeaders: true,
                emptyText: 'No items in the cart.',
                columns: [
                    { name: 'Product', dataIndex: 'productName', flex:
    1 },
                    {
                        name: 'Quantity', dataIndex: 'quantity',
                        editor: {
                            xtype: 'numberfield',
                            allowBlank: false
                        }
                    }
                ]
            }
        ],
        bbar: [
            '->',
            { text: 'Close', itemId: 'closeCart' },
            { text: 'Order Now', itemId: 'orderNow' }
        ]
    });
```

Within the grid, we have used the `cellediting` plugin that allows the user to tap the quantity column and use the plus or minus icons that Ext JS provides on the touch-friendly theme to adjust the item quantity. When the quantity is edited and the `edit` event fires on the grid, we immediately commit the change to the cart store, which is bound to the grid from the parent view model.

Note that there is no specific view model for this view. Instead, as we instantiated this window within the constructor of the main view, it'll inherit the main view model. This means that we can share the cart store with multiple components by having it high up in the view model hierarchy.

Let's move on to the cart view controller, as shown in the following code:

```
// app/view/cart/CartController.js
Ext.define('Alcohology.view.cart.CartController', {
    extend: 'Ext.app.ViewController',
    alias: 'controller.cart',
    listen: {
        component: {
            '#closeCart': { click: 'onCartClose' },
            '#orderNow': { click: 'onOrderNow' }
        }
    },
```

```
onCartClose: function() {
    this.getView().hide();
},

onOrderNow: function() {
    var vm = this.getViewModel();

    if(!vm.get('currentUser')) {
        this.fireEvent('loginrequired');
    } else {
        var order = vm.get('cart').toOrder();

        vm.get('cart').removeAll();
        vm.get('orders').add(order);

        Ext.toast('Order Accepted!');

        this.getView().hide();
    }
}
});
```

We wire up event handlers for the window's buttons by using itemId, which we defined in the view as the selector. The onCartClose method is straightforward, but the onOrderNow one is a little more interesting.

It first determines if the user is logged in by checking whether currentUser on the view model is null. If the user is not logged in, a loginrequired event will be fired; if you remember, we handled this earlier in the main view controller. If the user is logged in, we perform the following actions:

- Call the toOrder method from the cart store to get an Order model
- Remove all the items from the cart
- Add the new Order model to the orders store on the view model
- Show a toast notification to the user
- Hide the cart window

All of this results in the cart being moved to an order. In a comprehensive e-commerce application, this is the bit that will be replaced by credit card capturing and payment processing, but we've taken the simple approach here, that is, composing various calls to other classes to perform the action we need.

As previously discussed, the cart view doesn't have its own view model because it inherits from its parent, so we'll now move on to the final view in the application; the account window.

The account window

The account view is a window that contains several subcomponents (such as login, register, and past orders). Let's take a look at the lengthy, but straightforward code for it:

```
// app/view/account/Account.js
Ext.define('Alcohology.view.account.Account', {
    extend: 'Ext.Window',
    xtype: 'account',
    layout: 'fit',
    controller: 'account',
    modal: true,
    resizable: false,
    header: false,
    onEsc: Ext.emptyFn,
    width: 800,
    autoHeight: true,
    frame: true,
    items: [
        {
            xtype: 'container',
            layout: 'column',
            items: [
                { xtype: 'login', title: 'Login', columnWidth: 0.5
},
                { xtype: 'register', title: 'Register',
columnWidth: 0.5 }
            ],
            bind: { hidden: '{currentUser}' }
        },
        {
            xtype: 'container',
            layout: 'column',
            items: [
                { xtype: 'register', title: 'Register',
columnWidth: 0.5 },
                {
                    xtype: 'panel',  title: 'Past Orders',
                    columnWidth: 0.5, items: [
```

```
                              { xtype: 'pastorders', bind: '{orders}' }
                    ]
                }
            ],
            bind: { hidden: '{!currentUser}' }
        }
    ],
    bbar: [
        '->',
        { text: 'Close', itemId: 'close' },
        {
            text: 'Login/Register', itemId: 'loginRegister',
            bind: { hidden: '{currentUser}' }
        }
    ]
});
```

We've got two panels here, both set to use a `column` layout. One contains the login and registration forms and is shown when the user is logged out. Another shows the registration form repurposed as a way to let the user edit their profile details and the past orders. The second panel is only shown when the user is logged in.

The hiding and showing of components in the account window is accomplished by binding the `hidden` config to `currentUser` at the top-level main view model. Ext JS converts the user object to a "truthy" value, that is, either true or false. This is used to set the component's visibility.

Next, we have the `login` component, which is just an `Ext.FormPanel` with the relevant fields along with a little bit of explanatory text, as shown in the following code:

```
// app/view/account/Login.js
Ext.define('Alcohology.view.account.Login', {
    extend: 'Ext.FormPanel',
    xtype: 'login',
    items: [
        {
            xtype: 'fieldset', margin: 10, padding: 10,
            defaults: { xtype: 'textfield', width: '100%' },
            items: [
                { fieldLabel: 'Email', bind: '{email}', vtype:
'email' },
                { fieldLabel: 'Password', inputType: 'password' }
            ]
        },
```

```
        {
            xtype: 'container',
            padding: 10,
            html: 'If you've already got an Alcohology account,
                please enter your login details above. If not,
    please complete the registration form and join us!'
        }
    ]
});
```

Then, we have the `register` component, another form containing the fields that a user must complete in order to sign up:

```
// app/view/account/Register.js
Ext.define('Alcohology.view.account.Register', {
    extend: 'Ext.FormPanel',
    xtype: 'register',
    defaultType: 'textfield',
    items: [
        {
            xtype: 'fieldset', margin: 10, padding: 10,
            defaults: { xtype: 'textfield', width: '100%' },
            items: [
                { fieldLabel: 'Email', bind: '{email}', vtype:
    'email' },
                { fieldLabel: 'Password', inputType: 'password' }
            ]
        },
        {
            xtype: 'fieldset', margin: 10, padding: 10,
            defaults: { xtype: 'textfield', width: '100%' },
            items: [
                { fieldLabel: 'House Number' },
                { fieldLabel: 'Street' },
                { fieldLabel: 'Town' },
                { fieldLabel: 'County' },
                { fieldLabel: 'Postcode' }
            ]
        }
    ]
});
```

The final piece of the account user interface is the past orders component:

```
// app/view/account/PastOrders.js
Ext.define('Alcohology.view.account.PastOrders', {
    extend: 'Ext.DataView',
    xtype: 'pastorders',
    tpl: new Ext.XTemplate('<tpl for="."><div class="past-
order">',
        '<h3>Ordered on {date:date("m F Y")}</h3>',
        '<ul><tpl for="items">{name} x {quantity}</tpl></ul>',
        '<p>Total: &pound;{total}</p></div></tpl>'),
    itemSelector: '.fake',
    emptyText: 'No Previous Orders.'
});
```

Here, we use DataView with `itemTpl` configured to output all of the orders as well as loop through the items within this order. As none of the past orders are clickable, there's no detail view for orders to click on to. Therefore, we need to specify a fake `itemSelector`. Binding this component's store to the orders store on the view model was performed in the containing account window.

Finally, we have a simple view controller to handle interactions with the account window, as shown in the following code:

```
// app/view/account/AccountController.js
Ext.define('Alcohology.view.account.AccountController', {
    extend: 'Ext.app.ViewController',
    alias: 'controller.account',
    listen: {
        component: {
            '#close': { click: 'onAccountClose' },
            '#loginRegister': { click: 'onLoginRegister' }
        }
    },

    onAccountClose: function(btn) {
        this.getView().hide();
    },

    onLoginRegister: function() {
        this.getViewModel().set('currentUser', {
            email: this.getViewModel().get('email')
        });
```

```
            this.getView().hide();
        }
    });
```

This is standard stuff in onAccountClose, but in onLoginRegister, we perform a very naïve login action in which the currentUser gets set to an object with the e-mail address that the user entered for login or registration. As previously discussed, we're bypassing a full authentication system for simplicity, but this demonstrates the general idea, that is, perform an action that ends up with a user being set on the inherited view model. Once again, you'll see that we don't have a separate account view model as everything's passed up and down to the one that's defined on the main view.

Summary

This chapter's been a whistle-stop tour through a set of features and ideas that we should already be familiar with. It was a consolidation of the work we've done over the past few chapters and a demonstration of how to build an application with multiple views, but with a low level of complexity.

In the next chapter, we'll be moving on from full applications and looking at performance and debugging considerations involved in an Ext JS project. How can we design our applications to help developers when issues arise? How can we try and make sure our application feels responsive to end users? We'll also be looking at these questions in-depth in the next chapter.

10
Debugging and Performance

In previous chapters, we discussed the role of the architect as being one with many facets. From understanding client requirements to designing the code structure based on UI wireframes right down to coding standards and naming conventions, an architect will wear many hats during the lifetime of a project.

One of these hats is that of planning with knowledge of the technology at hand. In order to make sure that the users of a software platform have a responsive experience that won't result in frustration, we need to make sure that the design that's in place will load quickly and will promptly react to user input. With Ext JS, this means having an understanding of the right component to use at the right time, working with layouts in an efficient manner, designing your view model hierarchy to avoid overnesting, and so on. There are lots of things to consider.

Once the design is complete, there may be unexpected performance issues or bugs as development progresses. In these situations, the architect may take on the role of an expert problem solver, jumping in to apply their practical knowledge of the technology. Working with third-party developer tools to step through source code and profile areas of slow performance are key aspects to driving a project through to completion.

In this chapter, we'll cover these topics in the context of Ext JS and more:

- Working with browser tooling to debug and track performance
- Picking through the Ext JS source code
- Ext JS performance do's and don'ts
- Common pitfalls of Ext JS development

By the end of this chapter, we'll have the ability to work as project firefighters, jumping into situations that need fast, authoritative solutions before they spiral out of control.

In-browser debugging

We'll examine several features of the Developer Tools of the Google Chrome browser (firstly, stepping through code and debugging it). Why Google Chrome? Aside from the fact that it's my own browser of choice, its tools feel a little slicker than those in, for example, Firefox. Having said that, Firefox will allow you to do most of what we'll discuss in this chapter if you'd prefer to stick with Mozilla. At the time of writing this book, Chrome was at version 40, but most of these features have been around for at least a year.

During development, there will inevitably be situations in which we'll deal with code that doesn't work exactly as we'd expect, whether that's the code we've written, code from another member of our development team, or code in a third-party library (such as Ext JS).

When this happens, it's useful to be able to halt code execution and inspect the state of the application directly. This is exactly what the Chrome Debugger allows us to do.

> Documentation on using Chrome Developer Tools to debug JavaScript can be found at `https://developer.chrome.com/devtools/docs/javascript-debugging`.

We'll use the Alcohology app from *Chapter 9, A Shopping Application*, to show how a debugging session might play out.

Stepping in

Let's load up the Alcohology project in Chrome and navigate to a product, then pop up the Chrome Developer Tools by going to the **View** menu, then **Developer**, and **Developer Tools**. Select the **Sources** pane on the Developer Tools and you should end up with something like this:

The Alcohology app with Chrome Developer Tools

Let's imagine a theoretical situation in which something's not quite right when we add this product to the shopping cart. We'd like to drop into the code that handles the `click` event on the **Add to Cart** button, so in the left pane of Developer Tools, we use the file explorer to navigate to `/app/view/product/ProductController.js` and scroll to the `onAddToCart` method.

By clicking on the line number for line **54**, a blue indicator appears to show that we have set a "breakpoint" in the code at the beginning of the `onAddToCart` method. When code execution reaches line **54**, the debugger will pause execution and give us a chance to inspect the application state:

```
  ▶ 🗀 header             50        },
  ▶ 🗀 main               51
  ▼ 🗀 product            52
      🗋 List.js?_dc=disable   53       onAddToCart: function() {
      🗋 ProductController.js?_dc 54           var product = this.getViewModel().get('currentProduct');
      🗋 Application.js?_dc=disable 55
  ▶ 🗀 build/development/Alcoholog 56           this.getViewModel().get('cart').addProduct(product);
  ▶ 🗀 ext                58           Ext.toast('Product Added');
                         59       }
                         60   });
```

ProductController.js with a breakpoint (indicated in blue) on line 54

The breakpoint has been set, so the next step is to trigger the execution of this code and examine `onAddToCart`.

Breaking point

Clicking on the **Add to Cart** button will call the `onAddToCart` click handler and pause the execution on line 54. The whole line will become highlighted in blue to show the location we're paused on. This line of code grabs the current product from the view model and stores it in a `product` variable.

At this point, the highlighted line of code is yet to run and so the product variable will be undefined. Let's move on to the next line and examine the contents of product by clicking on the curving arrow in the right pane:

The "step over next function call" button highlighted in a red circle

This will skip the current line and move to the next, this time highlighting line 56 in blue.

At this point, the product variable will be set, so you can hover the mouse over it and a popup will appear showing its various properties and methods. As it's an instance of `Alcohology.model.Product`, which is `Ext.data.Model`, we'll see all of the properties and methods on the object provided by all of the classes in the inheritance chain.

Depending on the exact structure of the inheritance chain, some of these properties and methods will only be revealed by drilling down through the __proto__ property and expanding it.

The __proto__ property is an internal property on a JS object that points to the prototype of this object. Ext JS replicates classical inheritance by using JavaScript's prototypal inheritance. You can read about this in more detail at MDN `https://developer.mozilla.org/en-US/docs/Web/JavaScript/Guide/Inheritance_and_the_prototype_chain`.

The line 56 looks like this:

```
this.getViewModel().get('cart').addProduct(product);
```

Let's say we'd like to drill down into the `addProduct` method and investigate what's happening in here. The **Step in to next function call** button will let us do this (it's the downward arrow next to the **Skip over** button). The trouble is that it does exactly what it says, that is, steps into the next function call. Line 56 actually consists of three separate function calls:

- A call to `getViewModel` that returns the view model assigned to this view controller

- A call to get with the parameter 'cart' that returns the cart from the view model

- Finally, the call to `addProduct` with the product variable as a parameter

The result is that the first time we click on **Step In**, we'll end up in the Ext JS framework code for `getViewModel`. We then click on the **Step Out** upward arrow to return to line 56. **Step In** and **Step Out** again takes us in and then back out of `get`. Finally, on the third party of our little dance, **Step In** will take us into the source of the `addProduct` method:

Stepping in to the addProduct code

We can now examine how the product is used in this method and verify that the code is behaving as expected and if not, why not?

The repeated stepping in/out can be painful and confusing, particularly for new developers looking to use these advanced tools. As the problem-solving architect, we need to understand these quirks for both our own sake and to assist our team in debugging sessions. There are a couple of ways around this; we'll look at these next.

Black box and cut to the chase

Chrome has a feature known as "blackboxing", which tells Chrome to bypass a code file when debugging. This is exactly what we need in order to avoid the step in/out dance we saw earlier; by blackboxing the Ext JS source, Chrome will not step into this code.

It's easy to set up blackboxing. Just use the left-hand side file navigator to open the Ext JS source code, which in development builds will likely be something like this:

```
/ext/build/ext-all-rtl-debug.js
```

We also opened this file earlier as we stepped through the code, so we have an alternative method of getting it open in the central pane. When we've got the file in question, it's a simple matter of right-clicking on it and choosing the **Blackbox Script** option from the menu:

```
┌─────────────────────────────────────────────────────────────────────────────────┐
│ ▣ Cart.js?_dc=disable │ ext-all-rtl-deb...js?_dc=disable ×  │ »            ▶▤ ⫶⫶ │
├─────────────────────────────────────────────────────────────────────────────────┤
│ 56753                                                                             │
│ 56754                                                                             │
│ 56755    get: function(path) {                                                    │
│ 56756        return this.getStub(path).getValue();                                │
│ 56757    },                                                                        │
│ 56758                                                                             │
│ 56759                                                                             │
│ 56760    set: function (path, value) {                                             │
│ 56761        var me = this,                                                        │
│ 56762            obj, stub;                                                        │
│ 56763                                                                             │
│ 56764        |                                                                     │
│ 56765        me.getData();      Open Link in New Tab                               │
│ 56766                           Copy Link Address                                  │
│ 56767        if (value === u                         structor === Object) {        │
│ 56768            stub = me.g                                                       │
│ 56769            value = pat   Save                                               │
│ 56770        } else if (path   Save As...                                         │
│ 56771            obj = {};                                                         │
│ 56772            obj[path] =                                                       │
│ 56773            value = obj   Local Modifications...                             │
│ 56774            stub = me.g   Blackbox Script                                     │
│ 56775        } else {                                                              │
│ 56776            stub = me.g   Reveal in Navigator                                 │
│ 56777        }                                                                     │
│ 56778                                                                             │
│ 56779        stub.set(value)   Add Source Map...                                   │
│ 56780    },                                                                        │
└─────────────────────────────────────────────────────────────────────────────────┘
```

The options menu for a source file with the Blackbox Script option highlighted

A banner will appear at the top of the pane to indicate that the file has been blackboxed. This is a great way to simplify debugging sessions. As the Ext JS source code is more than 100,000 lines long, it can also speed up the process a great deal.

There are multiple methods of blackboxing a script. Refer to
`https://developer.chrome.com/devtools/docs/`
`blackboxing` for more information on the Chrome Developer
Tools documentation.

The second method of avoiding step in/out pain is to bypass the code in question altogether. If we know the source of the method we really want to debug, then why not just set another breakpoint there instead? In our previous example, it would have made more sense to set the breakpoint on line 9 of Cart.js, right inside the `addProduct` method. By clicking on the **Resume Script Execution** icon, represented by a blue right-facing arrow, we could have jumped immediately from the breakpoint in the `ProductController` to the one in the `Cart` class.

There's an adage in software development: writing code is easier than reading code. Taking the time to work through and understand code that others have written is a key skill that all developers should acquire, but it's of particular value to architects who are often in the position of evaluating existing code and understanding how it fits into a bigger picture.

Debugging and stepping through code is a key part of this, tracing the execution of different paths to build a picture of how the application is behaving.

Breaking and busting

At some point in the development of a project, a developer will inevitably be faced with an obscure error, which is raised from the depths of Ext JS when the application loads. This raises an issue with the way Ext JS sets up its caching mechanism. For example, a normal (if slightly naïve) request for a JavaScript file might look like this:

```
GET: /assets/javascripts/jquery.min.js
```

Out of the box, `Ext.Loader` will pull scripts like this:

```
GET: /ext/build/ext-all-rtl-debug.js?_dc=1420215165267
```

It appends a timestamp query variable to the request. This is designed to ensure that we always get the latest version of the script by bypassing browser caching mechanisms.

This can be very useful; however in our situation, it means that any breakpoints set in our code will be removed when the page reloads because Chrome thinks the file is different as the timestamp's different.

How can we resolve this? It turns out to be really simple; just open `app.json` in the root of an Ext JS project and search for the comment starting "this option is used to configure the dynamic loader". The comment contains various options to be passed to the loader, such as passing `true`, which "allows requests to receive cached responses". So, we can add the following code:

```
"loader": {
        "cache": true
},
```

Also, the cache-busting timestamps will be removed. Note the trailing comma. This is required to ensure the file remains as parsable JSON.

Caught in the act

Back to the situation in which errors pop up to surprise us. There may be an error that happens on page load, on user interaction, or because of some background job. It would be great to be able to catch errors as they happens so that we can poke around with the debugger and try and establish what went wrong.

Fortunately, Chrome provides a feature that does exactly this: "break on error", as shown here:

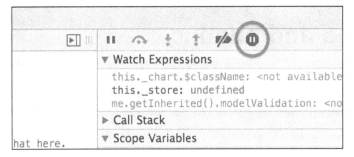

The "break on error" icon, highlighted by a red circle

Let's try a contrived example. Click on the "break on error" button and it turns blue, then open up the Alcoholology project's `Application.js` file, and add the following code to the launch method:

```
Ext.create('Ext.Panel', {
    html: 'Break on error test!',
    renderTo: 'myElement'
});
```

Save and reload the web browser. Chrome will immediately jump to the source of the error deep into the Ext JS code:

```
bootstrap.js    jquery.js    ext-all-rtl-debug.js ×  Cart.js
70059                   newNode = el.firstChild;
70060           }
70061           return returnElement ? Ext.get(newNode) : newNode;
70062       },
70063
70064       doInsert: function(el, o, returnElement, where) {
70065           var me = this,
70066               newNode;
70067
70068           el = el.dom || Ext.getDom(el);
70069
70070           if ('innerHTML' in el) {
```

Chrome's debugged paused on a line of code which is throwing an error

The original error thrown is `Uncaught TypeError: Cannot read property 'dom' of null`. This doesn't make much sense out of context. Now that we're in the code, we can see the surrounding variables and work out exactly what was null, in this case, the `el` variable.

We can also use the **Call Stack** panel in the right-hand pane to jump up through the call stack to the code that originally initiated this code path and view all of the code calls in between. This is great in complicated scenarios to let us trace the root source of an error:

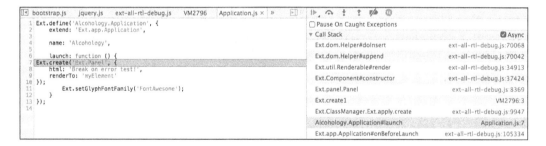

Alone, none of this will help us solve the problem. Being able to see the error, the state of the application when it was raised, and the path through the code to the original call site, all in combination with an understanding of Ext JS and a bit of intuition give us a smoking gun to resolve this issue.

The el variable, short for "element" is null, and looking back at our code in the launch method shows that we set our panel to renderTo an element called myElement. Using the **Call Stack** pane, we can step down to the constructor and do some detective work:

- Ext.create will call the constructor for the panel; we can see this by clicking on Ext.panel.Panel in the **Call Stack** pane.
- This in turn calls the render method on the Ext.util.Renderable mixin. It passes the value of the renderTo config as an argument.
- Within the render method, this argument is called container.
- The render method calls Ext.DomHelper.append with a container argument, which the debugger shows to be null.
- This indicates that the container variable is being manipulated elsewhere within the render method.
- Tracing back, we find the culprit: container = me.initContainer(container).
- The initComponent contains the line container.dom ? container : Ext. get(container).

All of this leads us to the root source of this particular error: the string myElement is passed to Ext.get. As we haven't added an element with this ID to the HTML page, Ext JS cannot find it. This means that the panel doesn't have a valid container to render to and causes an error to be thrown.

The ability to undertake this kind of investigation can be the difference between a project that meets its deadlines and one that stalls due to unexpected issues. Diving deep into the code in this way is an essential skill to avoid roadblocks and keep your developers moving.

Performance in Ext JS

As architects, we'll start a project with a lengthy list of requirements from the client that need to be implemented for them to be satisfied. There'll be explicit things such as "login feature" and "mobile friendly", but there are requirements that are not included in this list that nonetheless are unavoidable requirements for every client.

One of these is that the application should perform well. This is a catchall term that could include:

- Responsiveness of UI elements
- Initial application start up time
- Remote requests such as load/save

A slow application is a key source of user frustration and the first step to diagnosing any issues of this nature is to collect information.

Let's look at the various ways in which Chrome Developer Tools can help us and address common problems using Ext JS.

Network performance

As we've seen in our examples, many Ext JS applications will communicate with a backend API service in order to read and write data. If user feedback shows that remote requests are unresponsive, we need to first diagnose the calls that are causing problems. Chrome can help us here.

With the Developer Tools open, click on the **Network** tab and refresh the page. We get a list of all of the resources requested as the application loads; we can filter this by clicking on one of the headers at the top of the pane. Here's the Alcohology application filtered to "XHR" or Ajax requests:

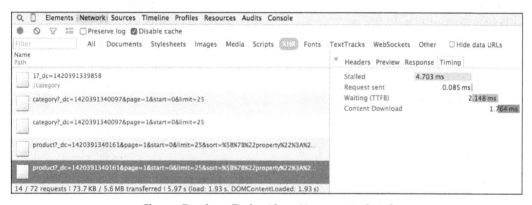

Chrome Developer Tools with an Ajax request selected

In this example, one of the requests has been selected and a breakdown of timing details in shown on the right-hand side. While the Alcohology application has a very fast response time, it serves as a good illustration of how to analyze network performance.

 More details about the **Network** panel can be found at
`https://developer.chrome.com/devtools/docs/network`.

How does this help us? If the remote server is slow, then as frontend developers, there's not much we can do about this; other than keeping our remote requests to a minimum, we're stuck with what's available. Here's one example that we can act on in order to speed things up.

Note the "stalled" entry in the timings. This is often caused due to the limit that browsers impose on the number of connections that can be active to one origin (such as a domain or subdomain) at a time. When this number is exceeded, the browser will block any new requests until a connection becomes available. This knowledge gives us several opportunities for optimization.

Make fewer requests

The no-brainer approach to this problem is to simply request fewer things from the server and Ext JS gives us several ways to do this. First up is a technique we used in the Alcohology app (use an icon font such as FontAwesome instead of image icons). This means that we'll only have to download one font file rather than multiple icon files. The glyph config on menu items and buttons gives us a really easy way to use this feature and negate the need to use bitmap images for icons.

Next up is nested data. This is an approach that we used in the Questionnaire component, but one that needs to be used carefully. By setting up model associations, we can request data for the whole hierarchy and populate our data model all at once, rather than per mode type.

For example, for the Questionnaire component, we could have loaded the questionnaire, the steps, and the questions in three separate requests, but by bringing it all down at once, we avoided the two remote requests. There are two caveats to this idea; firstly, the server needs to support nested data; secondly, the size of the nested data maybe much larger and therefore result in a slower response time. Multiple separate requests might result in better perceived performance, so application of this concept strongly depends on the situation, speaking of the perception of performance, and so on.

Perceived performance

There are some cases in which we can't improve the load time of certain aspects of an application, for example, it could be report generation where the number crunching involved is a long-running operation.

In these cases, we need to do what we can to improve the user's perception of performance and assure them that the action they're undertaking is underway and will finish soon.

In Ext JS, one key mechanism to do this is `Ext.LoadMask`. It's used by Ext JS internally in several situations:

In the previous example from the Ext JS Kitchen Sink, a grid with a paging toolbar will automatically use `LoadMask` while waiting for the server to return the next page.

The advantage to the user is that while they have to wait, they're at least being told that they have to wait. Without `LoadMask`, they'd have hit a button and received no feedback that the server was thinking about the request.

We can leverage `LoadMask` in our own code by creating a new instance when we need it, but it's more likely that we'd use it on an existing container and leverage the fact that many Ext JS components have `LoadMask` functionality baked in.

We can use event domains, which we discussed back in *Chapter 2*, *MVC and MVVM*, as one way of hooking into remote requests and masking our components:

```
listen: {
    store: {
        'products': {
            'beforeload': function() {
                this.lookupReference('list').mask('Loading...');
```

```
        },
        'load': function() {
            this.lookupReference('list').mask(false);
        }
    }
  }
}
```

In this code snippet that we added to the `ProductController` on Alcohology, we tell the `listen` config to watch out for `beforeload` and `load` events on the products store. The listener can use the "products" alias that we'd already set up on the products `store` class. When the `beforeload` event fires, we grab the product list view and call its mask method to show its `LoadMask`. When the server response returns and the `load` event fires, we call the mask method with the false argument to hide it again.

It's a simple and an unobtrusive way to wire up the loading mechanism and give the user that all-important feedback, showing that their actions have triggered an effect.

Load less

One very simple way to speed up the response of Ajax requests is to simply request less stuff! If the server supports paging, then any component powered by a store can immediately become more performant by requesting a single page of data rather than pulling it down all at once.

`Ext.PagingToolbar` can be linked to a store and placed anywhere in an application to provide a pagination UI:

```
bbar: [{
        xtype: 'pagingtoolbar',
        store: { bind: '{products}' },
        displayInfo: true
    }]
```

Here, for example, is how we'd begin to add a paging toolbar to the Alcohology application's product list view. It automatically takes on touch-friendly styling from the theme we used:

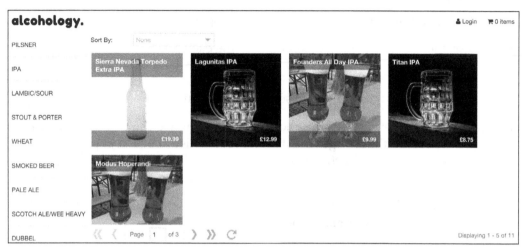

Alcohology's product list complete with paging toolbar

A more advanced version of this technique involves using the `Ext.data.reader.Reader.metaData` property or the `Ext.data.proxy.Proxy.metachange` event. This can be used to pass data from the server to the client, which is in turn used to configure the Ext JS application; a common example is to allow the server to specify the columns that a grid contains when it first loads.

This could mean that on initial load, the server omits a field and matching grid column, such as a description, which may contain a lot of data. The user could customize the grid via the column header UI to show it when they need it.

Optimistic updating

When saving a record to the server, we'd normally see the following actions:

- User clicks a button to save the record
- Ext JS displays a "saving" message
- Save completes and a "success" message is displayed

In some situations though, we can trust that the server is going to save successfully and cut the actions down to the following:

- User clicks on a button to save the record
- Save proceeds and a "saved" message is displayed

In this case, the save action happens entirely in the background and doesn't block the user from performing other actions. You can see this kind of behavior in many e-mail applications with the server interaction happening behind the scenes and an "outbox" to store messages that fail to send on the first try.

In the event that the server does raise some kind of error, we can display a failure message and rollback the changes that the user performed. The Ext JS grid includes UI to do this; it will highlight changed values with a red marker that can be cleared when we're sure the record has been successfully committed to the server.

This is an advanced technique that requires extra UI design work, but it can immeasurably improve your user experience.

Quick on the draw

In addition to ensuring that the way our application interacts with the server is always done in a timely fashion, we also need to be concerned with the speed at which the user interface renders and how quickly the browser draws the UI. There are a number of common pitfalls with Ext JS in this regard:

Overuse of panels

Panels have several features such as a header containing tool icons, the ability to be draggable, collapsible, and have docked items. In many situations, these features just aren't required. In this situation, a container is a much better choice. It's more lightweight in memory and the markup it generates.

Overnesting

Overnesting of containers and panels, particularly those implementing border layouts, are a very common source of performance issues, particularly if the user needs to move between various screens containing over-nested components. Ext JS needs to perform lots of calculations to build a viewport and the layout process is particularly expensive. Every time we find ourselves adding a new component to the hierarchy, it should cause us to stop and re-evaluate.

We also need to think about how a deep hierarchy could affect cases in which we are querying our component structure. With a more complex component tree and a more complicated DOM, any operations to fetch either components or elements from the application will be slower. In many cases, this slowdown will be marginal; in some cases, it'll be a critical consideration when improving your application's performance.

Deferred rendering

When creating a container or panel with a card layout, by default the layout will immediate render all components within each card. This is usually unnecessary because the user will only see the first card to begin with. Instead, we can use the deferredRender configuration option on the card layout to render items only when their parent card becomes active. This reduces the initial render time, therefore, the time until the application can respond to user input.

Another similar approach involves grids. Ext JS allows you to load a large server response into a store and attempts to display it on a grid, but in situation with thousands of records, the store causes memory usage to balloon and the browser will struggle to keep things smooth with such a large number of DOM nodes making up the grid rows.

The solution is to swap out a standard store for Ext.data.BufferedStore. This uses an enhanced paging mechanism to preload pages of data in advance. Meanwhile, the grid will automatically use Ext.grid.plugin.BufferedRenderer and as the user scrolls through the grid entries, the backing BufferedStore will automatically load in new pages of data while removing old pages. It does this seamlessly, so the user has no idea that the rows are being loaded from the server on the fly. The BufferedRenderer will also dispose of DOM nodes from old nodes as they scroll past, removing the memory burden of such a large amount of data.

All of these techniques have their place. They are also useful tools to be aware of at the start of the architecture process. If a client asks whether the application can handle 10,000 records in a datagrid, we now know that a buffered store can deliver the goods. On the flipside, we need to be conscious of premature optimization; there's no point implementing a buffered store when we're only dealing with a handful of records.

Analyzing performance

Dealing with performance issues is initially a problem of intelligence gathering. There can be multiple reasons why an application feels slow, and the feedback of users often doesn't help. Describing a part of the app as "sticky" just isn't a great way to diagnose the root cause. We need to get firm facts and figures in front of us before we can hope to find a solution. While we'll look at metrics such as rendering and response times, there are many considerations that must be taken into account, such as memory usage and user perception. These topics are left as an exercise for the reader.

The Chrome Developer Tools come to the rescue again. This time, we'll look at two main features that help diagnose performance problems: profiles and the timeline.

> In general, there are two situations in which Ext JS applications feel slow: poor design decisions and over-complicated apps. Having said that, these techniques are invaluable when the problem does crop up and are applicable to any JavaScript technology.

The profiler can be found by bringing up the Developer Tools and selecting the **Profiles** tab:

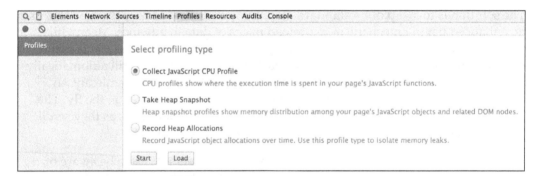

While there are several types of profiles that can be issued, we'll take a look at the CPU profile. In the preceding screenshot, we'd click on **Start** to immediately begin profiling. Here's a look at what happens when you click on a product in Alcohology:

Heavy (Bottom Up) ▼ 👁 ✕ ↻					
Self	▼	Total		Function	
9.1 ms	**0.40%**	**11.2 ms**	**0.49%**	**▼ getStyle**	
4.1 ms	0.18%	5.1 ms	0.22%	▶ isStyle	
2.0 ms	0.09%	2.0 ms	0.09%	▼ Ext.define.getStyles	
1.0 ms	0.04%	1.0 ms	0.04%	▶ Ext.define.cacheMissHandlers.borderInfo	
1.0 ms	0.04%	1.0 ms	0.04%	▶ Ext.define.cacheMissHandlers.paddingInfo	
2.0 ms	0.09%	2.0 ms	0.09%	▼ getLocalXY	
2.0 ms	0.09%	2.0 ms	0.09%	▶ Ext.define.sync	
1.0 ms	0.04%	2.0 ms	0.09%	▼ Ext.define.getStyle	
1.0 ms	0.04%	2.0 ms	0.09%	▼ Ext.define.getOverflowXStyle	
1.0 ms	0.04%	2.0 ms	0.09%	▶ Ext.define.beginLayoutCycle	
7.1 ms	0.31%	133.0 ms	5.87%	▶ Ext.define.doFire	
6.1 ms	0.27%	112.7 ms	4.98%	▶ Ext.Base.Base.addMembers.callParent	
4.1 ms	0.18%	24.4 ms	1.08%	▶ Ext.define.invalidate	
4.1 ms	0.18%	7.1 ms	0.31%	▶ Ext.define.setProp	
4.1 ms	0.18%	4.1 ms	0.18%	▶ setLocalXY	

The grid is ordered with the most time-consuming function calls at the top and each line can be expanded so that we can see the functions that were called in turn. The **Self** column shows the percentage of time spent in just that function's body; the **Total** column shows the time spent in that function as well as all of the functions it called.

While this part of the Alcohology application is performing just fine, this simple view of the heavily-used parts of code is a key avenue to diagnose serious performance problems. However, we can do more.

We've used Chrome Developer Tools to evaluate the performance of remote requests and now we've used them to track down hotspots in our code. What about a single view that could help us track the general behavior of our application and help us visualize the types of interactions that are slowing things down? This is exactly what the **Timeline** tab offers.

 This is a whistle-stop tour of **Timeline**. Refer to https://developer. chrome.com/devtools/docs/timeline for more details and full documentation.

By selecting the **Timeline** tab and clicking on the **Record** button, Chrome immediately begins recording every event currently taking place on the page. Clicking on **Record** again allows you to analyze the results:

Timeline allows you to filter down a timeframe of events and view each in turn, from user clicks to Ajax requests to URL changes and browser repaints. From the first event, we can trace down each subsequent event, viewing stack traces, detailed timings and warnings regarding problematic behavior.

Timeline is a powerful tool and you will need time and experience to use it to the fullest. It's time well spent; it can reveal clues that would be difficult or impossible to discover any other way. These clues can help resolve problems that would otherwise take days to tackle.

Summary

This chapter has given us a number of angles to approach two of the most important parts of building a successful application: fixing issues and adding polish. While explicit customer requirements form the main body of our work, we should always strive to make sure that our projects are performant and as bug-free as possible.

The Chrome Developer Tools are an invaluable weapon in our arsenal. By opening a window in the otherwise dark world of debugging and performance, we can take educated steps to quickly resolve issues. Stepping through our own code and that of the Ext JS framework becomes significantly easier with the power of breakpoints and the call stack explorer.

In the next chapter, we'll take our final step to building a well-rounded and robust application. While we are constantly working to build the best architecture we can, automated testing can provide a level of reassurance that takes the solidity of our work to the next level.

Code changes and refactoring can be done with confidence when our test suite can tell us if we've broken something with our latest amendments. Integration tests can provide assurances that our final application meets customer requirements and unit tests can encourage separation of code and ensure that our business logic is sound.

In the next chapter, we'll look into a variety of ways to implement these ideas and more.

11
Application Testing

Our role as architects isn't just to tick the boxes, send the application to the client, and forget about it. We have a responsibility, both from a professional perspective and a business perspective to produce software that tries to exceed expectations. A part of this was mentioned in *Chapter 10, Debugging and Performance*, in which we discussed the need to build an application that responded quickly to user actions. Now, we'll talk about building a robust application, one that stands up to scrutiny when it's under intense use.

What does it mean for an application to be robust? It means that if we click on a button, we see the expected result. If we try and enter an invalid e-mail address, we see a validation message. If we refresh the page, we find ourselves on the same screen as before. If the network connection drops out, remote requests get retried later. If we try and break the application, and so on, can we succeed?

The core of building a robust application is that the application should always behave as the user expects, even in unexpected circumstances. We must recognize that developers (and architects) are fallible and are unlikely to be able to account for every possible ramification of even a minor code change; this is where bugs arise and why the struggle for robustness is constant and ongoing.

We need a safety net for the fallible nature of coding. If we rename a particular method in the product list view, can we guarantee that it won't affect the shopping cart? We can use find and replace in our text editor, but we can never be 100 percent certain without refreshing the application and working through the functionality of the product list and the shopping cart to show that the customer requirements are still fulfilled.

A quality assurance process is a safety net of which automated testing is a key component. When working with Ext JS, there are a multitude of tools that we can use and a range of approaches to ensure that our applications are built in a way that is conducive to automated testing. To this end, in this chapter, we'll look at:

- The different types of test and when to use them
- Keeping Ext JS code concerns separate to promote unit testing
- Naming and coding conventions to assist with integration testing
- Testing tools for unit tests and integration tests
- Ext JS-specific testing tools

The goal in this chapter is to build an understanding of the advantages of testing, how to write Ext JS applications that are easy to test, and how to select and employ suitable testing tools. When we're done, we'll have covered all of the subjects an Ext JS architect needs to produce exemplary products.

Total testing

In this chapter, we'll cover two types of test, one at the detail level and one at the "big picture" level. The first, unit testing, is great for helping with the algorithms and calculations that often make up business logic; the second, integration testing, helps us make sure that customer requirements are met and the user experience is sound. Let's look at each in turn.

Unit testing

With unit testing, we unsurprisingly test a unit, a unit being an individual unit of code. This will generally be a whole class, but will focus on a single method depending on the circumstances. In a unit test, we'd be able to say something like this:

```
Create cart object
Add product #1 to cart
Add product #1 to cart
Assert that there is only one item in the cart
```

To set up the test, we add the same product to the cart twice. This should result in one line item with a quantity of two rather than two line items, each with a quantity of one. In the first test, we make the assertion that the cart count is equal to one, assuring us that adding to the cart won't add duplicates. The next test will check whether the quantity is incremented as expected:

```
Create cart object
Add product #1 to cart
```

```
Add product #1 to cart
Assert that first cart item has a quantity of two
```

It performs the same setup as the previous test, but then picks out the first line item in the cart and makes the assertion that its quantity is equal to two, one for each time the product was added to the cart.

Assert yourself

What's all this "assertion" business? It's simply a way of saying, "if this condition isn't met, something's wrong". In the previous examples, if the actual value and the expected value aren't equal, something's wrong. In most unit testing libraries, there are lots of different assertions, such as:

- Equal
- Less than
- Greater than
- Is it numeric?
- Does it contain the specified value?

Each testing library has its own flavor of assert methods. Some will use slightly different terminology (such as expectations or specifications). The terminology is less important than the principles behind unit testing, which is to put an isolated piece of code under intense scrutiny.

Integration testing

While unit testing focuses on a small piece of functionality, integration testing goes to the opposite extreme. Its purpose is to check whether all of the moving parts of the application work together correctly, replicating some of the actions that a real-world user would take.

For this reason, integration testing will often be described as UI testing because it acts directly on the interface. Let's say that we want to verify whether the detail window will show when a product is clicked on. We can do something like this:

1. Find the link for the product in question.
2. Simulate a click event on the link.
3. Verify that the DOM element with the product in question appeared as expected.

This is completely different to the kind of focus we had with unit testing in which we were drilling down to a single function or class in the code. Here, the actions we test will span multiple classes in the application, checking whether they're integrated and working together correctly.

Integration and differentiation

The nature of integration testing means that it operates on the same application that your users can see; the tests effectively load up a browser and simulate the path a user would take. However, rather than moving the mouse cursor manually in the same way as a user, integration test frameworks generally work by picking out HTML elements on the screen and allowing you to perform actions directly.

This is both good and bad. When a user negotiates a web page, they can generally spot the UI components they're interested in fairly quickly, but when the person writing the test comes to pick out this same component, they need a way of referencing it. The usual approach to this is to use CSS or XPath selectors. For example, to reference an element on the page with an ID with CSS and then XPath, use the following code:

```
#someElement
//*[@id="someElement"]
```

Also, another slightly more complicated code to get the first button in a container is as follows:

```
#container > button:nth-child(1)
//*[@id="container"]/button[1]
```

This goes some way in demonstrating a potential pain point of writing integration tests. What if the ID of `someElement` changes? It'll break the test, but it's a fairly simple fix. What if the ID of "container" changes? Well, not only will it break the previous example, but it'll also break any other tests that are looking for buttons or other elements within this `div`.

This is an ongoing problem with integration testing: the fragility of tests. Later in the chapter, we'll look at some methods to address this within Ext JS.

Testing tool time with Jasmine

Enough theory! Let's get our hands dirty with some practical examples using the Alcohology app from *Chapter 9, A Shopping Application*. First, we'll drill down into the guts of the application and build a unit test for some of the key business functionality. Then, we'll jump up to a high-level view and check whether our building blocks integrate correctly.

There are a wealth of tools we can use for both. The Ext JS framework has begun to build a set of unit tests to verify its behavior and cut out regressions in core functionality. To do so, Sencha has chosen the Jasmine library.

> Sencha has hinted that there'll be a big announcement surrounding testing alongside SenchaCon 2015. Given that they're already using Jasmine, we can hope that it'll be a good bet for Ext JS application testing in the future.

Jasmine is a behavior-driven framework, a term that relates to the way tests are described. Rather than using the "assertion" terminology, it uses the "expectation" format that we briefly mentioned earlier in the chapter. It asks us to specify behavior and expect a particular result. Here's the canonical example from Jasmine's documentation:

```
describe('A suite', function() {
    it('contains spec with an expectation', function() {
        expect(true).toBe(true);
    });
});
```

The `describe` method encloses one or more specifications, themselves declared in an `it` method, with expectations declared using the `expect` method. To translate the previous code to plain language, use the following command:

```
We have "a suite", which "contains spec with an expectation". This
expectation expects "true" to be "true".
```

Obviously, this is a contrived suite, as we'd hope that true would always be true! However, it should serve as a useful demonstration of the general syntax of a Jasmine test. Before we can get going and use this on our own application, we need to take a little bit of time to download and set up the Jasmine library.

Jasmine – installation and configuration

The simplest way of getting started with Jasmine is to download the latest version from the project's release page. At the time of writing this book, the current version is 2.1.3. Refer to `https://github.com/jasmine/jasmine/releases` for more information.

Extract the ZIP file and you'll see that the download includes some example specifications that we don't need; let's clear these out from within the new Jasmine directory:

```
rm MIT.LICENSE spec/* src/*
```

Now, we can move the Jasmine library to the root of the Alcohology project, assuming our current directory is now in the Alcohology project:

```
mkdir ./tests
mv ~/Downloads/jasmine-2.1.3 ./tests/jasmine
```

We can now fire up our application; if you've downloaded the project files, then the readme file will tell you to run `npm start` and it'll start the Ext JS project and the API server. Once this is done, we can open `http://localhost:1841/tests/jasmine/` `SpecRunner.html` in our browser to run the specs, as shown here:

The Jasmine spec runner before writing any specifications

In this screenshot, we can see the spec runner, but it's got nothing to do. We've got a little bit more configuration to do before we can start writing some specifications. Let's open up the `SpecRunner.html` file in an editor and tweak it to look like this:

```
<!DOCTYPE html>
<html>
<head>
  <meta charset="utf-8">
  <title>Jasmine Spec Runner v2.1.3</title>

  <link rel="stylesheet" href="lib/jasmine-2.1.3/jasmine.css">

  <script src="lib/jasmine-2.1.3/jasmine.js"></script>
  <script src="lib/jasmine-2.1.3/jasmine-html.js"></script>
  <script src="lib/jasmine-2.1.3/boot.js"></script>
  <script src="../../ext/build/ext-all-debug.js"></script>

  <script type="text/javascript">
    Ext.Loader.setConfig({
      enabled: true,
      paths: {
```

```
        'Alcohology': '../../app'
      }
    });
  </script>

  <script src="spec/Cart.js"></script>
</head>
<body></body>
</html>
```

This HTML file is really just a host for the Jasmine library, but it's also where we wire up Ext JS to work outside of the context of an application. By including the `ext-all` JavaScript file and reconfiguring `Ext.Loader` to grab any Alcohology classes from the correct directory, we can instantiate classes to test and Ext JS will automatically request the files we need from our application directory. All that's left to do is include the actual JavaScript specification files at the bottom of the head element. Here, we've already added a reference to `spec/Cart.js`.

With all of the setup out of the way, we can move on to writing some tests!

Make it happen

Earlier, we wrote some pseudocode to illustrate how to test the `addProduct` method on the cart store. Now, let's build out the real Jasmine specification that accomplishes this for real. We need to create a test suite with a cart store that'll be used as test subject:

```
describe('Cart store', function() {

  var cart;

  beforeEach(function() {
    cart = Ext.create('Alcohology.store.Cart');
  });
});
```

Our first suite is simply called `Cart store`. We have a cart variable that gets reassigned `beforeEach` specification is run. It's assigned an instance of the cart store via `Ext.create`. Thanks to our configuration in the previous section, `Ext.create` will use `Ext.Loader` to automatically pull in the relevant source code file, including any dependencies. By reinstantiating before every test, we can be sure that a test later in the suite won't be affected by the way an earlier test has manipulated the cart.

We can now sketch out the functionality we'd like to test. The following code goes after the `beforeEach` call:

```
describe('#addProduct', function() {
    it('should accept a Product model');
    it('should create a new CartItem line');
    it('should increment the quantity when adding an existing
Product');
    it('should not create a new CartItem when adding an existing
Product');
    });
```

If we refresh the `SpecRunner.html` page, then we'll actually be able to see something like this:

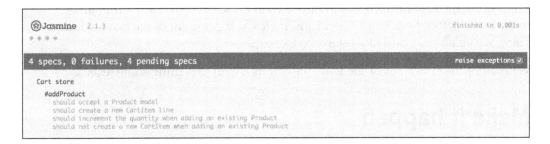

These specifications are just placeholders, but the fact that they show up in the runner is useful for developers practicing test first development. We can write a series of specification statements that describe the functionality we require, then the specs, and finally, the code itself. In this way, we're specifying the behavior we need and the code itself follows, and we can be safe in the knowledge that it meets our requirements. This can be a powerful methodology for an architect to spell out in detail how a class should behave.

Let's go through each spec one by one:

```
it('should accept a Product model', function() {
    expect(cart.addProduct.bind(cart, {})).toThrow();
});
```

We expect that if `addProduct` is passed, something that is not a product model, it will throw an exception. We pass the method to the expect call prepopulated with an empty object literal. As this isn't a product model — as expected — it throws an exception and satisfies the test as follows:

```
it('should create a new CartItem line', function() {
    var product = Ext.create('Alcohology.model.Product');

    cart.addProduct(product);

    expect(cart.count()).toBe(1);
});
```

When the product is added to the cart, we expect that it will cause a new line item to be created in the store. We simply check whether the cart count is as expected after adding a product:

```
it('should increment the quantity when adding an existing
Product', function() {
    var product = Ext.create('Alcohology.model.Product');

    cart.addProduct(product);
    cart.addProduct(product);

    expect(cart.first().get('quantity')).toBe(2);
});
```

After adding a product that's already in the cart, we expect that it will increase the quantity of the corresponding cart line. We pass in the same product twice and check whether the quantity is two, as expected:

```
it('should not create a new CartItem when adding an existing
Product', function() {
    var product = Ext.create('Alcohology.model.Product');

    cart.addProduct(product);
    cart.addProduct(product);

    expect(cart.count()).toBe(1);
});
```

This is a similar setup as the last test, but we are expecting that there will not be a duplicated cart line, but instead, there will be only one item in the cart.

With all of the specifications written, we can refresh the spec runner again:

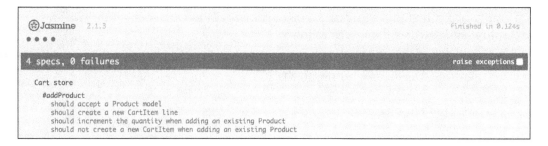

As you can see, the specs are all in green, indicating that they have passed successfully.

This is just a brief primer on unit testing with Jasmine, but it demonstrates the power available and the utility of testing in this manner. It gives us confidence in the code we've written and ensures that any additions to the `addProduct` method won't break the functionality that already exists.

Testing with robots

Now that we've covered a method of testing the fine detail of our code, let's look at a completely different way of running functional checks across the entire application. For this, we'll need a new tool: CasperJS. It allows you to drive a "headless browser"—one without any user interface—navigate around an application, and run evaluations on what we find. The first step is installation, which varies depending on the platform. Instructions for the same can be found at `http://docs.casperjs.org/en/latest/installation.html`.

When complete, we'll have a CasperJS command available to run.

With Jasmine, we were using the behavior-driven method of testing with expectations to verify the code. In CasperJS, we go back to using the assertion style of testing. Take a look at a minimal test script from the CasperJS documentation:

```
casper.test.begin("Hello, Test!", 1, function(test) {
    test.assert(true);
    test.done();
});
```

Pretty straightforward. The real magic comes when we combine this with CasperJS's ability to control the headless browser and interface with the web page that forms our application. Check this out:

```
casper.test.begin('Google search retrieves 10 or more results', 4,
function suite(test) {
    casper.start('http://www.google.com/', function() {
        test.assertTitle('Google', 'google homepage title is the
one expected');
        test.assertExists('form[action="/search"]', 'main form is
found');
        casper.fill('form[action="/search"]', {
            q: 'casperjs'
        }, true);
    });

    casper.then(function() {
        test.assertUrlMatch(/q=casperjs/, 'search term has been
submitted');
        test.assertEval(function() {
            return __utils__.findAll('h3.r').length >= 10;
        }, 'google search for \'casperjs\' retrieves 10 or more
results');
    });

    casper.run(function() {
        test.done();
    });
});
```

This looks a bit more exciting! Let's break down what's happening here:

1. Create a new CasperJS test suite.

2. Navigate to the Google home page.

3. Assert that the page title is as expected and that we can find the search box.

4. Fill in the search box and submit the form.

5. Then, when the page has loaded, assert that the URL is as expected and contains our search query as a parameter.

6. Assert that there are at least ten search results on the page.

Fantastic! This example shows how easy it's to use CasperJS to control a web page and how its testing features allow us to evaluate the content of the page and the behavior of an app.

The next step is to see how to use these features to test our own application, so let's hook CasperJS into our Alcohology project and get testing.

Up and running with CasperJS

Let's create a new subdirectory within our project at tests/casper and then create a new file in there called Sanity.js. We're going to write a couple of simple checks to make sure the application is loading correctly. Here's the starting point for the code:

```
casper.test.begin('Alcohology Sanity Checks', 0, function
suite(test) {
    casper.start('http://localhost:1841/', function() {
    });
    casper.run(function() {
        test.done();
    });
});
```

We kick off by calling the casper.test.begin method, which starts off a new test suite and takes three arguments: a description for the suite, the number of tests we expect should be run, and a callback function that is called when the suite is created. The callback gets passed on a test object on which we can call various assert methods.

We then call CasperJS's start method with the URL to our application. In order to trigger the test run, we call CasperJS's run method and when everything's complete, we call the done method on the test object.

The first test we're going to write will check whether the category menu on the left-hand side of the application is populated as expected. To do this, we'll look for the first menu item and check whether it contains the text we expect, but it complicates matters slightly when we're loading this content in with Ajax. We need to be able to wait for the page to load, select the relevant element, and check whether it contains the content we'd expect.

In order to select elements, we're going to use the CSS selector, and so on, but we need a mechanism to find the correct selector to use. Fortunately, Chrome Developer Tools will come to our rescue once more; if we right click on the **Pilsner** text in the top category menu item in Alcohology, then pick **Inspect Element**, the elements panel will display with the menu item's element selected.

Next, right-click on the element and click on the **Copy CSS Path** option:

The CSS select of this `div` tag will be copied to your clipboard and should look like this:

```
#gridview-1014-record-6 > tbody > tr > td > div
```

We can now use this with CasperJS:

```
casper.test.begin('Application sanity checks', 0, function
suite(test) {
    casper.start('http://localhost:1841/', function() {
        var selector = '#gridview-1014-record-6 > tbody > tr > td
> div';

        casper.waitForSelector(selector, function() {
            test.assertSelectorHasText(selector, 'Pilsner');
        });
    });

    casper.run(function() {
        test.done();
    });
});
```

After telling CasperJS to start and load the application's web page, we will use the `waitForSelector` method to wait until the specified selector appears on the page; by default, it'll wait for 5 seconds before throwing up a failure message. When the selector appears, the callback function is triggered and we use the `assertSelectorHasText` method to check whether the `div` tag has the correct text:

```
2. colinramsay@spaceghost: ~/Projects/personal/ext-js-app-architecture/9/alcohology (zsh)

ext-js-app-architecture/9/alcohology   master ✗                                    1d ⚑
▶ casperjs test tests/casper/Sanity.js
Test file: tests/casper/Sanity.js
# Application sanity checks
PASS Find "Pilsner" within the selector "#gridview-1014-record-6 > tbody > tr > td > div"
PASS 1 test executed in 1.905s, 1 passed, 0 failed, 0 dubious, 0 skipped.
Unsafe JavaScript attempt to access frame with URL about:blank from frame with URL file:///usr/loc
al/lib/node_modules/casperjs/bin/bootstrap.js. Domains, protocols and ports must match.


ext-js-app-architecture/9/alcohology   master ✗                                    1d ⚑
▶ █
```

Running our first CasperJS test

It's simple, but effective. If we'd broken something due to an amend in the code for the categories store, incorrectly bound the data to the view model, or some other minor change that cascaded to affect this key feature, then this test would immediately flag it up.

 CasperJS relies on another library called PhantomJS to drive the headless browser. There's an issue between the two in the current version that causes the `Unsafe JavaScript attempt...` message that you can see in the preceding screenshot; it's fine to ignore it.

We can do a lot more. Although the correct text is showing, the menu isn't just for display purposes, and when a user clicks on a menu item, it will load the products with this category. Can we create a CasperJS test for this?

Of course we can! Take a look at the CasperJS API documentation at http://docs.casperjs.org/en/latest/modules/casper.html#casper-prototype.

Alongside the `start` method, we have ones such as `fill` that allows you to complete form fields: `scrollTo`, which lets us move to a particular location on the page, and for our current purposes: `click`, it provides a means to click on an element specified by a selector. Let's build another test using `click` to run a more advanced set of steps, something like this:

- Load the application
- Click on the **IPA** category
- Select the **Lagunitas IPA** product
- Check whether the product window appear
- Check whether the correct product name and price appear

This is a much more comprehensive test that goes some way to demonstrating the power of CasperJS to replicate user actions and validate the behavior of our application. Here's the code:

```
casper.test.begin('Product walk through', 2, function suite(test)
{
    casper.start('http://localhost:1841/', function() {
        var categorySelector = '.categories-body table:nth-
child(2) td',
            productSelector = '.product-list .product:nth-
child(2)',
            windowSelector = '.product-detail',
            headerSelector = '.product-detail h1',
            priceSelector = '.product-detail p.price';

        // Wait for the categories to load.
        casper.waitForSelector(categorySelector, function() {
            // Click the specified category.
            casper.click(categorySelector);
        });

        // Wait for the category products to load.
        casper.waitForSelector(productSelector, function() {
            // Click the specified product.
            casper.click(productSelector);
        });

        // Wait for the product window to appear.
        casper.waitForSelector(windowSelector, function() {
            // Assert text for heading and price.
            test.assertSelectorHasText(headerSelector, 'Lagunitas
IPA');

            test.assertSelectorHasText(priceSelector, '£12.99');

            // Capture a screenshot.
            casper.capture('products-page.png');
        });
```

```
    });

    casper.run(function() {
        test.done();
    });
});
```

The comments in the code should make it pretty self-explanatory. After setting out all of the selectors we need, we wait for the categories and click on the one that we need. Next, we wait for the product we want and click on it before waiting for the product window to appear and asserting on its contents. For the final trick, we instruct CasperJS to take a screenshot, a feature that can be useful for debugging or further evaluation.

Running this code gives us the following screenshot:

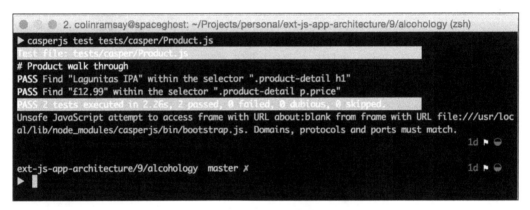

Success! We've simulated and validated a small user path through the Alcohology application, checking whether several moving parts of our project work in tandem as expected.

The eagle-eyed reader will notice that the selectors in this example look a little more friendly than the ones in the first example that we grabbed using Google Chrome. There's a very good reason for this and it relates to a set of ideas surrounding making your application easier to test.

Testability

As with many aspects of software development, there are many different ways of testing. Some will advocate a test-first methodology, where the tests are created first and the code will be written to satisfy these tests. Whichever method is used, we need to take steps to make sure our code can be tested. While this occasionally means adding in some helpful hooks and tricks that are only used to test, we should generally try to avoid this approach and look to write code that is naturally testable; this will often have the fortunate consequence of being better code too.

Sometime back, we talked about selectors and their relationship to testability. Let's look at the selector that Chrome Developer Tools gave us:

```
#gridview-1014-record-6 > tbody > tr > td > div
```

This is a very specific selector and the first part of it is using an ID that was autogenerated by Ext JS. As soon as we add or alter the component hierarchy of the application or change the records being displayed on the page, this will break and our CasperJS tests will fail.

We can increase testability of our application by ensuring that our test code is less brittle. In this case, we can leverage the CSS classes that we use to style our application. Back in *Chapter 9, A Shopping Application*, when we built the category list view, we set the `bodyCls` configuration option to `categories-body`. This gives us a great way to target the list that we know isn't going to randomly change.

Using it in addition with the `nth-child` pseudo-selector gives us a simpler and more robust version of our original Developer Tools selector:

```
.categories-body table:nth-child(2) td
```

In plain language, get the element with a class of `categories-body`, find the second child table, which corresponds to the second row, and grab its `td` cell element.

Using Chrome Developer Tools is still a great way to look at the HTML structure of the page and work out an optimal selector for each case, but it's rarely going to provide the most robust selector.

Should I or shouldn't I?

There's plenty of lively debate about how testing should inform your code, if at all. In the last example, we had a useful CSS selector that was already being used for styling, but in the event we hadn't already placed it there, should it have been added specifically to support styling?

In this case, it's a very minor change, so we probably don't have to feel that bad about it. We could even wrap it in a Sencha Cmd directive to ensure that it doesn't get included in production builds:

```
//<debug>
bodyCls: 'categories-body',
//</debug>
```

In general though, anything that adds complexity or maintenance overhead to our main code base just to improve testability should be avoided. Instead, we can look at ways in which the design of an application naturally promotes testability.

Earlier in the book, we talked about MVC and MVVM and how one of the benefits of such patterns is to promote the separation of code concerns. Throughout, we've used events to ensure that components can "fire-and-forget" and trigger actions without having an awareness of other parts of the system.

This is a key feature that gives an elegant, clear design combined with a side benefit of separation of components. We can pluck out individual views, render them alone on a simple page, and perform tests on a single component in isolation. As in our Jasmine examples at the start of the chapter, we can take a single model and instantiate it without having to worry about the user interface layers.

The beauty of good application architecture is that it provides an understandable application that immediately lends itself to testing. Although, integration testing is an important weapon in our arsenal, it's much more important to ensure that the various parts of the machine are well built before trying to fire the whole thing up.

Faking it with mocks

When it's up and running, our application still has one giant dependency: the server. During integration testing, this means that the server-side database needs to be primed with test data, and test suite will result in many requests being sent back and forth. In a large test suite, this can be slow and the database setup can be painful.

A common resolution to this problem is to bypass the server API altogether. When our application makes an Ajax request, we can hijack the XMLHttpRequest and feed the calling code some static test data instead.

To demonstrate this and show the flexibility of the technique, we'll create a small Jasmine test case that shows how to supply a product store with mock JSON data. Although, faking an Ajax request is really useful in integration tests, this will show off the technique in a succinct way that can be used in both unit and integration testing.

We'll be using a feature of Ext JS that isn't included by default: `Simlets`. The classes that implement `Simlets` are included in the `examples` directory of the Ext JS distribution, so all we have to do is open up the `SpecRunner.html` file from earlier in the chapter and amend it to instruct `Ext.Loader` to pull in the files from the correct location:

```
Ext.Loader.setConfig({
    enabled: true,
    paths: {
        'Alcohology': '../../app',
        'Ext.ux': '../../ext/examples/ux' // added
    }
});
```

All we've added is the line for the `Ext.ux` path. Now, we can build our Jasmine test, so let's dive straight into the code:

```
describe('Mocking Ajax', function() {
    var productStore,
        fakeJsonData = [{
            "id":1,
            "name":"Test Product",
            "price":"19.99",
            "description":"Test Product Description"
        }];

    beforeEach(function() {

        Ext.syncRequire('Ext.ux.ajax.SimManager');
        Ext.syncRequire('Alcohology.model.Product');

        Ext.ux.ajax.SimManager.init().register({
            'http://localhost:3000/product': {
                type: 'json',
                data: fakeJsonData
            }
        });

        productStore = Ext.create('Ext.data.Store', {
            model: 'Alcohology.model.Product'
        });
    });

    it('Uses fake JSON data', function(done) {
        productStore.load({
```

```
            callback: function(records) {
                expect(records.length).toBe(1);
                expect(records[0].get('name')).toBe('Test
    Product');
                done();
            }
        });
    });
});
```

Lots going on here! First, we set up a couple of variables, one to contain the `productStore` between tests and one containing our fake JSON.

In the `beforeEach` function call, we load in the `SimletManager` class and the `Product` model from Alcohology; `Ext.Loader` will pull in the files for us before allowing execution to proceed to the next lines. Next, we set up `SimletManager` by registering the URL to be intercepted and the data that should be returned instead of the normal server response.

This is actually all we need to set up a fake request; the rest of the code proceeds as if it were a normal Jasmine test in which we set two expectations after the product store loads, that is, there will be one returned record and its name will be set to `Test Product`, just like in the test data.

Running the test through the spec runner sees everything pass as expected and demonstrates the power of this technique. We can disconnect all of our testing from the backend and run independent of a database; test data is supplied directly in the tests and not in a database row somewhere on a server.

Continuous coverage

You've learned how to use a couple of different testing tools in this chapter, but what about when to use these tools?

When it comes to code testing, there's a metric known as "code coverage" that tells us the percentage of our code that is covered by tests. The first thought of a passionate architect starting a new project is that everything should be covered with tests, tests everywhere!

Realistically, there are things that we just don't need to test; as always, we should take a pragmatic approach. Configuration of components probably doesn't need to be tested; we don't need to test the return values from third-party code libraries; there are many examples.

Having said that, code coverage is a useful way to make sure that a certain level of testing is maintained in a project. For example, we might wish to have 90 percent test coverage of our model code and only 50 percent coverage on our controllers, which contain more boilerplate that doesn't need to be tested. The exact ratios will depend on the project, the developers, and indeed the architect.

There are many code coverage tools for JavaScript, one of which is Istanbul. It provides a comprehensive set of features to check code coverage in a variety of ways and reports on the level of coverage in a range of formats. You can find this on GitHub at `https://github.com/gotwarlost/Istanbul`.

When a project is well covered by unit tests and integration tests are in place to make sure the user experience remains consistent, we're left with one part of the puzzle: when to run these tests?

Of course, a developer should be running the relevant tests for the section of code they're working on, but in reality, a full test suite can take a long time to execute. In such cases, we can make use of something called **continuous integration** (CI).

Jenkins CI is an open source CI system (`http://jenkins-ci.org/`) and Circle CI (`https://circleci.com/`) is paid for, but with a free plan.

Whenever a developer pushes new code to the source control repository, a CI server grabs that code and runs the tests. This enables us to see when a developer has committed code that breaks the current build; it also gives us peace of mind that a successful CI build will be one that has passed our automated checks and is well on its way to production.

Summary

Testing is a huge topic with many different libraries, programs, and techniques vying for the attention of software architects. As with many facets of our role, there's never one correct answer and the most important thing is to settle on something that works for our particular project.

In this chapter, we've reviewed a range of different ideas and approaches to testing Ext JS and touched on the ways in which we can ensure our architectural decisions trickle down into making testing easier. The different extremes of test—from unit to integration—can always benefit when we isolate certain parts of the system under test, from remote requests through to separation of code concerns.

Testing is an essential, yet often neglected part of Ext JS application architecture and this chapter is only an overview. This, and the other topics covered in this book, must be used in combination and alongside a constant search for new ideas in order to truly master the concepts we've touched on.

Index

default sources 36
example 36

event handlers, CMS application
page, adding 103, 104
page, deleting 104
page, saving 104
page, selecting 103
using 101-103

events, webmail client 165, 166

Ext.DataView
using 159

Ext JS
about 10, 232
advantages 13
CMS application, implementing 90
data binding 91
model-view-controller (MVC) pattern 12
MVC concept 24
MVVM, using with 30
Sencha Cmd 13

Ext JS 3
benefits 29

Ext JS 4 4, 13

Ext JS 5 4

EXTJS-13933
reference link 201

Ext JS application
/build 46
/overrides 45
/packages 45
/resources 46
/.sencha 45
app.js 46
app.json 47
bootstrap.css 45
bootstrap.js 45
bootstrap.json 45
build.xml 46
exploring 44
index.html 46
SASS 46

Ext JS MVC
examples 25-28

Ext.Loader class 66

F

FontAwesome
URL 245

G

global state
drawbacks 57-59

H

Header.js file, webmail client
about 175-178
ViewController 178, 179
ViewModel 178

I

in-browser debugging
about 266
Alcohology project, using 266, 267
blackboxing 270, 271
breaking point 268, 269
code, stepping in 266, 267

integration testing
about 289
differentiation 290
integration 290

interface, shopping application
about 242, 243
custom event, handling with
main control 246-248
custom header, adding 244-246

Istanbul
about 307
URL 307

J

Jasmine
about 291
configuring 291-293
installing 291-293

testing, with 290
tests, writing 293-296
Java JAR
  URL 73
Jenkins CI
  URL 307
Jetty 62
JSHint
  URL 73

L

login form, shopping application 230
login view, webmail client 170, 171

M

main view controller, monitoring dashboard
  about 126, 127
  redirectTo method 128
  routes, implementing 128
  routing 127
main view, webmail client
  about 172, 173
  ViewController 174, 175
  ViewModel 174
Messages.js file, webmail client
  about 182, 183
  ViewController 184-186
  ViewModel 183, 184
mixin, questionnaire component 221, 222
mixins 53-57
model-view-controller. *See* **MVC**
monitoring dashboard
  application design 106-109
  application template, building 121
  building 105, 106
  components, building 129-134
  constant evaluation 134
  dashboard view controller 136, 137
  dashboard view model 135, 136
  data 122
  data structure 110
  flexibility 118
  main view controller 126

pragmatism 118
requisites 109, 110
subpages 141-145
testing 119-121
user interface 114-117
view 125, 126
Web, controlling 140
web logs subpage 137-139
Web view model 139, 140
MVC
  about 22
  implementing, to Web 23, 24
  illusion of choice 29
MVVM
  about 30
  event domains 36
  inter-communication 35
  main event 35
  starting with 30-34
  stores 35
  using, with Ext JS 30

N

navigation bar, questionnaire component 211, 212
Network panel
  URL 275

O

object-orientated programming (OOP) 4

P

packages 78
performance, in Ext JS
  about 274, 275
  analyzing 282-284
  fewer requests, making 276
  loading less 278, 279
  network performance 275, 276
  optimistic updating 279
  perceived performance 276, 277
PhantomJS 62

Thank you for buying
Ext JS Application Development Blueprints

About Packt Publishing

Packt, pronounced 'packed', published its first book, *Mastering phpMyAdmin for Effective MySQL Management*, in April 2004, and subsequently continued to specialize in publishing highly focused books on specific technologies and solutions.

Our books and publications share the experiences of your fellow IT professionals in adapting and customizing today's systems, applications, and frameworks. Our solution-based books give you the knowledge and power to customize the software and technologies you're using to get the job done. Packt books are more specific and less general than the IT books you have seen in the past. Our unique business model allows us to bring you more focused information, giving you more of what you need to know, and less of what you don't.

Packt is a modern yet unique publishing company that focuses on producing quality, cutting-edge books for communities of developers, administrators, and newbies alike. For more information, please visit our website at www.packtpub.com.

Writing for Packt

We welcome all inquiries from people who are interested in authoring. Book proposals should be sent to author@packtpub.com. If your book idea is still at an early stage and you would like to discuss it first before writing a formal book proposal, then please contact us; one of our commissioning editors will get in touch with you.

We're not just looking for published authors; if you have strong technical skills but no writing experience, our experienced editors can help you develop a writing career, or simply get some additional reward for your expertise.

Learning Ext JS 4

ISBN: 978-1-84951-684-6   Paperback: 434 pages

Sencha Ext JS for a beginner

1. Learn the basics and create your first classes.

2. Handle data and understand the way it works, create powerful widgets and new components.

3. Dig into the new architecture defined by Sencha and work on real-world projects.

Mastering Ext JS

ISBN: 978-1-78216-400-5   Paperback: 358 pages

Learn how to build powerful and professional applications by mastering the Ext JS framework

1. Build an application with Ext JS from scratch.

2. Learn expert tips and tricks to make your web applications look stunning.

3. Create professional screens such as login, menus, grids, tree, forms, and charts.

Please check **www.PacktPub.com** for information on our titles

PUBLISHING

Ext JS 4 Web Application Development Cookbook

ISBN: 978-1-84951-686-0   Paperback: 488 pages

Over 110 easy-to-follow recipes backed up with real-life examples, walking you through basic Ext JS features to advanced application design using Sencha's Ext JS

1. Learn how to build Rich Internet Applications with the latest version of the Ext JS framework in a cookbook style.

2. From creating forms to theming your interface, you will learn the building blocks for developing the perfect web application.

2. Easy-to-follow recipe steps through practical and detailed examples, which are all fully backed up with code, illustrations, and tips.

Ext JS Data-driven Application Design

ISBN: 978-1-78216-544-6   Paperback: 162 pages

A step-by-step guide to building a user-friendly database in Ext JS using data from an existing database

1. Discover how to layout the application structure with MVC and Sencha Cmd.

2. Learn to use Ext Direct during the application build process.

3. Understand how to set up the history support in the browser.

Please check **www.PacktPub.com** for information on our titles

www.ingramcontent.com/pod-product-compliance
Lightning Source LLC
Chambersburg PA
CBHW062058050326

40690CB00016B/3135